An OPUS book

THE POLITICAL DEVELOPMENT OF THE BRITISH ISLES 1100–1400

OPUS General Editors

Christopher Butler
Robert Evans
Alan Ryan

OPUS books provide concise, original, and authoritative introductions to a wide range of subjects in the humanities and sciences. They are written by experts for the general reader as well as for students.

The
Political Development
of the
British Isles 1100–1400

ROBIN FRAME

Oxford New York

OXFORD UNIVERSITY PRESS

1990

Oxford University Press, Walton Street, Oxford OX2 6DP

Oxford New York Toronto
Delhi Bombay Calcutta Madras Karachi
Petaling Jaya Singapore Hong Kong Tokyo
Nairobi Dar es Salaam Cape Town
Melbourne Auckland

and associated companies in
Berlin Ibadan

Oxford is a trade mark of Oxford University Press

First published 1990 as an Oxford University Press paperback
and simultaneously in a hardback edition

British Library Cataloguing in Publication Data
Frame, Robin
The political development of the British Isles, 1100-1400.
— (Opus)
1. Great Britain, 1154-1399
I. Title   II. Series
941.03
ISBN 0-19-219202-7
ISBN 0-19-289183-9 (pbk)

Library of Congress Cataloging in Publication Data
Data available

Typeset by Colset Private Ltd, Singapore
Printed and bound in Great Britain by
Biddles Ltd, Guildford and King's Lynn

For my Father and Mother

Preface

NOWADAYS, we often hear, British history (in the wider sense) is all the rage. Even so, there still does not seem to be much of it in print. While spending the last few years trying to view the medieval British Isles as a whole, I have sometimes felt that I was engaged in an odd, not to say foolhardy, activity: why, if the job was worth doing, had it been so rarely attempted before? The picture I have discerned, and now place before the reader, is therefore bound to be idiosyncratic. My hope is that, by setting familiar things in a less familiar context, the book may prompt fresh questions, and also convince others that there is more to the past of this complex region than can be regimented into the neat categories 'English history', 'Scottish history', 'Irish history', and 'Welsh history'.

The book springs from a deep well of indebtedness. It owes much to my time as an undergraduate at Trinity College, Dublin, where, thanks to James Lydon, I first learnt something about medieval Ireland, and first became aware of medieval Scotland. In the TCD of a quarter of a century ago, English constitutional history had an honoured place, and Stubbs's *Charters* enjoyed an Indian summer. I took the late Jocelyn Otway-Ruthven's special subject, 'The Great Liberties of England, Ireland, and the Marches of Wales in the later Middle Ages'. This was, it must be said, an exercise not without its austerities; it was also a bold and unusual adventure in comparative history (though, typically, she never for a moment thought to market it as such). More recently, the boot has been on the other foot, and I have gained a great deal from the Durham undergraduates who have studied medieval Scotland, Wales, and Ireland with me: if the book has lucid moments, the credit is theirs. I am grateful to the Research Foundation of the University of Durham, which elected me Sir Derman Christopherson Foundation Fellow for 1987–8; although my year as Fellow was chiefly devoted to another project, it enabled me to bring the text of this book within sight of completion. Several colleagues at Durham have been patient in responding to my apparently idle questions, and generous in lending me books. Michael Prestwich, amidst the manifold cares of a modern departmental chairman, somehow found time to read the entire typescript in a final search for slips and obscurities. Rees Davies, whose work must inspire all students of the medieval British Isles, has encouraged the undertaking from the outset, and has by precept and example sought to revive an author who sometimes flagged. He also read the book in draft; at more than one point his comments blew away the mental fog that threatened to envelop me, and pointed a way forward. The errors and blemishes that remain (and, in a book that amounts to a sustained act of trespass on the academic patches of others, there may be many) are of course my own responsibility. My last and greatest debt is, as ever, to my wife and family—for their patience, and occasional salutary impatience.

ROBIN FRAME

Durham
August 1989

Contents

List of Maps

List of Genealogical Tables

Introduction

To the geographer, archaeologist, or student of prehistory, the British Isles may appear a natural, or at least convenient, area of study; for the historian of the early Middle Ages, too, the lines of demarcation between English, Welsh, Scottish, and Irish history often seem beside the point. Yet until recently, despite the publication of G. W. S. Barrow's *Feudal Britain* as long ago as 1956, it was unusual to find historians of the following centuries setting out to cross more than one, let alone all, of those frontiers. If old academic habits die hard, few seem more durable than the convention, enshrined in the syllabuses of History departments in English universities, that 'British History' means to all intents and purposes 'English History', and that (save for a nod towards Henry II's expedition to Ireland, Edward I's conquests in Wales, or the Anglo-Scottish wars of the later Middle Ages) everything else is best left for historians of the 'Celtic Fringe' to contemplate in modest seclusion. Irish, Welsh, and Scottish scholars for their part have often seemed happy enough to cultivate their gardens in isolation not just from the English but from one another. Historical writing has as a result tended to set in moulds that can prove very hard to break.

Over the last few years signs of discontent with this state of affairs have multiplied. Like many shifts in the perceptions and priorities of historians, this may not be unrelated to changes in the surrounding world. Since the late 1960s, the 'Irish question' has resurfaced after several decades when it seemed (improbably enough) to have been buried. Scottish and Welsh nationalism has impinged sufficiently on the consciousness of English politicians for schemes of devolution to be mooted. Economic and social changes have sharpened political divisions between the regions of England itself. Entry into the European Economic Community has raised fundamental questions about the sovereignty of the British state. And post-war immigration has made topical the problems that attend relations between diverse ethnic groups who inhabit the same territory. All this has provided a reminder that the United Kingdom, despite its tradition of centralized government, is a highly complex, even problematical, political fabric.

Historians are sensitive to the charge of casually reading the past in the light of the present. But the effect of the recent emergence (or re-emergence) of public issues of such moment may be salutary, since it serves to draw attention to significant and neglected aspects of the medieval past. During the period 1100–1400 the British Isles formed a political sphere of great complexity, and were closely integrated with continental Europe. Not only that, the origins of enduring political forms, relationships, and tensions may, with more or less conviction, be discovered in these centuries. For instance—to touch only on some of the most obvious developments—England and Scotland acquired their familiar geographical dimensions, together with the aristocracies and parliaments that were to remain until 1707, and the rudiments of the legal systems that have come down to the present day; through a long-drawn-out, yet spasmodic process Wales was tightly bound politically and administratively to England, while keeping its cultural distinctiveness; and English power was extended for the first time into Ireland—a venture that had enough success to create lasting legal, governmental, and cultural patterns, but did not unify the whole island under a single political authority.

Historical perceptions are not, however, guided merely by readily identifiable changes in the exterior scene; scholarly advances and alterations in academic fashion (themselves, it is true, often shaped more subtly by the modern world) also have a part to play. In the nineteenth and early twentieth centuries political history was concerned above all with the gestation, birth, and growth of the nation-state. (Since the phenomenon itself was viewed almost as part of the natural dispensation, the biological metaphors may be thought to fit.) The history of kingdoms such as England and (to a lesser degree) France, which achieved and maintained a measure of unity in the Middle Ages, was a subject for celebration. By contrast the experience of countries which were never unified, or which gained unity only to lose it again, was deemed unsatisfactory: writings about Germany (notably), or indeed Ireland, were marked by a need to explain the 'failure' to tread the appointed path. A further effect of this vision of the past was to focus attention on the political units that appeared to be the ancestors of the later states of Europe: with hindsight a solidity was attributed to them that was denied to other political spheres, which may have been equally real in their own day. Often the historian, having defined to his own satisfaction the interests of his nation, did not hesitate to pass summary judgement on distant generations for promoting or obstructing them.

Recently we have been made more aware of the tentative and shifting quality of medieval political structures. The states familiar to us, far from being part of a predestined order, developed slowly and messily in competition with a range of possible alternatives. French history, for instance, has come to be seen as the sum total of the histories of the 'empires' of dukes and counts, which in certain cases (Normandy is the most obvious) stretched beyond the boundaries of what we know as France. It was only gradually that the Capetian kings outstripped rival powers and in doing so drew the outlines of a territorial kingdom. The historian, especially of the twelfth century, has learnt to live in a world characterized by permeable frontiers across which the interests of the nobility readily spread, and by powers of varying types whose fields of dominance ceaselessly expanded, contracted, and overlapped. He must adjust his focus to take in vast multi-national empires, kingships marked by great unevenness of control from region to region and period to period, and principalities that cannot be categorized as consistently within or without the control of superior authorities. It is no longer adequate to write a political history identified with the fortunes of one or other of the national kingships.

At first sight these points may seem less relevant to the British Isles than to France or Germany. The early appearance of a powerful English monarchy, together with the emergence of its stable Scottish counterpart, suggest a neatness that is frequently missing elsewhere. But this impression can be treacherous: at the beginning of the twelfth century political arrangements in Britain and Ireland were still fluid and provisional—a point that is better appreciated when the archipelago is seen as a whole. To suggest this is not to claim that the British Isles form an area of historical study that is innately more valid than others: in fact it is highly artificial. Despite Edward I, no unitary monarchy of the orbit of Britain emerged in the Middle Ages; moreover the political history of the region was for long periods interwoven with that of France, and to some extent of Scandinavia. Hence it is far from the purpose of this book to argue that the usual lineaments of English, Irish, Welsh, and Scottish history should be erased, and replaced according to some new prescription, which might seem to afford greater freedom of manoeuvre, but which could in the end amount to a more unnatural form of tyranny. Its aim is to offer a complementary, rather than an alternative, perspective. A view that takes in the British Isles as a whole may highlight themes and relations that otherwise are only dimly visible; it can help to pin-point similarities and differences, and prompt questions that might otherwise remain unasked; above all, it should have the capacity to set well-known features in an unfamiliar context.

There are few settled conventions for writing about the history of the British Isles. This is stimulating, but also alarming: I have had to proceed by trial and error, mapping the scene (so to speak) while hastily passing through it. In that sense the book is experimental, and the map no doubt idiosyncratic and well furnished with empty spaces and wrong turnings. For reasons that should be apparent from the foregoing paragraphs, I have not assigned separate chapters to individual countries; each chapter deals with an aspect of the whole subject, and the book may be read as a sequence of essays. Naturally the reader will look for organizing themes. Two stand out. The first, inevitably, is the impact on the British Isles of the dominant power within them, represented (in the first part of the book) by the Anglo-Norman aristocracy, church, and monarchy, and (in the second part) by their successor, the English state. The expansion of that power, the responses it encountered, and the limits that were placed upon it form an important thread in a somewhat winding story. But the English impact was uneven; nor of course was it the sole, or always the most significant, influence on the political history of the region. So comparisons and contrasts between the different parts of the British Isles form a second prominent theme. Discussion of the two goes forward throughout the book. For convenience, they might perhaps have been more rigorously separated: but that would have pulled apart too many things that belong together.

PART ONE

Ascendancy and Assimilation, 1100–1270

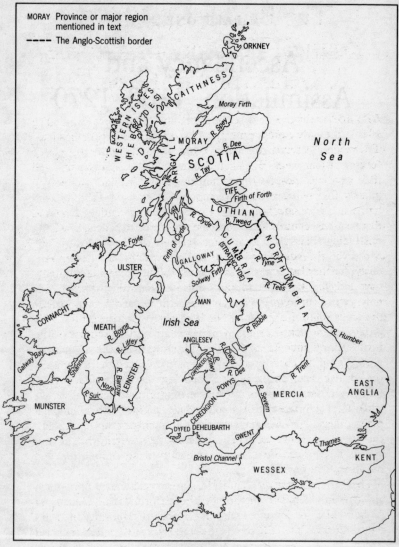

Map 1. The British Isles

1. The British Isles in 1100: Political Perceptions and the Geography of Power

ANYBODY who tries to describe the political make-up of the British Isles in the early twelfth century will soon encounter complications. The modern observer can hardly avoid approaching the past with a scheme of four lands—England, Scotland, Wales, and Ireland—and their associated peoples already imprinted on his mind; and he will quickly find evidence that contemporaries too could think in such terms, and were sometimes eager to arrange history and myth around these national entities. Such a scheme would not, of course, be wholly misleading. Parts of it bear some relation to the facts of power. Moreover, the existence of words and concepts has to be taken seriously, for they had a way of gaining the solidity they might initially have lacked. The Capetian kings, for example, ruled directly over only part of northern France, and the term *Francia* did not include the lands south of the Loire: but it mattered that the writers who publicized the French kingship in the twelfth century could associate it with the old province of Gaul—an idea towards which it gradually grew. Yet, if the observer allows his eye to dwell a little longer upon the British Isles, he may well conclude that the four-nations framework can obscure as much as it illuminates. This was an age when local and trans-national political associations were often paramount, the national hesitant and fragile. The shape into which political structures would ultimately settle was less certain than it may appear in retrospect. So it is with some of the many complexities and paradoxes that we begin.

The reader of twelfth-century historians can distil from them an agreeably familiar picture of the British Isles. William of Malmesbury, for instance, who like Henry of Huntingdon maintained the traditions of Bede and the *Anglo-Saxon Chronicle*, travelled widely around the libraries of English cathedrals and religious houses, gathering up the English past and handing it on to the Normans. In his *History of the Kings of the English* and its sequel, the *Historia Novella*, he produced a connected account from early Anglo-

Saxon times to 1142. He displays a clear perception both of the kingdom of England and of its neighbours: the English rulers whose deeds he recounts dealt with kings of the Scots to the north, kings of the Britons (Welsh) to the west, and—now and then—Irish kings across the sea. William's contemporary, Geoffrey of Monmouth, composed a largely legendary *History of the Kings of Britain*, in which he sought to stimulate and satisfy the curiosity of the Normans about the peoples they had come to dominate. His story of the division of Britain between the three sons of the Trojan Brutus suggests an island that readily falls into the component parts, England, Wales, and Scotland. Half a century later, Gerald of Wales could write books specifically about Ireland and Wales and their inhabitants, and plan to follow them with a description of Scotland too. These national units are, however, of limited and unequal value for the purposes of political description.

The idea of an English kingdom was a potent one. It owed much to Bede, who related how Pope Gregory the Great in 597 had sent the mission of St Augustine to the *Angli* ('English'). This concept of a Christian English people was important because it could embrace the various Anglo-Saxon kingdoms within the island of Britain; it also had the effect of excluding the Britons, who, according to Bede, were guilty of resisting Augustine's authority. The sense of a national identity, in the form of a province of the universal Church, had thus already taken a firm hold among the learned when the Wessex kings expanded their power during the ninth and tenth centuries. Alfred and his successors appropriated it, and gave it a political substance it had not possessed before. In time it incorporated the Scandinavian elements in the population of the midlands and north, and it was part of the legacy that fell first to Cnut and then to William of Normandy in the eleventh century. William became 'king of the English'; he had close links with Canterbury, where Lanfranc, the successor of Augustine, personified the ecclesiastical side of English unity. The combination of a developed idea of a kingdom and an established, effective kingship made England unusual; it differed not just from France but even more from Italy, where monarchical structures had collapsed in the tenth century, and the notion of a kingdom was kept alive primarily by the lawyers, whose documentary formulas required it.

Ireland too had a sharply etched, though differently constituted, identity. It owed much to the fact that men had long understood that the country was an island, and one which had remained outside the orbit of the Roman Empire and Germanic invasions. It also sprang from the sense of a shared Christian past, expressed above all in the cult of St Patrick. This awareness had been preceded and nourished by an ancient cultural unity, represented and consciously fostered by a hereditary class of lawmen, poets, and historians, to which the clergy became in part assimilated. The raids of the Vikings and their settlements in the east and south had led to a sharpening among the learned classes of the sense of being Irish, and Christian, in contrast to the pagan outsider. Their view is displayed in the early twelfth-century compilation *The War of the Gael with the Foreigners (Cogadh Gaedhel re Gallaibh)*, which presents the Viking age as a national struggle to defeat the invader. In reality, however, Ireland had been, and remained, politically fragmented. Power lay in four or five pro-vincial·dynasties, which had not yet smothered the pretensions of a number of other royal kins, among them the Norse rulers of Dublin. The major kings competed for the rank of 'king of Ireland', which court historians and poets dangled before them. (*The War of the Gael with the Foreigners* was actually written to promote the claims of the contemporary O'Briens, whom it portrays as leading a general resist-ance to the Vikings.) Although by 1100 the Scandinavian enclaves were Christian and had been to a large extent absorbed into the economic and political life of the island, which they greatly quick-ened, the absence of a single ruling house meant that there was no all-embracing political structure within which a blending of tradi-tions could occur. Whereas in England there was a rough harmony between the idea of the kingdom and its actuality, in Ireland the dissonances are more apparent.

For the political historian Wales is in some ways a more awkward concept than Ireland. To the east it lacked defined boundaries; indeed in Bede's day north Wales was associated with the British kingdom of Cumbria or Strathclyde, which had only slowly been dismembered by Northumbrian and Viking attack and through expansion by the kings of Scots. Like the Irish, the Welsh had many kings. Although the rise of large overlordships was a feature of the tenth and eleventh centuries, the resulting kingdoms were fissile: it is hard to discern the progress towards political unity that patriotic historians once took for granted. In Wales, as in Ireland, national consciousness had more to do with a common language, culture, and view of history than with political organization. The Welsh saw themselves as descendants of the Britons; their sense of identity is also apparent in the use of the term *Cymry* ('people of one region'). But not until the late twelfth century did native rulers begin to describe themselves as kings or princes of 'North Wales' or 'South Wales'; they did so in the context of dealings with the English Crown, which promoted a clearer sense of territorial rule. Awareness of the British past, both real and imaginary, was specially relevant to the clergy, who were anxious to resist Norman encroachment. The *Chronicle of the Princes* (*Brut y Tywysogyon*) occasionally presents the wars of kings of the eleventh and twelfth centuries as part of a national resistance to the intruder. But whether the horizons of such leaders and their warbands stretched much beyond their own interests and networks of alliance may be questioned. The chronicle itself hovers on the brink of irony when it tells how Gruffydd ap Rhys, king of Deheubarth, in 1116 'gathered round him many young hotheads from all sides, lured by a desire for booty or by an urge to restore and to renew the Britannic kingdom'.[1]

What we can scarcely help thinking of as Scotland is still more problematical. The lands north of the Tweed and Solway included areas of Gaelic, English, and Norse speech, and lacked the comparative cultural homogeneity of Ireland and Wales. Since the ninth century there had been in northern Britain a powerful dynasty, descended from Kenneth mac Alpin (d. *c*.858), producing kings 'of the Scots'. The terms 'Scot' and 'Scotland' bristle with ambiguities. *Scotus* originally meant a Gael, or Irishman, and referred to the settlement of parts of western Scotland from north-east Ireland in the fifth and sixth centuries. Kenneth's rule had been over an agglomeration of Gaelic and Pictish population groups in the north and west; and in the twelfth century the term *Scotia* still normally meant the regions north of the Forth. By 1100, however, the descendants of Kenneth were based in the south and east, having established a firm grip on English-speaking Lothian. The paradox is visible in th. ecclesiastical sphere. Donald Bán (d. 1097) was the last king of Scots to be buried on Iona, at the island church of the Irish St Columba. Donald was a throw-back; the dynasty's religious associations were by this time much more with the cults of St Andrew in Fife and St Cuthbert at Durham, reflecting the shift in the geographical basis of its power. As a kingdom Scotland was still very much in the making. The authority of the kings of Scots was barely nominal in Galloway or Moray; in Argyll or Caithness, as of course in the Isles, it faded out in the face of a world of virtually autonomous chiefs under the loose overlordship of Norway. It was only gradually that the kings expanded their power, identified all northern Britain with themselves, and gave the inhabitants of their ethnically diverse lands a common identity as subjects of a *rex Scottorum*.

Effective as the English kingship was by 1100, and significant as concepts of Ireland, Wales, and Scotland may appear from a later standpoint, it would clearly be ill advised to allow a political study to be shaped entirely by such a matrix. Indeed twelfth-century writings themselves suggest other arenas within the British Isles that call for attention. William of Malmesbury represents the main English chronicle tradition; it was a southern one, which drew its logic from the success of the house of Wessex and the church of Canterbury. There was as yet, for obvious reasons, no school of historiography associated with Scotland. What did exist, however, was a northern tradition visible in such works as the *Historia Regum* (attributed to Simeon of Durham), the chronicle of John of Hexham, or the *Chronicle of Melrose*. This tradition was far from separate: the *Historia Regum* drew on southern sources such as the Worcester chronicle, and Bede was of course basic to northern and southern writings alike. It is also true that works connected with Durham distinguished between England and Scotland, especially when dealing with the resistance of Scottish bishops to the claims of the archbishop of York. None the less in the pages of these historians there is little feeling of an Anglo-Scottish political border. Scottish kings rub shoulders with Northumbrian lords; the interests of religious houses and secular magnates readily cross the Tweed; all share a devotion to Cuthbert, whose translation in 1104 was attended by Alexander, brother and eventual successor to Edgar, king of Scots. The gap between the north and the rest of England (like that between the lands north and south of the Forth) was in most respects more marked than that between England and Scotland. It is evident in Geoffrey of Monmouth. Although Geoffrey could adopt a tripartite arrangement of Britain, the division that frequently occurs in his work is a simpler one, along the line of the Humber. It appears, for instance, when the brothers Belinus and Brennius share the island, the former taking the south and the latter ruling from the Humber to Caithness. In the later stages of the *History* Geoffrey has the beleaguered Britons holding the regions south of the Humber against the Anglo-Saxons who have occupied the north.

Sources from the west are also thought provoking. The *Chronicle of Man and the Isles*, written at the Cistercian abbey of Rushen on the Isle of Man, like the Welsh *Chronicle of the Princes*, draws the reader into a maritime arena that has received less attention than it deserves, partly because documents are few, and partly because its future was limited. The kingdom of Man formed part of the wider realm of the Isles which was subject to Norway. It was the hub of a Norse–Celtic orbit of power and plunder that took in Dublin, Anglesey, the Hebrides, Caithness, Orkney and Shetland; its pull was also felt strongly in much of Ireland and Wales as well as Galloway and Argyll. Its significance is clear in the *History of Gruffydd ap Cynan*. Written towards the end of the twelfth century, it tells the story of Gruffydd, ruler of north Wales, who had died in 1137 after a stormy career lasting more than sixty years. The details are often sparse or dubious but the importance of Ireland is beyond doubt. Gruffydd is said to have been born in Dublin; in his old age he gave gifts to Irish churches. His ancestry on his mother's side was part Gaelic and part Norse. For him, as for many of his kind, Dublin and Leinster were places of refuge and a source of armed support. His alliances and enmities spanned the Irish Sea just as they traversed Irish, Welsh, Scandinavian, and Norman society. For much of Gruffydd's career the most powerful Irish ruler was Murchertach O'Brien (Muirchertach ó Briain) of Munster (d. 1119). He too cut a figure in this seaborne world. In 1094 he drove out the current Norse king of Dublin, and within two or three years his own nephew was ruling on the Isle of Man. The phase ended in 1098 when King Magnus of Norway sailed into these southern extremities of his realm. Magnus not only asserted his authority in Man and the Isles; he exacted services from the men of Galloway, and also helped to put an end to Norman expansion along the coast of north Wales.

The involvement of the Norwegian king serves as a reminder that the British Isles, as well as resisting our attempts to divide them into neat political units, were not self-contained. The Normans, while they interested themselves in the traditions of England and Wales (and later of Scotland and Ireland), were conscious of their identity, and moved within their own political sphere, as the *Ecclesiastical History* of Orderic Vitalis, one of the most prolific of early twelfth-century chroniclers, shows. Orderic, who was born of a Norman father and an English mother, grew up in the Welsh borders, but went on to spend the greater part of his life as a monk at St Évroul in southern Normandy. Within the larger unity of Latin Christendom which was his primary home, he inhabited an Anglo-Norman world without internal frontiers; the kings, knights, and clergy whose deeds he records ranged through much of Britain as well as Normandy and the adjacent provinces. The same contours are apparent in the writings of Robert of Torigni, a monk of Bec who went on to be abbot of Mont-Saint-Michel, on the borders of Normandy and Brittany, from 1154 to 1186. Robert wrote in the Norman tradition of Dudo of St Quentin and William of Jumièges. For him Norman history had expanded to incorporate Britain: not only does his narrative take in the activities of the Normans on the other side of the Channel; he had assimilated the works of Geoffrey of Monmouth, Henry of Huntingdon, and others. Geoffrey's *History* has its own contemporary resonances. He has Sir Bedevere governing Normandy for King Arthur, and places his eventual burial in the city of Bayeux, which his grandfather is said to have founded. The *History of Gruffydd ap Cynan* also strikes a relevant note when it presents Rollo, the ancestor of the Norman dukes and kings, as a kinsman of Gruffydd's Norse mother.

The variety and complexity of perceptions reflects an age of overlapping political spheres which were subject to constant reshaping. Attitudes and attachments might be formed within ancient units such as the kingdom of Northumbria, which had once stretched from the Humber to the Forth, or within a newer construct such as the Anglo-Norman realm. These were not necessarily less significant than the embryonic national entities with which they coexisted; nor were men confined by one set of associations that took emphatic precedence of all others. It follows that any attempt to present the political history of the period as though it were set in a single mould is bound to distort. But perhaps one broad distinction, crude though it may be, serves to bring a number of essential features into focus: between southern and midland England on the one hand, and the remainder of the British Isles on the other.

In an age when the ability of rulers to control territory remained limited, the dominance of the English kings over the region that lay south and east of a line running approximately from Exeter to Chester and the Humber was remarkable; nowhere else in northern Europe was royal power so effectively institutionalized over so large an area. The most basic things favouring concentration and stability of authority were the relative absence of the obstacles physical geography can present to government, and the agricultural wealth available to be tapped. Openness to political and religious influences from the Continent was also helpful. Royal power was manifested in a network of shires, and in the dense distribution of boroughs, each with its mint where the regal silver coinage, which owed much to Carolingian models, was struck. Within this region was a smaller core where kingly control was even more intensive. Most of the royal estates of the late Anglo-Saxon period lay around and south of the Thames; this inner heartland of the monarchy contained London, the wealthiest borough, Canterbury, the ecclesiastical capital, and Winchester, the ancient centre of the Wessex kings, where their treasure was stored. But, although royal power faded somewhat as it moved outwards from Wessex and Kent, it did not decline steeply until it reached the Severn and the Humber.

The northern and western parts of the British Isles, by contrast, while they contain extensive cultivable districts (which were to play a prominent part in the history of kingship in Ireland and Scotland), are characterized by upland, bog, and lake; they also have long coast-lines in relation to their land mass. If lowland England encouraged the precocious development of central administration, the north and west favoured looser, more fragmented lordship. Control there was less firmly territorialized; frontiers tended to be zones of competition rather than lines of demarcation; and political supremacies, like raiders, showed few signs of stopping at the sea coast.

On the face of it, the contrast is nicely symbolized by the capture of York by King Eadred in 954. York was closely linked to Norse Dublin, from where some of its kings had come. The event looks like the triumph of the expanding land-empire of Wessex over a realm that spanned the sea. But the fall of York did not herald the reduction of the north to the condition of the southern heartlands of the monarchy; to the English kingdom of the century before 1066 York, the most northerly borough and mint, remained an outpost in a region that had yet to be assimilated. As in Roman times, it monitored a vast area containing a number of significant powers, which included the king of Scots; and it was still readily drawn into a Scandinavian orbit, though now by way of the North Sea rather than the Irish Sea. If in Northumbria what met the southern eye was a collection of powerful individuals and kins rather than an Anglo-Scottish border, to the west the position was equally fluid. The northern part of the old kingdom of Cumbria or Strathclyde had been absorbed into the sphere of the kings of Scots, who used it as an apanage for members of their family (Duncan, the future victim of Macbeth, presided over Strathclyde before becoming king of Scots in 1034); but we know almost nothing of what their rule—if it may be so described—amounted to. 'English' Cumbria, its southern part, was subject to raids by Northumbrians and Scots. But its local lords were hardly controlled by any outside power; the agonizing of historians over whether it 'belonged' to England or Scotland has an anachronistic aroma.

During the decades after 1066, when the north frequently presented a threat to the Conqueror and Rufus, southern direction began to acquire additional firmness. The castle and cathedral at Durham emerged as a base for royal influence sixty miles north of York, and in 1080 Robert Curthose, the Conqueror's eldest son, established the first castle at Newcastle upon Tyne. As aristocratic colonization spread, the Pennine lordships were beginning to take shape, as was the tenurial map of the future Lancashire. In 1092 William Rufus built a castle at Carlisle and provided for its security by encouraging settlement in its vicinity. Despite such developments, the Norman kings had only a limited grip on the north, which remained remote from their normal habitat. Rule north of the Humber still meant local alliances bolstered by occasional visitations and tribute-taking.

Beyond England lay a multiplicity of kings, inhabiting a vast arc of land and sea where the main political features were incoherence and fluidity. The kings of Scots, it is true, were an exception, in that they had a firm, though restricted, territorial core and a comparatively stable dynastic history. Their proximity to Northumbria and Cumbria made them intermittently threatening to English kings based far to the south. If—as happened temporarily between 1136 and 1157—they had absorbed the far north of England, they would have created a power-base which, while still inferior in size and wealth, might have faced the rulers of lowland England with a serious rival. Wales lacked an equivalent of the Scottish kingship. Its terrain was hostile to political consolidation except on a local level. The eastern borders were close to the English royal heartlands, and had long been vulnerable to English incursions which deprived kings in Gwent or Powys of the resources that were vital if their authority were to grow. Power clustered most readily in the coastal lowlands of Gwynedd and Deheubarth, which were separated by intractable mountain ranges. As Gruffydd ap Cynan's career shows, a successful

Welsh ruler had to concentrate on moving skilfully beyond Wales as well as building a political system within it. Ireland's greater size and economic possibilities allowed the emergence of kings whose resources and geographical impact may have outstripped those even of the kings of Scots. But they were a less stable phenomenon. Ireland lacks a seat of economic and political gravity as decisive as that formed by the English, or even the Scottish, lowland zone. The nearest equivalent—the rich and central lands of north Leinster and Meath with their outlets on the Boyne and Liffey—was a region over which a number of dynasties contended. The secret of the great, though transitory, repute of the O'Briens lay in their ability to dominate both this area and the wealthy Shannon basin where their origins lay.

The contrast between the weight and concentration of kingly power in lowland England and the weaker, more splintered kingship of the west and north finds a reflection in the way the English kings portrayed themselves. From the tenth century the West Saxon rulers claimed a general authority over the other kings of Britain. An early example comes from 934, when King Athelstan led a campaign to the north, taking hostages from the king of Scots. At Nottingham he issued a charter, recording his grant of Amounderness (the region north of the Ribble) to the archbishop of York, in which he describes himself as 'king of the English, elevated by the right hand of the Almighty, which is Christ, to the throne of the whole kingdom of Britain'; among the witnesses were the Welsh kings, Hywel, Morgan, and Idwal, who presumably were present in his army.[2] Such titles are common in later charters: we find Aethelred II in the 990s calling himself 'ruler of the English and governor of the other adjoining nations round about', 'emperor by the providence of God of all Albion', and 'king of the English and governor of the whole orbit of Britain'.[3] So too were instances of attendance and service by other kings, the most famous being in 973 when King Edgar was rowed on the Dee at Chester by six (or eight) sub-kings from Wales and Scotland.

To accept this picture of the English kingship at face value would of course be to swallow Anglo-Saxon propaganda whole. Like some grander imperial vistas, it was highly contrived: the Byzantines, for instance, presented the messy surrounding scene as a neat hierarchy of subordinate rulers in obedience to Constantinople. Similarly, Anglo-Saxon documents may tell us more about the outlook of the kings and clergy who produced them than about the control that was exercised in practice. Dominance over rulers in Wales was asserted spasmodically, sometimes in the face of a contrary pull from Ireland. We have recently been warned against interpreting all dealings between the West Saxons and the house of Kenneth mac Alpin as submissions by the latter to the former, when in fact they may have been closer to alliances. Our knowledge comes from southern English sources, and some details are preserved only by twelfth-century chroniclers who may have given distant incidents a gloss appropriate to their own day. It is difficult to obtain an accurate impression of the role of the Scottish kings in their own environment, which remains almost wholly silent.

Yet to deny significance to the authority claimed by the English kings would be perverse. It was rooted in a real disparity of power between the West Saxons and the other dynasties of Britain. Appearances by one ruler at the court of another were themselves redolent of subordination: in the Gaelic Irish tradition, which was an important part of the background of the Scottish kings, the term 'to go into the house of' was a synonym for submission; even before 1066 estates in England were earmarked for the support of the northern rulers on their journeys south. It is difficult to imagine the English rulers paying court to, or serving in the armies of, Welsh or Scottish kings. If this English ascendancy found practical expression only now and then, the same was true of the lordship wielded by the rich German kings of the period over their Slav neighbours. The conventions existed; they might fall into disuse; but on the English side they would not be forgotten, and in favourable circumstances might be given additional content.

The reigns of William the Conqueror and William Rufus saw recurrent challenges on the outskirts of the kingdom, which led the kings into forceful assertions of their overlordship. The career of Malcolm Canmore, king of Scots from 1058 to 1093, was punctuated by submissions; the most comprehensive took place in 1072 when the Conqueror led an army to Abernethy and imposed his will on him in the midst of his own land. After Malcolm was killed on a raid into the north of England in 1093, his sons, Duncan II and Edgar, were dependent on Rufus's support against their uncle, Donald Bán. In a Durham document, Edgar speaks of himself as king 'by the grant of my lord, William, king of the English, and by paternal inheritance'.[4] In 1099 his status as a sub-king was made abundantly plain when he carried a ceremonial sword at Rufus's court. In Wales English authority was manifested as much in response to the activities of Norman barons as of native kings, but the result was a similar intensification of lordship. English power had, as it happened, been strongly asserted on the eve of the Conquest. In 1063 the future King Harold had put an end to the threat posed to the west midlands by Gruffydd ap Llywelyn, who had presided over one of the short-lived associations of north and south Wales. North Wales had then been shared by two native rulers who became tributary to Edward the Confessor. In 1081 William I journeyed as far west as St David's, where he almost certainly gave his blessing as overlord to Rhys ap Tewdwr of Deheubarth. At the time of Domesday Book, Norman power was shown by the fact that Rhys was said to hold south Wales of the king at an annual rent of £40, while north Wales was now held for the same sum, not by Gruffydd ap Cynan, then in exile in Dublin, but by Robert 'of Rhuddlan', the earl of Chester's kinsman and chief adjutant.

Norman domination had another significant face. The crystallizing of the idea of a kingdom of the English had owed much to the Church, and the interests of the West Saxon kings had remained closely intertwined with those of Canterbury. The early Norman archbishops, Lanfranc and Anselm, were acutely aware of the status and rights of their see, a matter that was readily linked with the king's position as overlord of Britain. Their main concern was to establish their authority over the archbishops of York. But the primacy question had far-reaching implications. York itself claimed authority in Scotland, where there was no archbishopric. In addition Canterbury was aware that the more widely it could command obedience outside the northern province, the more easily its primatial rank would be justified and enhanced. It advanced its claims in Wales, asserting its jurisdiction over St David's and Llandaff. As early as 1074 Lanfranc received a profession of obedience from Patrick, the second bishop of the Norse see of Dublin, who addressed him as 'primate of the Britains' (*primas Britanniarum*), a title that echoed 'the orbit of Britain' over which earlier English kings had claimed sway.[5] Lanfranc then took it upon himself to address admonitory letters about Church discipline to the king of Dublin, and even to Turlough (Toirrdelbach), the father of Murchertach O'Brien.

The immediate impact of Canterbury's involvement with Ireland was slight; it did not have high priority among the archbishops' many urgent concerns. But the connection was to be an important part of the background to Henry II's intervention there nearly a century later. That fact sums up the significance of overlordship in general. A potent idea, which required only a little practical sustenance, it could be given closer definition and wider application by a monarchy and aristocracy with the resources and inclination to do so. This was what happened during the twelfth and earlier thirteenth centuries, at a time when many of the political features familiar in lowland England expanded to take in large parts of the world that lay beyond.

2. Empires, Continental and British

THE Norman Conquest inaugurated four centuries during which the history of the British Isles was intertwined with that of northern and western France. The connection intensified and relaxed by turns; more than once it changed its forms. But until Henry VI lost his grip on Gascony in the early 1450s, it was an inescapable fact. Between 1066 and the fall of Normandy and Anjou to Philip II in 1204 the political and social web that stretched across the Channel was particularly tightly woven; it unravelled only slowly and incompletely over the next fifty years. The twelfth and early thirteenth centuries were a time of significant changes in the distribution and organization of power in the British Isles, visible in the development not just of the English but also of the Scottish monarchy. Those changes can only be understood when they are viewed against the background of cross-Channel political structures.

For all but twenty-five of the years from 1066 to 1204 the king of England was ruler of Normandy. The accession of Henry II in 1154 restored the Anglo-Norman link, which had been broken during Stephen's reign; it also created a vast dominion embracing in addition Henry's inheritance from his father, Geoffrey of Anjou, and the lands of Eleanor of Aquitaine, whom he had married in 1152. By the 1170s the incorporation of Ireland and the establishment of suzerainty over the king of Scots and the count of Toulouse meant that Angevin lordship, generously regarded, stretched from Connacht and the Scottish lowlands to the Pyrenees and almost to the Mediterranean. The notion that such a widespread supremacy meant 'imperial overstretch' and a dissipation of power springs more readily to the modern mind than it did to the contemporary one. The successful kings of the age—Henry I, Henry II, and Richard I—spent more time on the Continent than in England. The two Henrys each ruled for thirty-five years; they made, respectively, twenty-one and twenty-five Channel crossings. Virtual confinement to one side or the other—as experienced by Robert of Normandy, Stephen, or King John in his later years—signified failure and promoted discord. John's grasping stay in his British lands did lead to a deepening of royal control on

1. The Norman and Angevin kings, 1066–1272

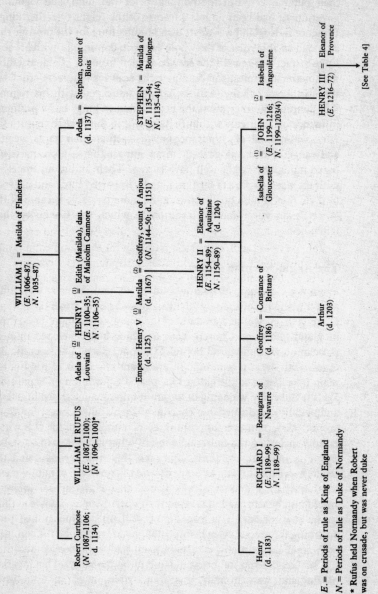

E. = Periods of rule as King of England

N. = Periods of rule as Duke of Normandy

* Rufus held Normandy when Robert was on crusade, but was never duke

their outer edges. But the political price was high, and vigour in government had been no less a feature of the reigns of earlier kings. Presence in England was on its own no substitute for the prestige that attended an able ruler of the whole Angevin dominions, with his ability to attract and reward the service of men from far afield, assemble multinational armies, and dominate the seaways that were crucial to the aristocracy, clergy, and merchants associated with his regime. The continental interests of the post-Conquest kings had a profound influence on their rule within Britain. But in the twelfth century the effect was not that of a hindrance or a distraction: their status, wealth, and range of contacts gave them an impact that a more narrowly based monarchy might well have lacked. Their ambitions, together with the need to protect far-flung lands, imparted force and urgency to their rule. Those qualities were the more palpable because of the West Saxon governmental tradition to which the Conqueror had fallen heir.

The Anglo-Norman realm

From the Conquest, Britain was linked to, and in many ways integrated with, one of the most dynamic powers of continental Europe. Duke William was in command of the energies of a vigorous aristocracy and reforming Church, both of which had developed in close association with the ducal house. The appearance of aristocratic lineages, with defined territorial interests and the habit of passing the main inheritance to the eldest son, placed a premium on expansion. For the duke, the widening of his area of dominance raised his status and, vitally, confirmed his control of men's allegiances; for those around him, it meant opportunities of enrichment for the whole family, including the cadets who might otherwise threaten its stability. The intimate connection between this military class and the Church—visible in gifts of property and the presence of family members in chapter and cloister—ensured that ecclesiastical interests would also benefit, and in their turn sharpen ducal and noble authority in new regions. The frontiers of William's influence had been enlarging for several years before 1066, notably through the conquest of Maine; his grip on Normandy itself had tightened, and with it his subjects' sense of being distinctively Norman. The invasion of England was, in that sense, an extension of an established pattern.

It had, however, another context. The connections of England with Normandy were many even before the Conquest. London and Rouen, leading economic centres of north-west Europe, were closely linked by sea and river. King Edward's reign (1042–66) had seen the appointment of French bishops to several English sees, and his donations to churches had included Rouen and Fécamp. Such links were accompanied, and advanced, by the association of the two ruling houses, sealed by the marriage in 1002 of Edward's parents, King Aethelred II and Emma of Normandy (who subsequently married Cnut). The Confessor had spent his youth in exile in Normandy, and in later life probably saw his kinsman, William, as his heir. His court attracted Norman warriors as well as clergy, among them the youthful Robert 'of Rhuddlan'. Hindsight may encourage us to place too much emphasis on the specifically Norman connection: there was interaction between England and the entire northern French littoral, and the Confessor's court was a cosmopolitan place where English, Scandinavians, Flemings, Bretons, and others mingled. But this scarcely defeats the point: William's army in 1066 was itself a mixed affair, in tribute to the spread of his reputation and recruiting-power during the previous decade.

Whether it is regarded from the Norman or the English side of the Channel, the emergence of the Anglo-Norman realm has a logic: the Conquest built upon an existing connection, and gave it primacy over the Anglo-Scandinavian link fostered by Cnut and his family, and eventually also over the maritime sphere of the west. In view of the economic, ecclesiastical, and political associations, and the proximity of northern France to the most developed parts of England, it is hardly surprising that the cross-Channel state came to possess a depth denied to some other dynastic unions of the period. It was—to compare it with the grandest contemporary example—far less superficial and clumsy than the linked kingdoms of Germany and Italy, whose rule demanded treks through the Alpine passes and the ability to cope with environments as different as the Slavonic frontiers and the cities of the Lombard plain. By contrast, the sea-crossings that punctuated the lives of the Anglo-Norman ruling groups were convenience itself, and the gap between English and Norman society barely perceptible.

The forces uniting Normandy and England were for several generations stronger than those that would have sundered them. The most obvious source of unity was the person of the ruler. Although William I at his death—whether out of respect for the convention that the eldest son received the lands the father had inherited while lands gained by military conquest or marriage were available to endow cadets, or because he was at loggerheads with his eldest son—divided the duchy and kingdom between Robert Curthose and William Rufus, there can be no doubt that the quarrels among his descendants were over the succession to the dominions as a whole. These formed their frame of political reference, as the moments of reconciliation show: in 1091 Robert and Rufus accepted that each was the other's heir; and Robert and Henry I came to a similar arrangement ten years later.

The unity restored when Rufus and Henry took control of Normandy in 1096 and 1106 respectively was not merely the product of the outlook of the royal house; it was promoted by powerful elements within the Anglo-Norman ruling class. By 1100 many aristocratic families held lands on both sides of the sea, and Norman religious houses had property scattered throughout England. For such interests, the separation of England and Normandy meant at best inconvenience, and at worst disinheritance. A story from 1101 preserved by Orderic Vitalis catches the difficulties well:

William of Warenne approached Robert, duke of Normandy, in great distress, and pointed out that he had suffered heavy loss on his account, since he had forfeited the earldom of Surrey which produced an annual revenue of a thousand pounds of silver for him; therefore, he asserted, it would be proper for Robert to become fully reconciled with his brother the king and intercede to secure the restoration of William's former honor.[1]

While by no means everybody of note was a major landholder in both Normandy and England, Anglo-Norman proprietorship, allied to a widespread maintenance of ties with places of origin, was a weighty influence for integration.

The management of the realm was something in which king, aristocracy, and clergy shared. Government reflected their cross-Channel character. The mobile royal household, with its military and clerical aspects, was the mainspring of the state. The king's constant migrations, on which he was accompanied by a large entourage, fostered coherence. He issued orders verbally or under the seal that had currency in all his dominions, gathered revenues into the chamber that formed part of the household, and dispensed justice in England and Normandy alike. His progresses could if the need arose become campaigns, in which case more of the magnates associated with his household would come to him in force, while his wealth would enable him to hire troops from the fringes of his lands and beyond. This central organization, which lay above the provincial structures of Normandy and England, was all the more effective for being peripatetic. It would be unwise to dismiss it as superficial: the unity it provided was little different, except in being far less shallow, from that which the French and German kings gave to the diverse regions over which each presided. The sea was not a serious obstacle to the exercise of a royal authority whose axis lay between London and Winchester on the one side and Rouen and Caen on the other, and which had Southampton and Portsmouth, Dieppe and Barfleur as its linchpins.

The shape of the Anglo-Norman realm confirmed lowland England as the main location of power within Britain. The cross-Channel state amounted to the union of the adjacent heartlands of the Norman dukes and West Saxon kings, and could give added strength to both. This is clear after Henry I had established himself on each side of the sea by 1106. For three decades he was the most effective overlord Britain had seen since the days of Athelstan and Edgar, and his rule in the outer areas had a depth which no tenth-century king could have matched. Having in 1102 defeated Robert's allies of the house of Montgomery-Bellême, whose interests stretched from Pembroke and Shrewsbury to Maine, he extended his power deep into Wales, rewarding men of his circle while retaining direct control of vital centres. Members of his administrative group, headed by Bishop Roger of Salisbury, organized and controlled south Wales. The baronial houses of Clare and Beaumont were among the bene-ficiaries, but these also included lesser men. Henry did not turn Dyfed into a single great lordship, but kept Pembroke in his own hands, encouraging a colonizing movement from across the Bristol Channel and planting a group of Flemings in the vicinity of Pembroke itself. Secular dominance was buttressed by the enlarge-ment of royal influence over the church in Wales, as is shown by the appointment of Bernard, the queen's chaplain, to the see of St David's in 1115. There was no attempt to re-establish Norman power along the comparatively inaccessible coast of north Wales; Henry's aim was not to conquer Wales but to ensure that both Norman and native aristocracies were responsive to him. Occasionally, as in 1114, a display of force was needed; but on the whole the Welsh kings accepted an overlord who was skilled at exploiting their divisions and attracting them to his court and the rewards of his service.

These events were paralleled by the growth of royal power in northern Britain. Here too men from Henry's circle were carriers of his authority as feudal settlement beyond the Ribble and the Humber continued. Many, such as Robert de Brus, to whom he granted extensive lands around the Tees, came from western Normandy and the Breton frontier, where his own interests before his accession had chiefly lain. The consolidation is symbolized by the appearance of a bishop at Carlisle, in obedience to York, in 1133, marking the detachment of Cumbria south of the Solway from the diocese of Glasgow. But Henry's influence was far from stopping at the Solway and the Tweed. Frontiers were porous, and the authority and security of a ruler measured by his impact beyond his territory. Unlike the first two Norman kings, Henry did not campaign in Scotland; but that was because he had no need to. In 1100 he had married Edith, or Matilda, a daughter of Malcolm Canmore. The queen's brothers were dependent figures. Alexander I (1107–24), who married Sybilla, one of Henry's illegitimate daughters, served him on the Welsh expedition of 1114. The future David I (1124–53) made his career at the Anglo-Norman court, becoming a prominent member of the royal circle, and acting as a justice in England. He was endowed with lands near Cherbourg in western Normandy and in Yorkshire, acts that symbolize his place among Henry's intimates. Henry also gave him the honor of Huntingdon, composed of a rich scattering of property mostly in the east midlands, by marrying him to Maud, a great-niece of the Conqueror, and steadfastly protected him against the claims of Maud's children by her first marriage. At about the same time (1113) Norman backing ensured that Alexander released much of Lothian and Strathclyde to him. Before and after he became king of Scots, David established his own men in southern Scotland; like himself, they were in many cases Henry's people too, the most striking instance being that of Robert de Brus, to whom he gave the strategic lordship of Annandale, fronting Galloway.

The advances of this period—involving the combined might of king, aristocrats, and churchmen—integrated western and northern Britain much more thoroughly with the English lowland core. One stimulus was Henry's need for security on the fringes of the British dominions from which he would often be absent: Pembroke, for instance, mattered because of the danger that its lords might find

2. The Scottish kings to 1286

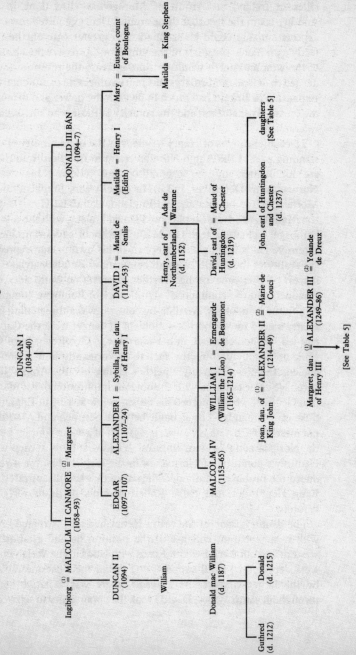

allies in Ireland, as Arnulf of Montgomery had done in 1102. Another lay in the fact that those around Henry required rewards, an expectation that could be satisfied with greater ease on the imperfectly assimilated outskirts of the kingdom. Moreover the absorption of the west and north would in time increase the revenues the king needed to defend, and enlarge, his more vulnerable continental lands. Expansion in Britain had much to do with the power and demands of the cross-Channel state, and the voracity of those who surrounded its ruler.

The achievements of Henry's time, and the impossibility of understanding part of the Anglo-Norman realm in isolation from the rest, are highlighted by the crumbling that followed his death in Normandy in December 1135. His sister's son, Stephen, count of Mortain, seized Normandy and England, excluding Henry's daughter, Matilda, to whom Stephen and David I, along with the rest of the baronage, had sworn fealty in 1127. The honor of Mortain included extensive lands in England; Stephen in his own person represented the reality of the Anglo-Norman connection. By his marriage to the heiress of Boulogne he had further interests on both sides of the Channel, and the commercial significance of Boulogne commended him to the Londoners. Matilda by contrast was a threatening figure. Henry's need for support at a moment of danger from the Capetians had led him to acquiesce in her marriage to Geoffrey, son of Count Fulk of Anjou, despite the fact that Normandy and Anjou were ancient enemies. Thereafter neither Henry nor the Anglo-Norman baronage came to terms with the obvious implication of the marriage, that Geoffrey would succeed his father-in-law as king of England and duke of Normandy. The struggle between Stephen and Matilda was not merely an English civil war; it was part of a wider conflict between the Norman and Angevin 'empires'. The worst blow to Stephen was Geoffrey's conquest of Normandy in the early 1140s, for it reintroduced the problems of divided allegiance that had disappeared when King Henry defeated Duke Robert and his partisans forty years before.

The disintegration of the realm Henry had reconstructed brought with it an apparent collapse of the position he had established in western and northern Britain. Lords with lands in the Welsh marches were deprived of royal support, and found their energies absorbed by the larger conflict. As a result, there was a native recovery throughout south Wales. David I took the opportunity to seize control of Northumberland and Cumbria. Newcastle upon Tyne and Carlisle were in his possession, and the latter became one of his usual residences; indeed it was there that Geoffrey and Matilda's son, Henry of Anjou (the future Henry II), went in 1149 to receive knighthood at his great-uncle's hands.

These events did not represent as catastrophic or straightforward a reversal as might seem at first glance. Although Anglo-Norman power in Wales shrank drastically, it retreated primarily from the areas, such as Ceredigion, where it had amounted to little more than loose overlordship. In those parts of south Wales where it had gained depth, above all through significant colonization, it held firm: centres from which recovery might be organized remained at Pembroke, Swansea, Carmarthen, Cardiff, or Brecon. The setbacks of Stephen's reign should not obscure the fact that Henry I and those whom he favoured had achieved the deepest and most durable penetration of Wales since Roman times. The change of fortunes in the north, for its part, was not without ambiguities. Where Malcolm Canmore had raided and taken tribute, David I stayed and ruled. His ability to do so sprang from the changes that had occurred in the region. The arrival of lay and ecclesiastical personnel, together with new castles and church buildings, betokened the emergence of a feudal society with the organization and stability to be taken over. It also mattered that David belonged to that same Anglo-Norman world: he presided over northern England less as an alien conqueror than as an alternative lord of an acceptable sort. His rule from Carlisle was a tribute to the successes of King Henry's reign, though it also hints at what was to become a familiar paradox: as Anglo-Norman rule spread out to the British peripheries, its features might be captured by neighbouring rulers, who could in favourable conditions exploit their gains to the disadvantage of the kings of the English.

The Angevin supremacy

The accession of Henry II to the English throne in 1154 restored the Anglo-Norman political link. But the realm ruled by Henry and his sons was very different from that of his grandfather. Its extent and diversity meant that, compared to the Anglo-Norman state, it lacked coherence. The dynasty's homeland was Anjou, which now formed a bridge between its northern and southern dominions. But it did not amount to a political centre of comparable weight to lowland England and Normandy, which were the most governmentally developed parts of the realm. Cross-Channel landholding revived on Henry's accession, but in general it continued to involve only Britain and Normandy, since Anjou, Poitou, and Gascony had their own customs, aristocratic circles, and ecclesiastical establishments—as well as their own disputed fringes.

It is not surprising that a long historiographical tradition has stressed the unwieldy character of the Angevin 'empire', and portrayed its rulers as engaged in an increasingly desperate struggle to maintain their monstrous assemblage of lands in the face of debilitating family quarrels and the relentless advance of the Capetian monarchy. The political elements common to their dominions amounted to little more than the unruly royal kin, together with the royal household and chancery. Such a unifying crust seems perilously thin in relation to the challenges of distance and diversity. Indeed Henry II's dispositions for the succession can be taken to suggest that he set little store by unity, for he intended to share his lands among his four sons (two of whom in the event predeceased him). Moreover the fact that the Angevins, unlike the Normans, did homage to the Capetians for some or all of their continental lands seems to diminish their stature.

Such an emphasis threatens to obscure the dynamism of the realm of Henry II and Richard I. It also provides an odd background to the expansion that took place within the British Isles. Recently, less pessimistic views of the Angevin polity have been offered. Growing awareness of the central position of the royal household in the political structures of the period makes it less easy to disregard the unity it provided. There was more exchange of personnel between the different parts of the realm, and more assimilation of custom (at least in England, Normandy, and Anjou) than was once imagined. And if—as has been strongly urged—John's defeat by Philip Augustus was the result of his own incompetence and a concatenation of unfortunate circumstances, rather than of an inherent imbalance between Capetian and Angevin resources, there is no reason to suppose that intermeshing could not in more propitious conditions have gone further. The dominions were effectively linked by sea, through royal centres of great commercial significance, from Dublin, Bristol, and Southampton to Rouen, La Rochelle, and Bordeaux. And although in the thirteenth century, the English nobility rejected newcomers

Map 2. The Angevin empire, c.1175

from Poitou, the hated Poitevin kinsmen, captains, and administrators of John and Henry III arrived in a climate of defeat and contraction that was peculiarly hostile to their reception.

Much of this remains controversial; we should not underestimate the difficulty of managing a large, composite realm in the late twelfth and thirteenth centuries, an age of written custom and bureaucratic growth, when provincial units were becoming more solid and self-aware. But it may serve as a warning against an unduly bleak presentation of the Angevin 'empire'. The history of the royal house itself should certainly be regarded in a more positive way. To dismiss the Angevin lands as a mere 'family assemblage' is less than helpful in the light of modern studies that reveal the essentially familial character of the Capetian 'state'; the two appear to have had much in common, not least in their stress on the integrity of the territorial core, and in the part played by cadets in penetrating peripheral regions. Angevin convention going back to the eleventh century favoured primogeniture for the main body of the inheritance. Henry II intended his eldest son, Henry (d. 1183), to succeed to Anjou, Normandy, and England: that is, to all that he himself had inherited from his parents. When he died in 1189, Richard, the elder of his surviving sons (who was already installed in his mother's duchy of Aquitaine), took the whole realm, and proved well able to dominate both his surviving brother, John, who was lord of Ireland, and the descendants of the middle brother, Geoffrey (d. 1186), who had become count of Brittany by marriage. Upon the childless Richard's death in 1199, the expectation was that John would take his place as ruler, not that there would be a partition between him and his nephew, Arthur of Brittany. If the family was noted for its quarrels, that itself might be read as evidence of its wealth and power: whereas the clan of Anjou squabbled from Meath to Gascony, the younger brothers of Louis VII sank to the level of local counts, or entered the Church (a fate reserved for Angevin bastards). The problem was that such quarrels were exploited by the Capetians, who gained both from their own comparative lack of dynastic friction and from the sophisticated propaganda-machine based in Paris, a glittering centre of learning that the Angevin lands could not begin to rival, which promoted their royal status and the idea of France.

The impact of the revival of royal power, manifested in the reunion of England and Normandy, was soon apparent within the British Isles. Henry II took remarkably little time to recover the ground lost since 1135. Though his expeditions to Wales between 1157 and 1165 neither crushed the Welsh kings nor wholly restored the position the Crown and marcher lords had held in south Wales, he took native submissions, asserted his authority over the marchers, and was probably well content to preside over the fairly stable balance between the two that had emerged by the early 1170s. His dealings with Scotland were even more decisive. By attending David's court at Carlisle in 1149 he had seemed to accept the legitimacy of his position there. This attitude was unlikely to outlast his accession: since a key part of his political stance was to present himself as the legitimate heir of Henry I, he was bound to reclaim the lands and rights his grandfather had possessed. Events played into his hands. The death of David's son, Earl Henry of Northumberland, in 1152 was followed by David's own death in the next year. In 1157, when the Scots were ousted from northern England in return for the restoration of the honor of Huntingdon, Henry faced only the young Malcolm IV. The degree to which the wheel had turned is illustrated by Malcolm's anxiety to be dubbed a knight by Henry, a reward he received only when he and his brother William—who had succeeded his father as earl of Northumberland, and was thus the chief loser in 1157—served Henry on his expedition to Toulouse in 1159–60. This satellite status, distasteful as it no doubt was to the Scottish royal house, was a true reflection of the underlying disparity of power between the two rulers. For Malcolm there was some compensation in the shape of the entry he was given into a wider world.

William succeeded in 1165 and remained king of Scots until 1214. Resentment over the loss of Northumberland helped to shape his outlook, while his whole-hearted membership of Anglo-French aristocratic society meant that, like David I, he was well placed to exploit any difficulties Henry might encounter. None the less he remained enmeshed within the Angevin web. When in 1173–4 Henry faced a rebellion, led by his eldest son and backed by the Capetians, William followed his grandfather's example and invaded the northern counties. His younger brother David (d. 1219), who now held the earldom of Huntingdon, played a leading role in raising the east midlands against the king. The rising was overcome and William was captured while besieging Alnwick. Henry then imposed upon him the Treaty of Falaise, which set forth the terms of his subordination as they had not been spelt out before.

This submission was typical of a period when custom was more and more being defined in writing, a process that was accompanied by the enlargement of royal jurisdiction. In the past, submissions and attendances by Scottish kings had been essentially personal; theoretical implications for the status of the kingdom of Scots had probably been distant from the minds of the parties. The Falaise agreement, on the other hand, involved William in doing fealty explicitly for his kingdom. This might be regarded as no more than an up-to-date English interpretation of the relationship that had always existed between the two rulers. But it is clear that the treaty was a consciously punitive affair. William had given grave offence to Henry, who was undeniably his lord for lands in England; otherwise it is unlikely that Henry would have bothered to disturb the usual state of affairs. His main concern was to chastise a recalcitrant vassal and exact guarantees for his future good behaviour. He took homage and hostages not only from the king but also from the leading barons of Scotland (who would thus have an interest in restraining their king); he insisted on the subjection of the Scottish church to the church in England; and, in accordance with feudal convention, he demanded that a number of William's castles in southern Scotland be rendered to him. He thus pushed his lordship into Scotland as none of his predecessors had done, and unwittingly gave future generations a starting-point for debate about the constitutional relationship between the two kingdoms.

Even though the treaty was without time-limit and bound the heirs of the parties, so long as William proved tractable Henry had little interest in enforcing it to the letter. He occupied only three of the five castles he was entitled to; in 1185 he restored Huntingdon to David of Scotland; and in the next year he forwarded William's marriage to his own kinswoman, Ermengarde de Beaumont. When in 1189 William attended the coronation of Richard I, who was eager to raise money for the crusade, he was allowed to purchase the abrogation of the Treaty of Falaise. The truth is that, while the treaty had tightened the constraints upon William, the relationship was throughout determined less by legal definitions than by circumstances, of which the chief was the immensely superior power of the Angevin monarchy. William was almost as much a satellite in the years after 1189 as he had been before. During Richard's reign he raised his northern claims as a petitioner rather than through military action. Under John he by turns tried to strike a bargain, fished for Capetian support, and made hostile gestures; but none of these tactics could evade the fact of English superiority.

If the ease with which the Angevins retrieved the mastery of Britain that King Stephen had lost is telling, even more so is the momentous spread of their authority into Ireland. Groups of minor lords from south Wales had infiltrated south-east Ireland from 1169, initially as hired troops of Dermot MacMurrough (Diarmait Mac Murchadha), the king of Leinster who had been driven into exile by Rory O'Connor (Ruaidrí Ó Conchobhair) of Connacht, the current over-king of Ireland. In 1170 they were joined by a more substantial figure, Richard de Clare, nicknamed 'Strongbow', lord of Strigoil (Chepstow) and heir to an earldom of Pembroke which Stephen had created and Henry had refused to recognize. Within a short time Strongbow had married Dermot's daughter, been established as his heir, and assisted him to capture Dublin, with its vital position both within Ireland and on the western seas. When King Dermot died in May 1171, Strongbow showed every sign of stepping into his shoes as ruler of Dublin, Leinster, and possibly more besides. The alarming growth of his power was what precipitated King Henry's expedition to Ireland in the following October.

Henry stayed in Ireland for six months. In that time he accomplished much: marking out Dublin, Wexford, Waterford, and their hinterlands as royal demesne; regularizing Strongbow's position as his vassal for the truncated lordship of Leinster; installing Hugh de Lacy as his representative, and giving him a title to Meath, both to protect Dublin and to block expansion by Strongbow; presiding over a synod of the Irish church; and taking submissions from most of the major kings save for Rory O'Connor. All this might, it is true, have rapidly melted away; when Strongbow and de Lacy left Ireland with their troops in order to support Henry against the rebels in 1173–4, the conquest faltered. But in the event both lords proved doughty colonizers, while the passage of Leinster to the king on Strongbow's death in 1176 enlarged the royal interest in Ireland at a critical time. The half-century that followed saw an intensification of the activity of Anglo-Norman military and economic entrepreneurs in the southeast, and its extension into Munster, eastern Ulster, and even Connacht.

This expansion seemed to fly in the face of the agreement, usually known as the Treaty of Windsor, which representatives of Rory had made with Henry in 1175. Under it, Rory was accepted as a sub-king and as overlord of the Irish outside the royal lands and the lordships of Leinster and Meath, to which Henry's barons and knights were to be confined. It is improbable that Henry, well used to the fleeting nature of political balances in Wales, viewed the agreement with quite the solemn constitutional expectations invested in it by later historians. Even as a medium-term measure it was based on doubtful premisses. There was scant hope that Rory, especially now that he was shut out of Meath, would be able to discipline the resentful kings inhabiting the vast arc, broken by mountain and flood, that makes up the north and west of Ireland; by the 1180s he was scarcely able to manage his own kin. In this situation the colonizing lords were unlikely to be kept within the territorial limits of 1175. As early as 1177 Henry's own attitude had shifted; at the Council of Oxford he publicized his intention to assign Ireland to John, and also made speculative grants of large areas of Munster to Anglo-Norman lords. The latter action can at a pinch be seen as saving rather than breaking the 1175 agreement, which contained a clause promising Rory the assistance of Henry's people against any Irish kings who would not obey him—for the O'Briens, long-standing enemies of the O'Connors, had been specially recalcitrant. But there is no disguising the fact that, in the absence of a much more effective native over-kingship, the Anglo-Normans could not be kept within the bounds of the Treaty of Windsor, and that the Angevin kings had little option but to respond appropriately.

This brief summary has given events the emphasis favoured by most Irish historians since the 1940s. Reacting against older inter-pretations, which viewed Henry II as a greedy expansionist, they have presented the movement that by the early 1200s had carried Anglo-Norman power as far afield as Kerry, Athlone, and Coleraine as baronially driven. The Crown has been portrayed as reactive, defensive, and strictly limited in its ambitions. These shifts in inter-pretation have been helped by the reassessment of an earlier episode. In 1155 Pope Adrian IV issued the privilege *Laudabiliter*, permitting Henry to enter Ireland and assert his lordship with the object of forwarding church reform. One chronicler tells us that the king toyed with the idea of an expedition because he saw Ireland as a possible endowment for his youngest brother, William—only to be dissuaded by his mother. The events of 1171 might thus be seen as the fulfil-ment of a long-delayed ambition. But most scholars now agree that the obtaining of *Laudabiliter* was the work of Canterbury, which was trying to persuade Henry to support its claims to authority in Ireland, which had finally disintegrated in 1152, when the previous pope gave the Irish church four archbishops, including one at Dublin. There is indeed some evidence that Henry's council rejected a scheme put up by influential ecclesiastics. The dangers presented by the empire-building of Strongbow were to succeed where clerical promptings had failed.

Much of this is no doubt correct, and salutary. But it tends to ignore the difficulty of separating 'defensive' and 'aggressive' impulses when considering imperial regimes (whose expansion commonly takes place in response to threats, real or imagined). It also rests on a distinction between the interests and activities of monarchy and aristocracy that is not easy to sustain. The Angevin kings did not extend their power into Ireland in a fit of absence of mind, let alone reluctantly. In Ireland, as in Wales, there was of course tension at times between kings and individual lords, but on a broader view expansion and exploitation by Crown and aristocracy went side by side. The original intruders from south Wales were attracted by Ireland partly because conditions in their homeland were no longer friendly to their traditional enterprises; one of those conditions was the power of Henry II, who not only denied his favour to Strongbow, but also entered into agreements with Rhys ap Gruffydd, lord of Deheubarth, rather than backing marcher expansion. By crossing to Ireland, Strongbow and those around him did not escape Henry's influence, which followed them rather in the manner that Henry I's authority had penetrated south Wales itself two generations before. Just as Henry I had enlarged and deepened the royal presence on the northern shore of the vulnerable Bristol Channel, so his grandson took a grip on the other side of the Irish Sea, across which dangers had frequently come. The expedition of 1171 signalled the beginning of the end of the maritime free zone in the west, and the emergence of a second Angevin lake: the message is clear in the passing of the Scandinavian cities of south-east Ireland into the hands of the Crown.

These events had, from the royal point of view, positive aspects that are too often ignored. *Laudabiliter* was not used by Henry in 1171–2, but the negotiations of 1155–6 must have confirmed the belief that there was an English title to Ireland which needed only to be activated: the king did not hesitate to make grants to his own people, or to act as overlord of Irish kings. His retention in his hands of the Viking regions of eastern Ireland led naturally to the expectation of revenue, as did his feudal lordship over Anglo-Normans and his tributary lordship over native rulers. The royal centres of Dublin and Waterford (soon joined by Cork, Limerick, Athlone, and others) served as collecting-points and nuclei around which a system of administration would grow. From the accession of King John there is evidence of Irish treasure flowing into the royal coffers in England, Normandy, and Poitou; no doubt it had already been contributing to his income before 1199, for that was one of Henry's objects in passing the new dominion to his youngest son.

Ireland brought with it another very obvious boon: it made available a large, untapped area within which royal patronage might operate; moreover it did so at a time—a century after the Norman Conquest—when the scope for making grants of land in England had become very restricted. The puzzling neglect of this aspect of the infiltration of Ireland may spring from the enduring image of those who benefited from it as adventurers and renegades who belonged to the marches rather than the court, a distinction as problematical as that between the interests of Crown and aristocracy. The early wave of invaders from south Wales came from a region that had long felt the impress of royal authority. Strongbow himself was, like his Clare ancestors, at home close to the monarch as well as in the marcher penumbra. Nor is it too much to say that, from the moment of Henry II's arrival in Ireland, the major figures who gained property there came from the inner circles of the household and administration. The pattern is especially clear in 1185, when John was sent to take possession of his lordship. His expedition was supervised by Rannulf Glanvill, the justiciar of England. Two youngish, upwardly mobile figures from Rannulf's East Anglian set were introduced to Ireland as a result: Theobald Walter, the ancestor of the Butlers, and William de Burgh, ancestor of the Burkes, both of whom became landowners in Munster. Two more senior men, Bertram de Verdon and Gilbert Pippard, who belonged to the élite group who served Henry II in war and government in England and Normandy, also accompanied the expedition; their families became major landowners in Meath and Louth as a result. For none of these men did the acquisition of Irish property mean the abandonment of interests or curtailment of connections elsewhere: links with the court played a major part in the history of the Butlers and the Burghs over many generations, while the Verdons, in common with other families, maintained properties and active careers on both sides of the Irish Sea for decades. The colonization of Ireland had much in common with Norman colonization in Britain, and indeed with the earlier expansion of Normandy itself; it took its impetus from the union of a dynamic aristocracy and monarchy. We should not forget that the penetration of both Wales and Ireland was at its most effective when kings were strong, not when they were weak.

The impressive span of Angevin lordship in the British Isles in the later years of Henry II is visible in the chronicle of Roger of Howden, a secular clerk in royal service. In 1177, for instance, Roger describes Henry's distribution among his men of northern castles, including those of Roxburgh, Edinburgh, and Berwick, which he held under the Treaty of Falaise. He continues:

then the king went to Oxford, and in a general council held there he made his son, John, king in Ireland, by the grant and confirmation of Pope Alexander. At the same council the king was attended by Rhys ap Gruffydd, sub-king [*regulus*] of South Wales, Dafydd ab Owain, sub-king of North Wales, who had been given the king's sister [i.e. half-sister] in marriage, Cadwallon, sub-king of 'Delvain', Owain of Cyfeiliog, and Gruffydd of Bromfield.[2]

He continues with a detailed record of grants and appointments in Ireland, followed by a description of the return of the papal legate, Cardinal Vivian, from Ireland to England, stating that he then received Henry's permission to travel on to Scotland, where he held a council at Edinburgh. Other passages record Howden's own mission to Galloway in 1174, and reveal Henry's role in the dynastic quarrels of the princes of a province still far from fully absorbed into the Scottish kingdom. Though Howden's position meant that he was unlikely to pass up the chance to dwell on the part the Angevin court played in the political life of distant regions, Henry's reach and drawing-power cannot be gainsaid. He had as firm a base in Ireland as his grandfather had possessed in Wales. The Angevin metropolis had thrust decisively into a region where Anglo-Saxon and Norman political power had been minimal.

The making of the Scottish kingdom

The inferior status of the Scottish rulers, on which the main stress has been placed so far, did not prevent them from expanding their own control within northern Britain. By 1266 their kingdom had come close to achieving the dimensions of Scotland as we know it: the kings of Scots may be said to have 'made' Scotland in much the same sense that the Wessex monarchy, with the help of some finishing touches from the Normans, had created a kingdom of England. Their success, like King David's ability to rule the north of England between 1138 and 1153, owed much to men and techniques imported from the Anglo-Norman world—advantages that flowed in more readily precisely because of their satellite position. This was not an unusual or isolated phenomenon; we shall encounter parallels, albeit on a smaller scale, when we consider the more transient regimes of thirteenth-century Welsh princes in Chapter 5.

The spread of Scottish royal authority had similarities to that of its Norman and Angevin counterparts. The kings moved forward, impelled by the need to secure themselves against challenges, and to provide for the new aristocracy, which was a chief engine of their power. But there were also differences. Around 1100 Scotland was much less 'complete' than England. Until about 1215 opposition not infrequently came from segments of the royal kin itself, whose members found support in the unassimilated north and west. Moreover the Anglo-French court nobility were not displacing older aristocratic groups as comprehensively as the Normans had done in post-Conquest England: the king's control depended partly upon his ability to draw traditional figures into his service and, ultimately, to facilitate the merging of old and new. Thus the enlargement of the area of royal authority involved two processes, which often overlapped: the obtaining of a tighter grip on accessible regions, through the implanting of king's men and the development of administration; and the attachment of peripheral societies more effectively to the centre, through—initially—military force, diplomacy, and the growth of ecclesiastical structures. The result was a kingdom that, far more than England, was marked by varying intensities of royal rule.

Under David I and Malcolm IV the geographical expansion of the king's control was limited. It was most striking in the south-west, where the establishment of Anglo-Norman lordships such as Annandale and Cunningham, and the foundation of a Flemish colony around Lanark, heralded colonizing ventures significant enough to provoke native risings in Galloway in 1160 and 1174. It was William the Lion's reign that saw a more substantial extension of royal influence, especially northwards to the Moray Firth. Most of the evidence for this post-dates 1174; it may be that the spread of Henry II's power into Lothian under the Treaty of Falaise had the effect of encouraging William to devote his energies to the outer parts of his

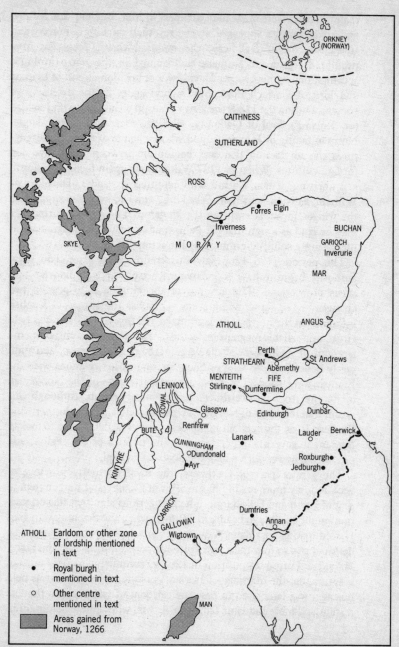

ORKNEY
(NORWAY)

CAITHNESS

SUTHERLAND

ROSS

Forres Elgin

Inverness

BUCHAN

SKYE

M O R A Y

GARIOCH
Inverurie

MAR

ATHOLL

ANGUS

Perth

STRATHEARN

St Andrews

Abernethy

MENTEITH

FIFE

LENNOX

Stirling

Dunfermline

COWAL

Glasgow

Renfrew

Edinburgh

Dunbar

BUTE

Lauder

Berwick

CUNNINGHAM

Lanark

Dundonald

Ayr

Roxburgh

Jedburgh

KINTYRE

CARRICK

Dumfries

GALLOWAY

Annan

Wigtown

ATHOLL Earldom or other zone
of lordship mentioned
in text

• Royal burgh
mentioned in text

○ Other centre
mentioned in text

Areas gained from
Norway, 1266

MAN

Map 3. Scotland in the twelfth and thirteenth centuries

realm. Grants were made to newcomers in Mar, Buchan, and Moray; and royal burghs appeared at centres such as Elgin, Forres, and Inverness. As in Galloway, the outward thrust seems to have prompted resistance: William campaigned in the north in 1179, accompanied by his brother David, whose position as earl of Lennox and lord of Garioch made him a vital agent in the extension of control. During the 1180s the king struck up an alliance with Lachlan (or 'Roland'), lord of Galloway, who had married into the Anglo-Norman family of Moreville, and whose change of name neatly captures the interaction that was beginning between the native and foreign cultures. When in 1187 William was again faced by a northern uprising, it was Roland who captured its leader, Donald mac William, a distant kinsman of the king, who had gathered support on the fringes for an attempt on the kingship. The general turbulence may be read as a sign that the behaviour of provincial magnates was increasingly being determined by the actions of the centre.

The period 1196–1266 saw this trend gather pace, and royal authority begin to have a decisive impact on the Scandinavian outskirts of Scotland. The advance of the kings was helped by two changes in the surrounding scene. One was the spread of English influence in the north of Ireland: from 1227 eastern Ulster was held either by a reliable magnate or by the Crown itself, thus curtailing the freedom of manœuvre available to Hebridean dynasties, and indirectly benefiting the king of Scots so long as his relations with the English were good. The other was the recovery of the Norwegian monarchy from its twelfth-century political trough. Although this meant that the kings of Norway were more active in the Northern and Western Isles, thus encouraging local rulers and candidates to look to Bergen, it gave a sharper focus to the politics of the region, and provided a power with which the Scots could deal.

The greater part of Caithness, the most northerly province of Scotland, lay more readily in the orbit of Orkney and Bergen than in that of Perth and Edinburgh. The first serious sign that this orientation might be changed came in 1196–7, when the Scandinavian Earl Harald rose against King William. He attacked Inverness, only to be defeated and to find the king exploiting rival candidates against him. Harald recovered his position in 1202 by submitting to William, and it seems that the marriage of Harald's granddaughter, who was held hostage, was later used to pass the earldom of Caithness to the less distant and more biddable family of Angus, who appear holding it in the 1230s. This amounted to light, indirect rule through diplomacy and the promotion of acceptable interests. But in the southern part of the province royal power acquired somewhat greater firmness, without ever approaching the depth it had in the land of burghs and sheriffdoms south of the Spey. From the time of Harald's rebellion the baronial house of Moray (*de Moravia*) rose to dominance with royal backing; by the 1230s they were using the title 'earl of Sutherland', signifying the region's separate identity from Caithness. Sutherland provided a base from which the Scottish church infiltrated Caithness and challenged the influence of the Norwegian bishops of Orkney: a rising against the imposition of tithes by Bishop Adam in 1222 is another sign of the penetration of the far north by the Scottish court. When Alexander II visited Inverness in 1236, he was entering a region far less detached from royal Scotland than it had been forty years before.

There was also a marked advance of the king's authority in the west. In 1197 William the Lion had founded a burgh at Ayr, establishing a royal centre well down the Clyde in a region already embraced by the lordships of the new nobility. Early in the thirteenth century the Stewart lords of Renfrew and Dundonald pushed their power north and west into Bute and Cowal. At this stage Galloway itself remained a virtual principality. But when Alan son of Roland died in 1234 with no legitimate son to succeed him, Alexander II acted forcefully to prevent his bastard son from seizing the inheritance with Manx and Irish support. Instead Galloway was divided between Alan's legitimate daughters, all of whom were married to members of baronial families; it is no coincidence that the royal sheriffdoms of Dumfries and Wigtown first appear at this period. Even more than in the north, the story was of the emergence of smaller political units which were more responsive to the centre.

The mid-thirteenth century saw the removal of Norway from the Western Isles and the deepening of royal control in Argyll, a region which, like Caithness, while it might be part of mainland Scotland, was inextricably involved with the political system of the adjacent islands. The Hebrides in theory belonged to the kingdom of Man and the Isles, itself tributary to the Norwegian king. In reality they were a patchwork of lordships mostly shared among the descendants of the maritime warlord, Somerled (d. 1164), who had also dominated Argyll. Under Alexander II Scottish power reached outwards. The king campaigned in Argyll in 1221–2, and the bishops of Argyll played a part similar to that of the bishops of Caithness. The Scottish expansion was paralleled by a more active attitude on the part of the Norwegian Crown: Islesmen were attracted to Bergen whenever possible, and the archbishops of Tröndjeim asserted their rights over the bishopric of the Sudreys (Sodor and Man). In 1248 Haakon IV sent a fleet into the contentious waters around Scotland; and in 1249 King Alexander died during an expedition to Argyll and Skye. By the 1260s Alexander III had hopes of bringing the Norwegians to agree to a settlement. The death of Haakon on an expedition to the Isles in 1263 was followed by the Treaty of Perth (1266), in which King Magnus transferred the realm of Man and the Isles to the Scots, in return for a payment of 4,000 marks and an annual rent of 100 marks as a recognition of past Norwegian lordship.

By this stage the Scottish kings had created, not so much a homogeneous kingdom, as a supremacy over local rulers of varied power and styles. Royal authority operated unevenly. At one extreme—as in Lothian, Fife, and much of Strathclyde—it was relatively intensive, with a close mesh of burghs and sheriffdoms. At the other—in most of the highland zone—it amounted to a loose presidency over distant lords, who no longer had an alternative allegiance. In between these poles were areas, from Carrick to Mar or Buchan, where significant royal centres existed within districts controlled by earls who were now mostly of mixed Anglo-Norman and native descent. The apt comparison may be less between the kingdoms of Scotland and England, than between Scotland and the empire of the English Crown in England, Wales, and Ireland.

The English sphere in the earlier thirteenth century

After 1204 the Angevin supremacy was a shadow of its former self. The loss of Normandy removed the region with the firmest ties with England, while the loss of Anjou severed the dynasty from its original roots. On the Continent, John and Henry III were left only with such lands south of the Loire as they could hold on to; and control of Poitou, with its strategic port of La Rochelle, was rapidly eroded by the Capetians during the 1220s. The eventual effect of these losses was to produce a political order more focused on England. But this did not happen overnight. Links with north-west France remained close, and, until the failure of Henry III's campaign in Brittany and Poitou in 1229–30, a significant group of barons shared his hope that

England and Normandy would soon be reintegrated. Thereafter Henry's own outlook remained that of a ruler who regarded Europe as his destined stage.

The hostility provoked by the 'foreigners' who thronged his court helped a more clearly English magnate community to crystallize. Its emergence has caught the attention of historians, distracting them not only from the surviving cross-Channel connections but also from the wider British and Irish scene. As the broad context once provided by the Angevin empire fades, the lines of demarcation between English, Scottish, and Irish historical writing seem to harden. This is a pity, for unity and assimilation, in a variety of guises, are among the more striking features of the earlier thirteenth century.

The loss of Normandy and Anjou did not inaugurate an age when kings, deprived of much of their continental inheritance, devoted themselves—as some later commentators have felt they ought to have done—to forming their insular lands into a more fully integrated state. Rather as William the Lion pursued his claim to Northumberland, John and Henry III set out to recover what they had lost in France. Yet John, under pressure of events, was an extremely active British overlord. Some of those discommoded by his failures—such as Strongbow's heir, William Marshal, earl of Pembroke, lord of Leinster, and of Longueville—had interests in Wales and Ireland, which drew the insecure king's attention to those areas. Moreover his search for the resources to fund a recovery on the Continent, together with his mere presence in England, led to a high level of governmental activity in outlying areas, such as Ireland and the far north of England, which drew them forcibly into the political cauldron. Henry III too, for all his familiar inadequacies, was in his middle years (*c*.1236–*c*.1257) active, and even effective, on the wider British stage. One of the most revealing moments came in 1245, when his Welsh expedition, which in many respects foreshadowed the more famous campaigns of Edward I, saw the shipment of supplies gathered by his Irish administration, and an attack on Anglesey led by the justiciar of Ireland, who had among his leaders of contingents King Felim O'Connor (Fedlimid Ó Conchobhair) of Connacht. This was a far cry from the days when enemies of Anglo-Saxon and Norman kings could find a safe hiding-place in Dublin.

The power of the English monarchy and the political assimilation of the British Isles are visible in many ways, some of which will be analysed more closely in the chapters that follow. The spread of direct rule is apparent in the scattering of royal centres as far afield as Newcastle upon Tyne, Carlisle, Chester (which came into Henry's hands in 1237), Montgomery, Carmarthen, Drogheda, Athlone, and Limerick; its dynamic quality is shown by its extension for the first time to Flint and Degannwy (1241–7), and in the growth of a more closely meshed shire organization in Ireland. Another measure of royal control is the lordship the king exercised over an aristocratic society that incorporated not merely England, but also the Welsh marches and much of Ireland; this superiority was expressed in rights over marriage and wardship which were now as effective in Pembroke or Munster as in the Home Counties. Moreover, the circle of those in homage to the king of England did not stop at the Anglo-Scottish border, since a significant (and increasing) number of major Scottish landholders had English property. The Crown's rights over the Church also stretched far beyond England. Royal approval was necessary for the election of bishops in Wales and Ireland. The bishoprics and canonries of the province of Dublin were colonized by royal servants as readily as those of English dioceses, and in time of vacancy the Crown could expect to exploit the temporalities of sees as far away as St David's, Connor (in Antrim), or Cloyne (in Cork).

Extending beyond these administrative and feudal aspects of rule was the king's lordship over other kings and ethnic lords. His relations with Welsh and Irish rulers fell into a similar pattern, though for obvious reasons dealings with the former were closer and more frequent than with the latter, who normally met royal authority in the guise of the justiciar of Ireland. While there might be argument, notably in the case of the princes of north Wales, about the implications of his overlordship, the overlordship itself was rarely challenged. In 1244–5 Dafydd ap Llywelyn of Gwynedd, oppressed by the weight of English authority, sought papal recognition as 'prince of Wales'. But, after his death in 1246, two of his nephews shared his lordships, in due obedience to Henry III. In 1258 Brian O'Neill (Ó Néill), the main Irish lord in Ulster, set himself up as 'king of the kings of Ireland'[3]—only to be defeated and killed by the local settlers of Down in 1260. Normally, however, royal authority was taken for granted: kinglets and princes looked to the king for justice and patronage, and responded to his military summonses. So too, quite often, did the kings of Man. Although they are commonly described as subject to the king of Norway, their position was not defined by some immutable law, but depended on practical considerations; with north-west England and eastern Ireland firmly under English control, they naturally looked as much to Westminster as to Bergen. The eventual Scottish acquisition of Man flew in the face of this fact, and was achieved largely because Alexander III did a deal with Norway at a time when the English polity was disrupted by the Barons' Wars: the Scots had good reason to agree to the annual rent that recalled the Norwegian title to the island.

The status of the Scottish monarchy is more problematical. There is no 'right' answer to the question whether Scotland was an autonomous kingdom: the theoretical position was ambiguous, and lent itself to contrary interpretations by the parties. In practice the king of Scots remained the king of England's inferior. There were moments, as in the 1260s, when English weakness allowed him considerable freedom of manoeuvre. There were long periods when relations between the royal houses were amicable—Alexander II's first wife was Henry III's sister, and Alexander III's his daughter—and his dependent status was not stressed. There were times too, as during the minority of Alexander III, when he welcomed the backing of his powerful neighbour against his own enemies. There is no doubt, of course, that the Scots would have preferred to cast off English claims definitively: Alexander II sought papal permission to place his kingship on a more elevated plane by acquiring the right to unction with holy oil as enjoyed by the kings of England and France at their coronations; and his second marriage, to a French bride, was a gesture of defiance. The English for their part might threaten to resurrect the Treaty of Falaise, or even to invade. But, given the disparity of power, there was little advantage for the Scots in trying to force legal issues; while the English, whose chief concern was security and stability, knew attempts at definition were likely to sour a relationship that was best kept in repair by diplomacy, and by threats that were veiled rather than naked. The Scottish kings, with their broad area of action, their own legal system, and their own regular foreign contacts, were on a different level from even the most powerful Irish, Welsh, and Manx rulers. But they too lay within the orbit of the English Crown, which was given additional strength by the cross-border lords. If there were two kingly empires in the British Isles, in important respects the greater incorporated the lesser.

The power of the king of England was manifested in a variety of ways. He could afford to allow, and indeed encouraged, the holding of property within his territories by the peripheral rulers. Llywelyn ab Iorwerth of Gwynedd (Llywelyn the Great), his son Dafydd, and Gruffydd ap Gwenwynwyn, the lord of southern Powys, all held land in English shires. Reginald, king of Man, was tied to John and Henry III by a knight's fee in County Louth and an annual stipend from the Dublin exchequer. The O'Connors of Connacht held districts within the king's Five Cantreds near Athlone. The Scottish kings remained vassals of the English for lands in England. In 1237 the death of Alexander II's cousin, Earl John of Huntingdon and Chester, leaving only sisters to succeed him, meant the break-up of the honor of Huntingdon, which had been for so long associated with the Scottish royal house. Relations were then set on a new footing by the Treaty of York, in which Alexander abandoned the ancient claim to Northumberland, and was given instead the the honor of Penrith in Cumberland, for which Alexander III did homage to Henry III.

Attendances at court also testify to the pull of the English Crown. In 1240 Felim O'Connor visited Henry III; Henry sent him home 'in safety, happy and cheerful'.[4] In the same year the king was attended at Gloucester by Dafydd ap Llywelyn, whom he knighted and who wore 'the small circlet that is called *garlonde*, the insignia of the principality of North Wales, submitting himself moreover in everything to the king of England'.[5] In 1246 Harald Olafsson, king of Man and the Isles, 'was knighted, as his father had also been, by Henry, king of England, who bade him farewell with much honour and rich gifts'.[6] The Scottish kings too were not-infrequent guests in England. The most splendid of such journeys occurred in 1251, when the ten-year-old Alexander III came to York to marry King Henry's daughter, to receive the accolade of knighthood from his new father-in-law, who provided lavishly for the ceremonies, and to do homage. The homage was for his English lands. But Henry also tried to insist on homage for the kingdom of Scotland. If, as we are told, Henry was rebuffed by the boy-king, a point had been made by each side.

Contemporaries were not unaware of the span of English overlordship. In 1235 Henry married his sister to the emperor Frederick II. The St Albans chroniclers, Roger Wendover and Matthew Paris, made much of the imperial aspects of the English kingship, recalling the first marriage of Henry II's mother, Matilda, to the emperor Henry V; adding a saintly dimension by relating (rather impudently in the circumstances) that the mother of Matilda had been a daughter of St Margaret, queen of Scots; and emphasizing the range of the authority of the Norman and Angevin kings, and the variety of peoples over whom they had ruled. Wendover stressed that the kings of England had 'in these parts . . . the kings of Scotland and Wales, of Ireland and the Isle of Man, in subjection to them'.[7] His words carry echoes of the tenth-century *orbis Britanniae*; but they were more than slippered antiquarianism.

3. The Aristocratic Nexus

No agent of political assimilation was more significant than the Anglo-French aristocracy which spread itself with varying degrees of density throughout much of the British Isles. Its expansion was a protracted affair. In England the process was relatively swift: far advanced by the time of Domesday Book (1086), it was to all intents and purposes completed during the reign of Henry I. In Wales occupation took place by fits and starts from as early as 1067; but there were repeated setbacks, and the gains were not fully secure until Edward I's conquest of north Wales in 1282–3. In Scotland, despite the presence of Norman influences in the eleventh century, the settlement of the new ruling groups seems to have begun only when the future David I was given his apanage in Lothian and Strathclyde around 1113, and it continued into the thirteenth century. In Ireland, where the start was postponed until 1169, the areas of settlement and domination carried on enlarging for most of a century, though in the absence of an equivalent of 1282–3 they never achieved the same stability as in Wales. The character and sheer extent of the diaspora are caught in the marriage in 1296 of James the Stewart of Scotland to Egidia, the sister of Richard de Burgh, earl of Ulster and lord of Connacht. James held lands and castles on both sides of the Clyde, and had a sphere of influence reaching into Kintyre; Richard ruled the Ulster coasts and held land in all the provinces of Ireland. The Stewarts were descended from Alan's son of Flaald, steward to the Breton bishop of Dol, to whom Henry I had given the lordship of Oswestry in Shropshire; Alan's third son, Walter, had attached himself to King David around 1136. Richard's family came from Norfolk, and had begun to make its way in Ireland at the time of John's expedition of 1185. The couple were endowed with lands around the River Foyle, where Burgh lordship even at this late stage was still advancing.

The long time-span, together with the varied settings and circumstances, must raise questions about the appropriateness of seeing this aristocratic expansion as a single phenomenon. Its modes differed from place to place and from period to period. England saw the quick dispossession, by force or the threat of force, of the Anglo-Saxon ruling class by a Norman élite operating under the tight control of a powerful monarchy. In Wales and Ireland the native aristocracies also felt the edge of the sword; but their expropriation was less rapid and complete, and is often portrayed as mainly the work of barons and knights who displayed a spirit of independent enterprise. The advance into Scotland offers further contrasts: it was shaped by native kings who were themselves turned towards the Anglo-Norman world, and involved the gradual insertion of newcomers alongside or above existing élites rather than their crude dispossession—patterns which led, through time, to a successful blending.

Such distinctions are more than a little over-simplified, and should not be allowed to obstruct the view of aristocratic expansion as a whole. In England, below the upper levels of the nobility, marriages blurred national divisions and assimilated the thegnly element of Anglo-Saxon society to the emerging knightly class. In the north there was a more striking survival of native kins: the Nevilles, for example, so influential in the later Middle Ages, were of English descent. In Wales and Ireland, too, marriage and other forms of contact blunted the edges of political and cultural difference between natives and foreigners. Several baronial families of the Welsh March, such as the Mortimers, had high-born Welsh women among their ancestors; and the great-grandmother of Richard de Burgh was a daughter of Donal O'Brien (Domnall Mór Ó Briain), king of Thomond (d. 1194). Moreover, as we have seen, the royal court played at least as large a part as freebooting ventures in shaping aristocratic careers in these regions. Scotland for its part knew friction and war as well as peaceful integration, as the history of Galloway or Moray shows; and the virtual absence of chronicle sources may conceal the violent aspects of the penetration of castle-building lords into parts of the south. We may also think—as we consider England south and north of the Humber, Scotland north and south of the Forth or Tay, Gwent and Ceredigion, or the valley of the Boyne and the lands across the Shannon—that the contrasts within countries might be as marked as those between them.

A second difficulty lies in the tendency of the aristocracy to acquire provincial colourings. In the twelfth century Norman lords, such as Robert of Gloucester, to whom William of Malmesbury and Geoffrey of Monmouth both dedicated their histories, took an interest in the English past; and the power of government in England made the barons whose lands lay mostly on the English side of the Channel all too aware of their common status as subjects of the king of

England. As early as 1200 those who had settled north of the Tweed were conscious of their shared position as men of the king of Scots; and a legendary history existed within which all the ethnic groups inhabiting his territories could find a place. The growth of a feeling of attachment on the part of newcomers to the spaces they occupied is illustrated in the verse account of the conquest of Ireland known as the *Song of Dermot and the Earl*: it depicts invaders from south Wales going into battle with the cry 'St David' on their lips. Identification was the forte of churchmen, who were eager to defend and build upon rights, real or spurious, that had been inherited from their native predecessors. Just as Lanfranc and Anselm squeezed every drop out of Canterbury's claims, so Anglo-Norman bishops of St Andrew's and St David's opposed them, vigorously (though unsuccessfully) pressing the metropolitan pretensions of their own sees.

The awkwardness created by such developments is apparent, for instance, in the debates of historians about the most suitable term to describe those who participated in the conquest of Ireland, a full century after Duke William's invasion of England. Are we dealing with 'Normans', 'Anglo-Normans', 'Anglo-French', or even 'Cambro-Normans'? Or would it be better—since English seems already to have been the first language of the majority and all, whatever their descent, were the people of the king of England—to follow Gerald of Wales in calling them, quite simply, 'English'? There is much to be said for this last suggestion. Yet it risks obscuring crucial ambiguities. William the Lion was accused of favouring only 'Frenchmen', and of placing the Scots in subjection; his 'French' followers were from the same stable as the 'English' who took part in the occupation of Ireland.

The strengthening of princely structures, and with them a sense of political identity, were indeed features of the period; they came readily to England, where the Norman aristocracy were established within an old kingdom with a pervasive royal government. But bonds of cultural and political association remained complex and many layered. Especially where they coincide with the political units of later times, provincial attachments have a way of monopolizing our attention. Significant as they were, they competed with other ties and perceptions. A region as small as Dyfed contained in the early twelfth century a jumble of languages and traditions—Norman-French, Flemish, English, Welsh, and perhaps Breton. These imperfectly blended ingredients were to transfer themselves to south-east Ireland a generation or two later. In 1200 the lord of Dyfed was William Marshal, earl of Pembroke (d. 1219). Marshal's vast lordships were scattered from Leinster across south Wales, southern England, and Normandy. As a landless youth his hopes had centred upon the noble and royal courts of England and northern France. Now his own ambulatory court was a prime focus for men of gentle birth and diverse origins. Its patronage had profound implications, even for those of lower status. Like other lords, Marshal gave the burgesses of his towns freedom to trade throughout his dominions. An inhabitant of Pembroke or Wexford, still conscious of belonging to an English or Flemish group huddled in a new environment, could at the same time move with some confidence on a trans-national stage. The Marshal holdings were exceptional in their wealth and extent. But they were typical of many other assemblages in that they stretched across more than one of the territories subject to the king of England; such internal divisions presented no serious problems to major lords. Even the boundaries between the dominions of different princes were inconveniences to be coped with, rather than insurmountable barriers: the Marshals contrived to hold on to their Norman lands even after King John lost his duchy to the French. Despite the existence of provincial sentiment and of xenophobia, there was an aristocratic freemasonry whose members were not confined by the frontiers that tend to have prominence in many writings on the period. Within the British Isles the aristocracy helped to foster, not only institutional and cultural uniformity, but also a web of connections that was of great political importance.

Trans-regional landholding

In recent years the phenomenon of 'cross-border' landholding has attracted attention, as historians have tried to reconstruct the arenas aristocracies inhabited, instead of working within national or regional boundaries that properties and careers often ignored. The obvious importance of the Anglo-Norman link has been a stimulus to such studies, and has led to the identification of approaches and techniques that may profitably be brought to bear within the British Isles. As we have seen, cross-Channel lords were significant both in binding England and Normandy together, and in encouraging their reintegration under a single ruler at the times when separation occurred.

Particularly in the first generation after the Conquest, lordships were sometimes divided at the Channel in a manner that suggests the convention that the eldest son inherited the original patrimony, while fresh acquisitions were used to endow a younger son. Robert de Bellême, the eldest son of Roger of Montgomery, earl of Shrewsbury (d. 1094), received most of the family's continental lands, while his brother, Earl Hugh of Shrewsbury, took the main English centres. But, in the nature of things, holdings in England soon passed out of the acquisition category, and anyway habits were never so clear-cut as this distinction suggests. Although lands might be divided between branches of a family, they had a way of coming together again, if only because of the frequency with which lines died out: when Earl Hugh was killed in 1098, Robert de Bellême reunited his father's lands, rather as William Rufus and Henry I reunited Normandy and England. Many other influences favoured the retention or acquisition of property on both sides of the Channel. A man whose interests were preponderantly in England might wish to keep up a connection, however slight, with his ancestral region. For a major baron the possession of lands or rents in England and Normandy made it easier to follow the royal court, a consideration that might also carry weight with the king who wanted his service. The Beaumont brothers, Robert, earl of Leicester and count of Meulan (d. 1118), and Henry de Neubourg, earl of Warwick (d. 1119), shared in properties on both sides of the sea. Robert intended his own twin sons to accept a division at the Channel, though Waleran of Meulan (d. 1166) was to retain some revenues in England. In the event, as their careers went forward from 1118 to 1141, both Waleran and Robert of Leicester (d. 1168) gained extensive interests on each side. When Waleran defected to the Angevins in 1141, Robert remained with Stephen, and shielded his brother's English property. And when Waleran later abandoned the Angevins for the Capetians, Henry II was careful to retain Robert in his service, partly by a promise of the restoration of his Norman lands.

Full-blown cross-Channel careers were open only to the very great; men of knightly rank tended to be rooted on one side or the other. But some of those in between might maintain active interests in both England and Normandy, especially if they were associated with one of the major aristocratic houses: the Beaumont sub-tenants, the

Harcourts and the Tourvilles, have been described as 'in a small way . . . the "cross-Channel barons" in the miniature Anglo-Norman *regnum* of the Beaumont honors'.[1] Any estimate of the depth of landholding connections must also include ecclesiastical property. The Norman barons were munificent monastic patrons. Quite apart from the spiritual advantages that flowed from gifts, the taking of a grip on a new area was materially assisted by drawing a favourite religious house into the venture: anybody who was dispossessed would find it particularly difficult to claw property back from the Church. The abbey of Séez, long connected with the Montgomeries in Normandy, gained interests in Sussex, where Roger of Montgomery, first earl of Shrewsbury, had lands; it also acquired property in the honor of Lancaster and in Pembroke, lordships held by his two youngest sons, Roger 'of Poitou' and Arnulf of Montgomery.

The Montgomeries are a reminder, if one is needed, that the occupation of Wales was an extension of the conquest of England, led by many of the same men. At the upper levels at least, the ruling groups in England and Wales continued to overlap; the term 'barons of the Welsh March' is deceptive if it is taken to mean that there was ever a set of major lords who were unique to Wales, homogeneous in outlook, and likely to act as one either in the March or beyond it. It is true that the subtenant class was composed for the most part of men who made (or lost) their lives in south Wales and the borders; they were the rock on which the marcher lordships were built. But, just as the general fate of Anglo-Norman enterprise in Wales depended on royal leadership and the vicissitudes of wider politics, so its local vigour had much to do with the performance of the leading barons.

A large proportion of the March was always in the hands of lords who were powerful elsewhere. They ranged from the Beaumont earls of Warwick in the twelfth century (lords of Gower), to the Clare earls of Gloucester and Hertford in the thirteenth century (lords of Glamorgan), and the Plantagenet earls and dukes of Lancaster in the fourteenth century (lords of Monmouth). Their possessions in Wales often came to them through the king's patronage, operating either directly or by way of the marriage market; and their holdings outside Wales made them more amenable to royal discipline. Lands in the marches naturally faced them with special challenges, while giving them ready access to military manpower, including that supplied by native Welsh lords. But most outbreaks of serious disorder in the

March—whether at the time of Henry I's clash with Robert of Normandy's partisans in 1101-2, of the Barons' War in 1263-5, or of Thomas of Lancaster's opposition to Edward II in 1321-2—were by-products of broader tensions. The region was a cockpit more because it was thoroughly infiltrated by the court nobility than because it was inhabited by unruly backwoodsmen.

Nor was it only the earls and greater barons who had interests outside the March. A second-rank family such as the FitzMartins of Cemais in Pembroke retained lands on the southern side of the Bristol Channel, and for a time also had property in Ireland. The Fitz-Warins of Whittington in Shropshire, who in some ways seem to epitomize the marcher ethos, are specially instructive. The deeds of Fulk FitzWarin III (fl. 1198-1258) are immortalized in the romance *The Legend of Fulk FitzWarin*, which was possibly committed to writing in the early 1260s. Interweaving fact and fantasy, it recounts his military exploits and wanderings, concentrating on his uprising against King John and his spell as an outlaw in 1201-3. The circumstances of his rebellion confirm the fundamental importance of the royal court: his behaviour was determined by John's denial to him of Whittington castle, which his father had acquired. During the 1220s and 1230s Fulk and his brother William constantly held royal commands and offices both in the marches and elsewhere. Nor were the FitzWarin interests confined to the Welsh borders. The family were substantial landholders in Berkshire; indeed Lambourn, rather than Whittington, seems to have been their chief seat. Fulk himself acquired interests as far afield as Yorkshire and Ireland through marriage. A later William FitzWarin was royal seneschal of Ulster in the 1270s, and his son, Alan FitzWarin (d. *c*.1327), was a proprietor in Berkshire and in the north of Ireland, and active on both sides of the Irish Sea.

The FitzMartins and FitzWarins provide examples, not just of the unity of baronial society in England and Wales, but also of its spread into Ireland. Thirteenth-century Ireland and its relations with England have yet to receive their historiographical due; we are still far from a full evaluation of the web of family ties and landholding that spanned the sea. But it is perfectly clear that in the first half of the thirteenth century many of the greater barons of Ireland had extensive lands elsewhere; of those who did not, several had some property outside Ireland, while others belonged to families whose interests were not primarily Irish. Leinster belonged to the Marshals until 1245. From 1190 to 1241 Walter de Lacy was lord of Meath, and a prominent landholder in Shropshire, Herefordshire, Gloucestershire, and other English counties; until 1204 he also held lands in Normandy. In Louth the chief lords were the Verdons (major proprietors in Staffordshire and the west midlands generally) and the Pippards (who had property in Oxfordshire and elsewhere). The holdings of these lords alone accounted for about one-third of the total area of Ireland, and more than half of the parts most firmly under English control. The proportion of Munster in the hands of lords with English lands was smaller. But, among the greater direct tenants of the Crown, the Butlers had property in Lancashire, Yorkshire, Norfolk, and elsewhere (to which they were to add substantially in the fourteenth century), the Worcesters in Suffolk, and the Valognes in Kent, Surrey, and East Anglia. The Burghs, who were to extend their possessions from Munster into Connacht and eventually Ulster, kept up their court connections from generation to generation; and when at the beginning of the fourteenth century Richard de Burgh inherited English lands from his mother's family, he quickly added to them by purchasing some of the Pippard properties.

Although the 1240s saw the partitioning of Leinster and Meath among heiresses, the effect in the short term at least was not to loosen the ties between England and Ireland. In Leinster the division produced four county-sized lordships and some smaller fractions. The successor lords included the Bigod earls of Norfolk and Marshals of England (Carlow), the Clare earls of Gloucester (Kilkenny), the Valence earls of Pembroke (Wexford), and the Vescys of Alnwick (Kildare). These lordships were valuable, and fully exploited through seigneurial administrations; now and then they figured in their lords' itineraries. It was only in the late thirteenth and early fourteenth centuries that further partitions conspired with deteriorating economic and security conditions to encourage disengagement. Meath, partitioned between the two granddaughters of Walter de Lacy, still amounted to two large and attractive lordships. One went to the Verdons, thereby increasing the Irish bias of their estates; the other passed to Geoffrey de Geneville, one of the continental nobles of Henry III's court, and brother of Jean de Joinville, the biographer of St Louis. For the rest of the century Geoffrey and the Verdons kept up Walter's itinerant habits, dividing their time between Ireland and Britain, and between their own affairs and royal service.

As in the case of England and Normandy (and England and the Welsh March), the connections are most apparent at the very top of the social scale. But while it was far easier for the higher nobility to exploit lands and keep up a role in more than one region, others did so too. They included some of the subtenants of the great Irish lordships, such as the Costentins of western Meath, who also held in Staffordshire and Lincolnshire, the Carews of Wexford and Berkshire, or the Pitchfords, who were associated with the Verdons both in the west midlands and in eastern Ireland. Baronial cadets might also gather property on both sides of the sea. William (d. 1233), the youngest son of the first Hugh de Lacy, and born of an Irish mother, carved out a lordship to the north of Meath, acquired manors near Denbigh through his marriage to a daughter of Llywelyn the Great, and held Britford in Wiltshire by the grant of Walter de Lacy. The fabric of ecclesiastical property and obedience likewise spread into Ireland. Among the beneficiaries were the Augustinian houses of Llanthony (at Monmouth and Gloucester), which were associated with the Lacys, and the Cistercian abbey of Tintern in Chepstow, which had the patronage of the Marshals.

The king had the same rights of wardship over the lands of his tenants-in-chief, whether they lay in Middlesex, west Wales, or on the Atlantic coast of Ireland, together with the right—within the limits of accepted good practice—to arrange and profit from the marriages of under-age heirs and of widows. He lorded it over a vast sphere of patronage that did not distinguish between England, Wales, and Ireland: when Henry III pushed one of the Marshal heiresses in the way of his Poitevin half-brother, William de Valence, he made William into a major baron in three countries. Scotland, of course, was different; the king of Scots exercised his own rights of patronage, and intervention from south of the Tweed took the form of influence only. But those who benefited from the generosity of the Scottish rulers might also be in receipt of the favour of the English king. The kingdoms were locked together by what was in a fuller sense a cross-border aristocracy; and the number of landholders in that category grew markedly between the reigns of David I and Alexander III.

From the outset the Scottish kings were able to control the Anglo-Norman migration into their kingdom. Although a few of those brought in by David were landholders in England (though not on the scale of Robert de Brus), most were not. Many were younger sons;

some were exiles from the honor of Huntingdon, which David forfeited to King Stephen. But there was no objection in principle to the holding of land in two realms whose rulers were usually at peace. Around 1138 Robert de Brus divided his lands, giving his elder son those within Stephen's orbit and his second son those within David's (the line of partition falling at the Tees rather than the Tweed). But this arrangement sprang from the difficulties of the immediate situation; it was not disturbed when English power was pushed north to its usual limits by Henry II in 1157; and the Annandale branch remained Anglo-Scottish proprietors until 1306, when a later Robert de Brus (Bruce) rose against Edward I. Similarly, the holding of lands on both sides of the border by William the Lion's brother and nephew, the earls of Huntingdon, posed no insuperable problems between 1185 and 1237.

The swelling of the ranks of cross-border lords was the product not so much of fresh grants by the Scottish or English kings—though important grants were made by the latter—as of the redistribution of land through marriage and inheritance. This in itself is significant: the higher nobility of much of thirteenth-century Scotland were in most respects part of the same aristocratic society that dominated the rest of the British Isles. Indeed some of the native families who were being absorbed into that society extended their interests beyond Scotland. The earls of Fife, who had received a charter regranting their ancient earldom as a fief as far back as David's reign, recruited foreign personnel in the same way as the royal house, and also acquired lands in Yorkshire. Likewise Roland of Galloway's marriage to the Moreville heiress expanded the family's interests. His son, Alan, held lands in Lothian, Cumbria (from where he imported tenants), Yorkshire, and the English east midlands; he also gained a title to large areas of eastern Ulster from King John, who was almost as much his lord as was William the Lion. Traffic the other way was also important. Just as the partitions of Leinster and Meath introduced new English families to Ireland, so the division of the Galloway and Huntingdon inheritances in the 1230s brought lands in Scotland to baronial houses—such as Forz, Balliol, and Hastings—whose Scottish interests had hitherto been small or non-existent.

It has been calculated that, at some stage during the thirteenth century, nine out of thirteen Scottish earldoms had English property, while seven out of twenty-two English earldoms had Scottish interests. A few magnates—such as Roger de Quincy, earl of Winchester and constable of Scotland (d. 1264), the Bruces, and the Balliols—had sizeable agglomerations of land on both sides of the frontier, and pursued genuinely cross-border careers. Most, however, had a primary association with one kingdom or the other: the earl of Fife was plainly Scottish, and Gilbert Marshal, earl of Pembroke (d. 1241), whose marriage to a sister of Alexander II brought him the lordship of Haddington, clearly English. But the dozens of tenurial complexities together amounted to a major overlapping. Nor were cross-border interests wholly restricted to the topmost levels, or to lay society only. Among the followers of Earl David or Roger de Quincy were men with lands or family ties in England and Scotland, while some lesser landholders had property athwart the Tweed or Solway. The former unity of Northumbria left traces in Durham's links with Coldingham Priory, and more recent royal and noble patronage had resulted in a number of religious houses in each kingdom—such as St Andrew's Priory at Northampton—having lands and rights in the other.

Baronial and royal politics

The dispersal across the British Isles of an aristocracy with its roots in northern France, and the unity of the society created by that process, are reflected in political events which, in order to be fully understood, need to be set in contexts broader than those instinctively employed by the historian concerned with a particular national or provincial unit. The reigns of John and Henry III provide valuable illustrations of this point, which could of course be exemplified by almost any major episode of the late twelfth and earlier thirteenth centuries.

We may take as a starting-point John's Irish expedition of 1210, an event that has (reasonably enough) interested Irish historians primarily because it marked a step in the growth of English law and administration in Ireland. From the point of view of contemporaries, however, this development—if they were conscious of it—would have seemed a mere by-product of a broader political crisis, whose epicentre was the royal court, and which had strong reverberations in Ireland because lords whom the king regarded with suspicion happened to have lands there. John went to Ireland in pursuit of William de Briouze (d. 1211), once his trusted agent, with whom he had recently quarrelled. William held extensive lordships in England and Wales; until 1204 he had also had property in Normandy; and in 1201 John had renewed in his favour a lapsed grant of the lordship of Limerick which Henry II had made to his uncle. One of William's daughters was the wife of Walter de Lacy. William sought Walter's protection, and was successful in gaining the support of his brother Hugh de Lacy, whom the king had made earl of Ulster in 1205. The relationship between the Lacys and the Briouzes was close, and is visible in more than one area: not only were they neighbours in the Welsh marches; they had dealings over property in both Normandy and Ireland. Their alliance, which John now perceived as hostile, was the more alarming to him owing to his fear of an even greater figure whose interests also extended across the entire northern sector of the Angevin lands. William Marshal's relations with the king had soured since 1204, largely because William's attempts to guard his Norman interests had drawn him into dealings with Philip Augustus. The end of the war in Normandy and his breach with the king led him to spend much of the period 1207–12 in Ireland, energetically exploiting his lordship of Leinster. Marshal had several times clashed with John's ministers at Dublin, and in 1210 the king clearly suspected that he might become part of a major conspiracy against him.

The particular configuration of royal and baronial interests thus meant that Ireland was briefly the stage where a wider political drama was played out. It ended with Marshal's submission, the temporary forfeiture of Walter de Lacy in Ireland and Britain, and the king's successful siege of the great Ulster castle of Carrickfergus, as Hugh de Lacy and the Briouzes fled across the narrow sea to Scotland. From Scotland Hugh and William de Briouze crossed to France. But William's wife and two of their sons were handed over to John by Duncan, earl of Carrick, to end their days (starved to death, as rumour had it) in prison at Windsor. The part played by Duncan highlights another aspect of the episode. He and his cousin Alan of Galloway supported John's Irish expedition; and they reaped a splendid reward, at least on parchment, in the form of charters granting them large coastal tracts of Hugh de Lacy's former earldom.

This complex skein of events shows that the waters between Britain and Ireland, like the English Channel, had become an Anglo-French aristocratic highway. Political integration of a new sort was taking place in the Irish Sea province. This is particularly clear from the *Histoire de Guillaume le Maréchal*, a verse biography committed to writing within a few years of Marshal's death, which offers a rare view of the political world as it appeared to the circle of a lay lord.

The narrative flows naturally from Normandy to Britain, to Ireland, and back again. Its points of reference are John's mobile court, with its outlying base at Dublin, and Marshal's equally peripatetic household. The *Histoire* also provides a view of the way in which association with a great aristocratic connection widened the horizons of lesser men. John de Erley, one of Marshal's household stewards, provided much of the information on which the biography was based. We see him busy on his lord's affairs, and present with him in Ireland. Such were the conditions in which the Erleys, like several other families, came to hold land of the Marshals on both sides of the Irish Sea. The strength and complexity of the ties of lordship, family, and property that grew between south-west Britain and southern Ireland at this period were to be reflected in the speed with which a dispute between Henry III and Earl Richard Marshal spread from England and Wales to Ireland in 1233–4. Partisans of the earl and the king assembled on the Curragh of Kildare, where Richard was fatally wounded. In the aftermath of the war a number of families, such as the Mariscos and Dunheveds of Somerset, who were connected with the Marshals on both sides of the sea, suffered periods of forfeiture.

There was also a significant interweaving of English and Scottish politics, which owed a good deal to the straddling of the border by baronial interests. It is most clearly visible in the 1250s, during the minority of Alexander III. Alexander's marriage to Henry III's daughter in 1251 had the effect of enlarging Henry's role north of the Tweed. Partly, it would seem, out of genuine concern for the young couple, he supervised Scottish government, attaching his daughter's guardians to the council and influencing its membership. The guardians, John Balliol and Robert de Ros, were both cross-border lords, so that they had a position in Scotland while remaining amenable to English discipline. The minority saw magnate feuds within Scotland. These have often been interpreted as a struggle between a 'Scottish' group of nobles, headed by Walter Comyn, earl of Menteith, and a rival group, led by Alan Durward, who were more English in their orientation and encouraged Henry to interfere in Scottish affairs. Curiously, this view of the matter appears to have its origin in the comments of Matthew Paris, writing at St Albans; it may be that Matthew, who interpreted the English politics of the 1240s and 1250s as a conflict between the English nobility and Henry's foreign courtiers, merely used a well-tried explanatory device to give a shape to events in Scotland. In reality, both factions seem to have turned to the English court when it suited them. Certainly the Comyn-dominated council, which ruled from 1251 to 1255, included a number of lords with English lands besides John Balliol and Robert de Ros. A revealing incident took place at the time when the Comyn group was ousted, with Henry's active help, in the latter year. Balliol and Ros, in whom he had lost confidence, fell with the rest, and the repercussions were not limited to Scotland. Balliol had held the post of castellan of Carlisle and sheriff of Cumberland. The king replaced him with Robert Bruce of Annandale, who had recently done homage upon inheriting from his mother an additional scattering of lands in England. At the same time Bruce became a member of the new Scottish council. The absence of a neat division between English and Scottish aristocratic society, and by extension between English and Scottish politics, could hardly be clearer.

Though only the king of England spanned the entire British sphere, it mattered that baronial society stretched throughout its individual parts, supplying a multitude of links that cut across local, provincial, and national boundaries. Just as the tenurial complexity of England itself was an agent of internal cohesion, so the mesh of aristocratic marriage and landholding was a powerful force for integration. Of course, political events might have a significance peculiar to one area (though this may stand out more clearly with hindsight than it did in the eyes of contemporaries). But most episodes of the period will also upon inspection turn out to have had a strongly trans-regional aspect—and there are moments when something close to a single politics of the British Isles may be discerned.

Uniformity and variations of lordship

By the thirteenth century all parts of the British Isles, with the partial exception of native Wales and Ireland and the Gaelic–Norse fringes of Scotland, were caught within an aristocratic web that was broken neither by the Irish Sea nor by the Anglo-Scottish border. This widespread society had, to a considerable extent, a common outlook and array of institutions. There were, of course, important regional differences. The variations arose from many influences that interacted in complex ways. Only a few of the more obvious can be touched upon here. Physical geography probably did most to decide the forms and extent of exploitation: at any period patterns of lordship in Surrey and in west Wales were likely to differ sharply. Aristocratic

rule in districts—whether in southern England or eastern Ireland—
that were occupied quickly and held for the most part in peace con-
trasted with the militarized, tribute-taking lordship found in the
Welsh and Irish borderlands. Differences also sprang from the character of the pre-existing political arrangements, which themselves
reflected the possibilities of the terrain. Lordship had to accommodate itself to intensive royal rule in lowland England, to a Scottish
kingship that was more limited both territorially and in governmental
sophistication, and to the fragmented, fluid power that marked Wales
and Ireland; such contrasts are imprinted on the resulting structures.
Finally, the chronology of occupation mattered. For example, the
early charters granting lands in Ireland diverge from their English
equivalents of a century before in specifying exact levels of knight
service; the contrast reflects the development in England during the
intervening period of a precise scheme of feudal military obligation,
monitored by the Crown. This is one manifestation of the climate of
definition in which expansion across the Irish Sea took place, giving
birth to the paradox—which will be more fully apparent in the next
chapter—that baronial lordship in distant Ireland was, formally at
least, more hedged about by royal authority than in the Welsh
marches, which had been colonized in an earlier age. Yet, despite
differences of emphasis and style, the uniformity of lordship is striking: variations observed recognizable limits, and occurred as readily
within kingdoms and lordships as between them.

Generally speaking, where royal authority was strong, landholding
patterns tended to be fragmented, and lordship in consequence relatively weak. Nowhere is this truism more apparent than in southern
and midland England. The distribution of land after the Conquest
had tended to produce a pattern of estates scattered in smallish lots,
and this fragmentation had increased over the succeeding generations, not least through the custom of dividing property among heiresses. In Earl David's time the honor of Huntingdon did not form a
consolidated block; it was made up of lands, revenues, and jurisdictional rights dispersed amongst those of other landholders great and
small over eleven counties in the east midlands and elsewhere.
David's knightly tenants were likely also to be the tenants of other
lords, just as he was himself. The sheer complexity of status and
tenure meant that allegiances were also complicated: few men of note
had a single overlord besides the king. There were some exceptions to
this pattern: for instance, castleries based upon the ancient rapes of

Sussex had formed large, compact units of lordship. Nor was there any guarantee that noble houses would not establish a practical regional dominance that might through time acquire the attributes of a great lordship. Several, such as the Beaumonts, who were centred on Leicester, got some way along this road during Stephen's reign. But the exceptions were few and for the most part politically insignificant; nor was royal authority weakened for long enough to allow an alternative distribution of power to become entrenched.

Minor equivalents existed elsewhere in the British Isles. The Scottish king's power was at its most intensive in the south-east, and particularly in Lothian, where there were many royal estates and hence also boroughs and castles, a dispersed pattern of tenures, and few big lordships east of Lauderdale. New men came into the area undramatically through royal patronage, gaining small parcels of land as forfeitures or heiresses made it available; there was no insertion of major barons between the Crown and the lesser landholding class. In Ireland, too, areas of intensive royal lordship emerged, notably in the regions of Dublin and Waterford, which Henry II kept as demesne. The County Dublin lowlands, like Lothian, contained a significant number of Crown tenants holding single knight's fees or fractional fees. Even in Wales, royal action, assisted by physical geography, made the castles of Carmarthen, and for a time also Pembroke, into centres on which clusters of smallish lords were dependent. These comparisons are not wholly ridiculous, for lowland England itself might be regarded as a Crown lordship of an unusually vast and effective sort. In practice, of course, they bring out the gulfs between the core region of intensive rule in England, its lesser counterpart in Scotland, and its still frailer equivalents in Ireland and Wales.

Beyond such regions lay rather different structures. The Welsh marches, much of the north of England, Strathclyde, and the other areas of Scotland beyond the royal heartlands, together with most of Anglo-Norman Ireland, were characterized by large, nucleated lordships. The Norman advance northwards on the whole saw the handing over of broad tracts of land to individual barons. This produced lordships such as Pontefract, Richmond, or Alnwick in the east, and the honor of Lancaster, Kendal, or Copeland in the west. Though it is easy to exaggerate their self-contained nature, they were undoubtedly closer to the common image of a feudal society than most of the lordships that existed further south. Many of them took their names from the chief castle which served as the lord's centre of command and collecting-point. It was there that the honor court, made up of his leading subtenants, met. The tenants formed communities that were more likely to display a common allegiance: when the Lacy family fell foul of Henry I and lost Pontefract, their vassals resisted the new lord put in by the Crown.

Similar patterns of organization appear in the areas of Scotland that lay in between the regions of intensive royal lordship and the receding fringes dominated by chiefs of Scandinavian and Gaelic origin. Lordship across the Solway mirrored that in English Cumbria. Brus at Annan, Moreville at Cunningham, or FitzAlan at Renfrew presided over compact lordships focused on their castles. The distribution of mottes brings out the contrasting models of lordship in Lothian and Strathclyde very clearly. Lothian seems to have had few; what castles there were tended to be royal, and were constructed in stone from an early stage. Strathclyde, on the other hand, was full of mottes, many of which can be connected with twelfth-century lords and their main subtenants; they clustered thickly on the frontiers of Galloway proper. In the north Earl David's lordship of Garioch, with its key castle and borough at Inverurie, lay on what were then the outskirts of royal Scotland. David settled the whole region with a thin stratum of vassals from Huntingdon and elsewhere in England, and also from within Scottish feudal society. Most had few external ties; they formed an honorial élite which, as in northern England, gradually incorporated those native landholders who managed to maintain their status.

The big lordships of Wales and Ireland were similar in many ways to those of England and Scotland, but the survival in both countries of unassimilated native aristocracies gave them additional facets. The lordship of Glamorgan affords a clear view of the resemblances and divergences. Its origins are no longer recoverable in detail. It began in the time of William Rufus, when Robert fitz Hamo took Cardiff (which was to remain its chief castle-borough and administrative centre) and apportioned its hinterland to men who had participated in his venture, which was probably launched by sea from across the Bristol Channel. Over the next two hundred years the lordship was expanded by fits and starts by his successors, the earls of Gloucester, until it reached the approximate dimensions of the old Welsh kingdom of Morgannwg. But the lordship of Glamorgan was always an uneven affair. The lord's authority operated most intensively around

Cardiff, where the tenants of the Vale of Glamorgan owed castle-guard, and those of the whole lordship suit at the honor (or 'county') court. Beyond this zone which had been occupied early and thoroughly lay an area of sub-lordships, held and defended by lesser castle-building entrepreneurs, such as the Turbervilles of Coety. Beyond that again stretched the upland lordships such as Senghennydd and Afan, which remained in Welsh hands. There Welsh custom was dominant; the lord of Glamorgan's role was that of an exactor of hostages and tribute—and then only when he was powerful enough to take them. In adverse circumstances the allegiances of the Welsh lords might be gathered in by the Lord Rhys of Deheubarth (d. 1197) or, in the thirteenth century, by the princes of Gwynedd.

Unevenness and varying forms of authority were likewise a feature of Irish lordships. As in Wales, the balance between feudal and native styles depended on the size of the lordship, the terrain it occupied, and the period under consideration. The south-eastern quarter of the island was occupied in the main by the lordship of Leinster, held at various times between 1171 and 1245 by Strongbow, the future King John, and the Marshals. Thanks to their grants, it became the home of a large group of knightly tenants, often described as the 'barons of Leinster'. Although the sheer size of the lordship led to its being organized around a number of centres—among them Kildare, Kilkenny, Carlow, and Wexford, where impressive stone castles were built—the honorial baronage formed a coherent community, most of whose members were to follow Richard Marshal in 1234, and pay the penalty for resisting the king.

This aspect of the lordship, together with the economic enterprise symbolized by its boroughs, is readily discernible in the records. Another is almost wholly hidden from us. Leinster included the southern ranges of the Wicklow Hills and the eastern sector of the midland bogs. There the lords of Leinster acted as patrons of Irish leaders. In some cases this may have spelt incorporation: William Marshal is known to have granted English legal status to a member of the O'Toole (Ó Tuathail) kin of Kildare. But other things hint at a duality of organization, which is confirmed by later events. After Dermot MacMurrough's death, Strongbow is said by the *Song of Dermot* to have granted local kingship in north Wexford, together with 'the pleas of Leinster', to his Irish successors, which suggests that they acted as heads of their own people under the new dispensation.[2] The continued presence of these 'lords of the wilderness' is scarcely visible—until they reappear in the record, as raiders, a generation after the partition of Leinster in 1247. But that such arrangements, akin to those of upland Glamorgan, existed is confirmed by evidence from Meath, where the payments in cash and kind due from the chiefs of the O'Farrells and others are preserved in fossilized form in early fourteenth-century valuations.

The contrast between lowland England, with its fragmented pattern of landholding and comparative lack of nucleated lordships, and the compact lordships of the rest of the British Isles, has long fascinated historians. Explanations have run upon two distinct lines. One would stress continuity with the past, presenting the extensive, nucleated lordship as a reflection of the territorial divisions and economic and political arrangements that existed in the west and north when the new aristocracy arrived. Thus regarded, the difference can become one between Celtic and Anglo-Saxon forms of organization. J. G. Edwards argued that the marcher lordships were composed of commotes or clusters of commotes (the commote (*cwmwd*) was the tribute-district into which Welsh kingdoms were organized), and that their exceptional judicial privileges should be seen as the mediatized rights of Welsh kings. Similarly, G. W. S. Barrow has linked the lordships on both sides of the Solway with the administrative districts of the ancient kingdom of Cumbria. Such forms of organization, in essence the support mechanisms of old chieftaincies, may once have extended throughout Britain (one school of thought would regard them as pre-Roman); in most of lowland England they had long since been obliterated by the rise of a unitary kingship with a powerful administrative and patronage system.

The alternative approach presupposes a greater mind and capacity on the part of kings and barons to remodel what they found; it also displays scepticism about the antiquity of arrangements for which the evidence is often preserved only in late sources (the texts of the Welsh laws, for instance, mostly date from the thirteenth century). The stress falls on the practical responses of powerful men to the problems and opportunities presented by distant, imperfectly assimilated regions. Kings of England and Scotland put trusted agents in charge of what to begin with were command-districts, in order to secure and advance their authority. By degrees such commands hardened into units of lordship, as the grantees brought in subtenants, built castles, and exercised jurisdiction. Such lordships did not necessarily respect past arrangements. Pontefract cut across old tenurial patterns. Glamorgan's fees and sub-lordships owed little or nothing to any pre-existing commotal structure. In Garioch Earl David gave the region a coherence and administrative identity that it had earlier lacked. Moreover, many of the 'privileges' of the marcher lords may be explained as the predictable accompaniments of feudal lordship in a frontier zone; there is no need to invoke a constitutional inheritance from Welsh kings in order to explain them. The emphasis should be placed upon positive action and present circumstances, rather than on capitulation to the weight of the past.

The truth lies in between these caricatures of the two positions. In southern and midland England the Norman kings inherited a region already thoroughly infiltrated by royal authority and marked by great tenurial complication; they enlarged that authority, and the granting of land after the Conquest changed tenurial dispositions while still preserving their complexity. Everywhere there was a dialogue between past patterns and present exigencies and ambitions. New rulers happily harnessed old districts and customs, giving them fresh emphases and often an additional sharpness; equally, they might weld existing units together or break them apart. The balance was likely to rest most decisively in favour of the past in regions where the hold of the newcomers was shallow—as in Ceredigion, which comes closer than most of Wales to the assemblage-of-commotes model proposed by J. G. Edwards. Continuity also tends to catch the eye in areas, such as Cumbria, where the configuration of plain, river valley, and hillside was bound to shape lordship, whatever the period.

The mixture of continuity and change is apparent in Ireland, which has yet to be brought fully within the debate. Henry II kept the cities and their hinterlands: County Dublin was, in effect, the area of the Norse kingdom of Dublin. Grants were often expressed in terms of the zones of authority of native lords who were being partly expropriated and subordinated to new authorities. Hugh de Lacy, for example, was given Meath 'as Murrough O'Melaghlin (Murchad Ua Máel Sechlainn) . . . best held it'.[3] But this did not mean that he or others took over going concerns with clear borders. The O'Melaghlins had been weak, exercising their authority within a fluctuating area over other Irish lords little less powerful than themselves. In reality Hugh was given a commission to conquer, settle, and organize as much of the region between the kingdom of Dublin and the Shannon as he could, and to dominate the remainder. Between 1172 and 1241 he and his son Walter, together with the subtenants they brought in, did just that: building castles throughout Meath; promoting boroughs at centres such as Drogheda, Trim, Kells, and Mullingar; and endowing religious houses. Much of this activity went on at sites which, like Kells, were already of ecclesiastical and hence economic significance. But the lordship of Meath in the mid-thirteenth century—with its society of vassals, its honor court at Trim, its growing number of stone castles and churches, and, in the eastern sector, its stable frontiers enclosing a largely English-speaking world of prosperous agricultural communities—was a far cry from the loose-woven realm that the O'Melaghlins had failed in practice to control. There was continuity of course; but the degree of innovation and reorganization is also striking.

Lordship in the twelfth and thirteenth centuries was at once homogeneous and remarkably flexible. Castles existed from the English south coast to the Moray Firth, and from Lincolnshire to beyond the Shannon. But their significance was infinitely variable: from quiet residence in a normally peaceful shire, to centre of command in a fast-developing barony, or to advance-post in a frontier region just starting to be brought under control. All lords of substance had knightly subtenants. But in one place they were men with many competing ties, while in another they might form a self-contained community with a real *esprit de corps*. Such tenants owed suit at an honor court. In southern England that court was by 1200 probably of little moment compared to the county court where they also owed attendance, let alone the royal courts where they received justice and served as jurors. But in Glamorgan, or Annandale, or Meath, it amounted itself to a shire court—and more besides, since the lord to varying degrees wielded judicial powers of a regal type. In Ireland and Wales, additionally, the lord's authority might reach out and, changing its modes of operation, absorb the leaders of a native society.

Such differences were taken in their stride by major lords whose interests frequently straddled more than one environment, with or without crossing the boundaries between kingdoms or provinces. Earl David coped both with the discrete honor of Huntingdon, lying within the ambit of the English monarchy, and the compact lordship of Garioch, on the outskirts of the influence of the less intrusive Scottish king. The Stewarts had estates in Lothian, as well as their compact Clydeside baronies of Renfrew and Dundonald, and their holdings in Bute and Cowal on the maritime frontier of Scotland. The manorial property of the Lacys in Warwickshire or Gloucestershire lay in a different setting from their border castle of Ludlow in Shropshire, or their lordship of Meath, with its regal status. Yet even within Meath itself there were sharp contrasts between the manorialized districts with their rich boroughs and the pastoral, largely Gaelic fringes. The aristocratic scattering that occurred during the two centuries after 1066 created a multitude of connections. It also ensured that custom, fashions in piety, the idioms of authority, and structures of lordship bore marked resemblances almost everywhere south and east of a line drawn from the Moray Firth to Galway Bay. The British Isles formed a single world through which the higher aristocracy moved with aplomb.

4. The Expansion of Royal Government

THE two centuries after the Norman Conquest of England saw the drawing of much of the British Isles within the framework of effective royal administration. The chief purveyor of government was the English monarchy, which built upon and modified its impressive Anglo-Saxon inheritance. English government grew in complexity and professionalism; it also expanded geographically by taking in, not merely the fringes of the kingdom itself, but also large areas of Ireland. In addition, at one remove, it had a profound impact on Scotland. The structures, styles, and reach of Scottish royal rule developed markedly during the twelfth and thirteenth centuries, and influences from south of the Tweed played a major part in their growth. This is not to claim that Scottish institutions derived wholly from England: the native Celtic past helped to shape them; there are hints, too, that the kings of the period were receptive to Capetian models as well as to Anglo-Norman ones. Nor did institutions that sprang from common sources always stay in step; they might follow contrasting paths and assume a different significance in the two kingdoms (on the whole Scottish government remained far less intrusive and bureaucratic than English). Nevertheless there is much to be said for viewing the development of administration in the interwoven realms as a single story. This is scarcely surprising, since the growth of government was closely connected with the spread of the aristocracy—a point that would hardly need to be made were it not for the enduring historiographical tradition that has presented kings and magnates as mutually hostile forces, and drawn a distinction between the advance of royal and aristocratic control that is in important ways misleading.

The expansion of government was not, of course, restricted to the British Isles, or to the two major monarchies within them; it was associated with economic and cultural changes that affected all Latin Christendom. Rising population favoured the colonizing and military ventures of lords and kings. The increased circulation of coin enabled rulers to mobilize resources and pay armies; it also promoted the business side of kingship, and encouraged the keeping of records.

At the same time the growth of literacy and education furnished monarchs with advisers and servants, who enlarged the part played by the written word in government, and whose habits of mind leant naturally towards precise definitions and the crisp assertion of rights.

The Church, which had a virtual monopoly of bookish education in northern Europe, was the seed-bed of important shifts in mentality. The reformers of the eleventh and twelfth centuries drew sharper lines between clerk and lay, and between secular and ecclesiastical authority. Canon law was collected and clarified, becoming an object of specialist study. Popes and bishops, in their ceaseless battles to uphold their privileges against kings, nobles, and one another, valued documents and legal expertise. Religious houses assembled their charters, inventing and retouching them where necessary. These things fed into the secular sphere. Since the personnel of royal and ecclesiastical administration were interchangeable, kings had access to similar skills. In order to uphold their authority in the face of what could appear an intolerable clerical assault, they defined what they saw as their own rights in written form: Henry II's demand in 1164 that the bishops swear to observe the Constitutions of Clarendon, which set out his view of Church–state relations, is a classic instance. Indeed the growth of royal legislation may have been inspired in part by a desire to give the customs of kings' courts the status that had been acquired by the canon law. Thus, paradoxically, the assertiveness of the Church gave added sharpness and confidence to the secular authorities with which the reformers had felt themselves at odds. Kings and nobles alike grew accustomed to a world where literacy and a widening range of technical accomplishments—which they often displayed in person as well as by proxy—were a vital ingredient of the successful exercise of power.

Such trends affected different societies to varying degrees. A wealthy region close to centres of learning would be more receptive than a remote upland fringe; and a strong, unitary kingship would have the advantage over a collection of competing minor dynasties. The English monarchy, with its deep roots in a rich land, had benefited from the economic quickening for a century before the Conquest; it continued to do so after 1066, when the connection of its rulers with France had both commercial and intellectual implications. The Scottish kings presided over a smaller and poorer kingdom. But the kingship itself was fairly stable, and was able to benefit from its connections with Anglo-French society. Other rulers were not immune from the currents of change. During the eleventh and twelfth centuries the greater Irish kingships grew in wealth and military capacity, and the association of kings with reforming clergy and the new religious orders brought some governmental modernization, and may seem to have presaged more. The principality created in thirteenth-century Wales by Llywelyn the Great and Llywelyn ap Gruffydd was likewise open to outside influences, and rested to some extent on the ability to exploit new wealth and techniques. In the event, however, the lesser rulers in Britain and Ireland failed to match the leading monarchies or withstand their power; their history is one of smaller advances, which were arrested and reversed. For that reason it is convenient to devote the present chapter to the administrative development of the dominant powers, and the next to a consideration of royal status itself, and the ways in which kingships flourished or withered in the face of opportunity and challenge.

English government in England and Wales

Anglo-Saxon government has been aptly described as a form of royal presidency over a hierarchy of communities—shires, hundreds, and vills—which were in most respects self-regulating: like all early medieval states outside Byzantium and Islam, the English kingdom was 'patrimonial' rather than 'bureaucratic' in nature. Such a truism may obscure its more remarkable features. The chief of these was the absence of a settled layer of provincial noble power between the king and the local communities, together with the many ways in which the centre penetrated the localities. Whereas in France around 1050 the king ruled a principality around the Île de France, beyond which he worked through alliances with other princes, some of whom were at least as wealthy as he was, in most of England he had a direct link to the next level of society. The two centuries after 1066 were to see great changes, but this characteristic of English government on the whole survived, and moulded administrative and political patterns.

South of the Tees royal authority in the kingdom of Edgar or Cnut was symbolized by the network of boroughs, which had originated in the programme of fortification undertaken by Alfred and his successors in the course of their wars against the Vikings. The boroughs were points of royal influence and profit. In each shire the king's representatives operated from a chief borough, where they held courts attended by the leading landowners. Justice was done according to customary procedures administered by these men; but it was done under royal supervision, and the king and his officials creamed off some of the proceeds in the form of a share in financial penalties arising from the major crimes that were emerging as 'pleas of the crown'. The boroughs also developed as economic centres. They had the protection of the king, who tried to confine trade within them in order to tap the wealth that accrued. The alliance of commercial privilege and royal power was sealed through the mints, located in boroughs, which facilitated both trade and the raising of revenue. Coining was a royal monopoly: although minting was not centralized, it was closely controlled by the monarchy, which provided the dies from which the coins were struck. Since the reforms of Edgar's reign, regular recoinings had taken place. Coin types were changed, and weight and metal content adjusted; the rhythm of recoining was at once an expression of royal authority and a source of income.

The combination of liquidity and a tough, if rudimentary, scheme of administration lay at the heart of the power of the English kingship. Its advantages also sprang from the fact that the West Saxon rulers, for all the antiquity of their lineage, were recent conquerors of much of England. Their expansion had taken place at a time of economic growth, when, moreover, contacts with the Continent were strong and Carolingian models available for emulation. The result was a kingdom whose lowland core was already well organized. Like the shires, the smaller districts of the hundreds and vills were familiar with corporate action. So too, of course, were local communities throughout Europe. But in England they were subject to an unusual degree of central direction, which helped to strengthen and preserve their identity and usefulness.

The local communities were harnessed by the king in various ways. A stable royal coinage and the threat posed by the Viking assaults in Aethelred II's reign facilitated the emergence of a system of general taxation. The geld, a land-tax which was used not so much to buy off the Danes as to hire troops to resist them, developed in the course of the eleventh century into a frequent impost of a sort scarcely known elsewhere in Europe. Its levying presupposed the ability of the king to apportion the burden among the population; this was done through the shires, hundreds, and vills, which served as the units of assessment. Taxation and military service were closely allied: it is often hard to be certain whether a medieval ruler was setting out to raise men, or the money to provide troops' wages. The shires and hundreds formed the basis for the assessment and imposition of military obligations, from the familiar duty of the king's subjects to perform army service, to Aethelred's demand for helmets and byrnies (mailed tunics). The local communities were also the vehicle through which the king's direction of peace-keeping—along with the geld, probably the most striking feature of English royal authority— proceeded. The king frequently intervened in, and voiced ordinances about, matters that concerned him. There was, for instance, a drive against cattle-rustling—a highly significant intrusion by the Crown in a society where great wealth was on the hoof. He also imposed on the population at large the obligation to form itself into groups, notionally of ten, who were to take responsibility for the conduct of their members and the pursuit of wrong-doers. Just as taxation and army service involved a dialogue between the centre and localities, so the security groups (or 'tithings') were supervised by royal officers at the level of the hundred and the vill. The habit of inquisition was also familiar, as communities were quizzed about the extent of royal lands and rights, or the activities of disturbers of the peace.

The effectiveness of late Anglo-Saxon government did not depend upon a large central organization; indeed the absence of records and departmental structures is apt to strike the modern mind as odd. It was an age when vital commands were still transmitted verbally, and when even important property transactions were symbolized by the ceremonial handing over of objects in the presence of witnesses whose memories served as authentication. Royal additions to, or amendments of, custom were also declared orally: the laws of kings are known, not from official texts, but from versions compiled by the Church. The king did issue charters, or 'books', in which he granted land or relieved it of customary obligations. Some charters may have been written by their recipients. Certainly the small amount of writing the king needed could be accomplished by a handful of clerks working from his chapel under the supervision of a chancellor; even these did not spend all their time at court, but might fulfil other functions such as that of envoy. In its lack of elaboration, English central government was no different from the most powerful regime in Europe, that of imperial Germany.

This brief summary is bound, of course, to over-simplify. The geld can hardly have been assessed and collected without records; it seems certain that pre-Conquest documents, similar perhaps to the cadastral surveys of the Carolingian age, lay behind Domesday Book; in that respect, if in no other, England was less innocent of bureaucratic forms of control than other north European kingdoms. Nor was the scheme of local communities regular. Even within the region of shires, boroughs, and mints (which did not extend north of York), the pattern of territorial organization and royal involvement was broken by, for instance, islands of ecclesiastical privilege such as the liberty of St Edmund at Bury or of St Etheldreda at Ely. Nor was the monarchy immune from the threat that large noble supremacies, capable of shutting out central government, might emerge: the eleventh-century earldoms of East Anglia or Mercia came close to doing just that. Nevertheless, the kingdom's heartland was probably the largest area of relatively uniform royal administration in the West at the time when it fell into Duke William's hands.

The government of England during the two centuries that followed must be one of the most intensively studied subjects in European, let alone English, history. Two very different reasons for this stand out. One is the remarkable survival of royal records, of finance from the mid-twelfth century, and of the chancery and central courts from the start of the thirteenth. The other is the proprietorial fascination of Victorian and Edwardian scholars with the history of the British constitution and civil service. Whether their interests lay in the origins of parliament or in the nuts and bolts of administration, they found much to their purposes in the wealth of evidence from the Norman and Angevin periods. Despite the obtrusiveness of some regrettable kings stubbornly wedded to the Continent, a period that saw stately exchequer accounts, the origins of the Common Law, and Magna Carta into the bargain was likely to be painted in positive colours.

Predictably, the tone has altered in recent years. Waning confidence in the virtues of government in post-imperial Britain, a deep hostility to 'bureaucracy', and a reluctance to construe quantities of neatly inscribed parchment as evidence of efficiency, can shape modern writings as surely as more optimistic assumptions informed those of earlier generations. But more reserved appraisals have arisen from advances in scholarship as well as shifts in fashion. An influential agent of change has been recent work on the Anglo-Saxon period. As understanding of the capabilities of pre-Conquest government has grown, hard questions have had to be asked about the effectiveness, and in some cases the novelty, of what succeeded it. To compare an unusually coherent early medieval government, which has left scant evidence behind it, with a well-documented administration of a more bureaucratic type is a task fraught with pitfalls. There is a danger of idealizing the former, whose outlines only are visible, and underestimating the latter because its own records reveal the messiness, expedients, and abuses that attend government in action.

The Norman kings maintained the direct links with the shires. Except in the Welsh borders, the post-Conquest earls did not dominate the counties from which they took their titles; like other proprietors, they held lands scattered in many places. The role of the sheriff as the king's main local representative continued, and was regularized and enlarged. Only during Stephen's reign, when he and Matilda, in their search for support, created earldoms lavishly, was this situation seriously jeopardized. The restoration of central authority under Henry II saw a return to former patterns before the new distribution of power could become ingrained. The Inquest of Sheriffs of 1170, which resulted in the removal of more than half the sheriffs of England, confirmed the point that they were royal officials without a proprietary interest in their offices. Whereas in the later Middle Ages sheriffs were normally members of the gentry community of the shire, in this period they were on the whole outsiders. They varied greatly in background and status; what they tended to have in common was a strong connection with the king. The term 'baronial sheriff', often used of some of the grander figures who held office under the Normans and Angevins, is misleading if it is taken to suggest that such men represented a magnate class, in some sense standing apart from the court. The men associated with the royal household included established curial figures and those with their way to make through service; the selection of sheriffs from their ranks amounted to an effective penetration of the localities by the centre; and, since the sheriff was castellan of the castle at the borough from which the shire was administered, he held the chief symbol of power in his area.

Royal control also expanded geographically. In the Anglo-Saxon period the far north of England remained unshired and the Welsh borders uncertainly controlled. It has been pointed out that, whereas the tenth-century rulers who extended their authority from Wessex into the midlands had refashioned administrative boundaries and established a fairly neat and uniform organization, the Norman and Angevin kings did nothing of the sort in the regions they absorbed.

Shires emerged hesitantly in the north in the course of the twelfth century; the honor of Lancaster and the territories of Cumberland, Westmorland, and Northumberland remained federations of large lordships, which in many cases acquired immunity from some of the multiplying aspects of royal government. Similarly, there seems to have been little will to iron out anomalies further south: tiny Rutland, which had been part of the dower of Edward the Confessor's queen, was allowed to gain and keep the status of a county. But the contrast is not between an effective monarchy, capable of innovation, and a line of less ambitious and rational rulers. The contexts were very different. The expansion of Wessex amounted to the absorption of neighbouring regions into what remained a nucleated and manageable area. The attention of the post-Conquest kings had to be spread over vast and scattered lands which could only be managed by accepting their diversity. Not only that, they ruled at a time when populations were larger, and boundaries and customs more deeply etched. Administrative meddling in the interests of regularity and institutional homogeneity was not on their agenda, and might well have been counter-productive.

In fact royal control as the king understood it spread impressively between the 1090s and the 1240s. Sheriffs appeared in northern England, operating from new castles and boroughs such as Carlisle and Newcastle upon Tyne. The see of Durham, with its episcopal castle, was held by curial bishops such as Rannulf Flambard and Hugh de Puiset. In the time of Henry II the northern sheriffs included administrator–barons such as Rannulf Glanvill and Gilbert Pippard. The royal stake in Wales and the marches grew spasmodically and suffered setbacks. But from the 1220s it began to gain a stability that was only temporarily shaken thereafter. Henry III recovered Carmarthen and Cardigan from Llywelyn the Great in 1223; he built a new castle at Montgomery from 1228; and in 1237 he took Chester into his hands. Chester, which was a great liberty, became the seat of a royal justiciar; the other centres were controlled by castellan-bailiffs. Like the twelfth-century sheriffs, these officers tended to be men with strong court connections. The increased reach of direct royal authority is perhaps best attested by its political reverberations. In the north, the shrieval organization went hand-in-hand with regular circuits of royal justices from the later twelfth century; there were also frequent visitations by King John, especially during the years after the loss of Normandy. This new intrusiveness was one reason why northern barons and knights were in the forefront of the opposition to the Crown in the years 1214–17. Similarly, the mid-thirteenth century stands out as the time when the special privileges of the Welsh marcher lordships took a more defined form; they did so in part at least because they were facing challenges from a royal authority whose tentacles were stretching ever more effectively into south Wales and the March.

A second area of growth was in the scale of central government, which during the twelfth century made its first, limited moves away from the king's person and towards departmental structures and the habit of record-keeping. It was not unique in doing so: the Norman kingdom of Sicily (with its governmental legacy from the Islamic and Byzantine past) saw similar developments, as—more tardily and to a lesser extent—did Capetian France. The early arrival of administrative kingship in England owed a good deal to the centralized character of the Anglo-Saxon legacy, supplemented by the tradition of strong (if distinctly unbureaucratic) ducal rule in Normandy. It was further encouraged by the fact that the monarch was not only often absent from the realm, but also under pressure to exploit English wealth in support of his continental wars and alliances.

As elsewhere, the expansion of central organization is first apparent in the area of finance. In the earlier part of Henry I's reign, exchequers (called after the chequered cloth on which reckoning was done) can be traced in England and Normandy. The English exchequer was charged with extracting accounts from the sheriffs and other officials who received and spent money locally. It did not manage the royal finances as a whole; that role was played, if at all, by the chamber, which travelled with the court, gathering and spending funds originating in any of the royal lands. But it was in this specificity that the exchequer's importance lay, for it came to be the hub of administration when the king was out of the country. It is in the exchequer that signs of bureaucratic rule can first be glimpsed. The earliest surviving pipe roll, containing the audited accounts of the king's sheriffs, dates from 1129 to 1130 and is the first of a sequence that survives almost unbroken from 1155 to 1834. The order and clarity of the roll suggest that it was one of an established series. Fifty years later, the *Dialogue of the Exchequer*, a handbook compiled by Henry II's treasurer, Richard fitz Neal, shows that the exchequer was the seat of procedures in which its experts took a pride: government had become literate, numerate, and self-conscious.

The manifold character of fiscal exploitation under the twelfth-century kings made the need to keep track of business acute; possibly the growth of the record-keeping habit in turn facilitated fiscal inventiveness. One of the characteristics of the period was the Crown's involvement in a host of arrangements with families and communities. The exercise of the king's rights as feudal lord meant making deals over the reliefs payable by heirs upon their succession, and over wardships and marriages. As aspects of government proliferated, the sale of exemptions and the agreement of fines also generated a host of debts. The royal Forest, a Norman novelty, created its own world of penalties and privileges. In addition, the reigns of Henry II, Richard I, and John were a time of experiments in taxation: the king by turns used knights' fees and movable property as the basis of assessments. He and his ministers were engaged in an often ruthless search for resources, and were past masters at driving the hard bargain: the records of King John's exchequer and chancery reek of bureaucratic profiteering. At the same time as the forms of financial exploitation were multiplying, older sources of income tended to dry up. The geld is the prime example. It was still raised in the early years of Henry II; but by that time levels of assessment were fixed by custom, and an accumulation of exemptions (which were a useful form of patronage) had reduced its yield. During the 1160s the decision seems to have been taken that it was no longer worth the political price of its levying, let alone of an attempt at a universal reassessment.

The Norman and Angevin rulers have been stigmatized as fertile in devising opportunities for casual profit, rather than single-minded in reforming or replacing general systems. But, given the entrenchment of customary practice, this is scarcely surprising; it was better to contrive and innovate piecemeal than to assault vested interests by trying to remodel a familiar landscape. And, although administrative growth, outstripping the emergence of agreed conventions of behaviour, presented an unpleasant face, in this area the post-Conquest kings were enlarging an existing feature of English government rather than bringing in wholly new styles. Aethelred II gained his bad reputation partly because of his fiscal and military demands; and there are intriguing similarities between the promises of amendment made by his successor, Cnut, on the subject of royal exploitation of rights of lordship over individuals—for instance, in the matter of heriots (reliefs)—and those in the coronation charter of Henry I and even in Magna Carta.

In the judicial field, the monarchy showed itself capable of considerable feats of organization, even though the growth of royal justice was not the result of a conscious design. The period *c*.1160–*c*.1240 saw the custom of the king's courts develop into the Common Law of England. The stealing of the scene by the royal courts was a complex business. The king had long played a part in repressing serious crime, and taken a slice of the profits. In addition, the Norman rulers had heard cases between their greater subjects in their own courts, while the shire courts had dealt with disputes over property among the tenants of different lords. The regulation of questions of title and succession to land, the most contentious matter in feudal society, had, however, been accomplished very largely in the honor courts. Between the reigns of Henry II and Henry III jurisdiction ebbed away from the courts of the honor and shire, and flowed instead to the royal courts, held by the king himself or by his justices sitting either at Westminster or in the counties.

The emergence of the Common Law was promoted by various things. The network of local communities and the habit of central involvement with them gave royal justice a tradition and an administrative structure within which to work: the shire, for instance, remained vital as the venue of the courts held by the itinerant justices. The complexity of tenurial patterns was also important. Since men tended to hold land of several lords, and tenants-in-chief were also usually subtenants, the number of cases crossing the boundaries of honorial jurisdictions was large, and the space for a royal role broader than in a kingdom made up of self-contained lordships. The familiarity of lords and their richer tenants with honor court, shire court, and king's court was a powerful antidote to regional variations in custom. Expansion arose from a combination of supply and demand; its extent and speed would have been inconceivable without the existing integration of king and kingdom.

The capacity and inclination of the Crown in the time of Henry II to play an interventionist part had much to do with the presence in the royal circle of men whose education equipped them to grasp ideas about royal jurisdiction and to formulate procedures. It also sprang from political conditions. The legitimacy of Henry's position as heir of his grandfather was expressed through his ability, apparent in his attitude to the Scots and to the Church, to assert the rights Henry I had exercised, or was believed to have exercised. More mundanely, he also had to restore royal authority in the aftermath of Stephen's reign. These circumstances fostered a habit of enquiry, a sense of urgency in repressing disorder, and a need to make the existing courts work swiftly and effectively. There was a rapid development of the Crown's criminal jurisdiction. In the Assize of Clarendon of 1166 royal justices were commissioned to visit the shires to receive indictments of criminals 'presented' by panels from the hundreds and vills. Travelling judicial commissions had been known in the time of Henry I; from now on they became a regular feature of English government. The justices in eyre were also charged to investigate all sorts of infringements of royal property and authority; the linking of such tasks with a brief to deal with serious crime gave emphasis to the king's responsibility for the peace of the kingdom.

It was the effort to stimulate other courts that led to what was once interpreted as an attack on baronial jurisdiction. Political harmony depended not least on the resolution of the perpetual disputes within the landed classes over property and inheritance. By insisting that nobody should 'answer for his freehold'—that is, have his title to land or rights challenged in court—without a royal writ (which had to be returned by the sheriff with a note of the action taken), the Crown sought to make the honor and shire courts work properly. Since the implication was that, if they did not, the case might be taken to the king's courts, the scope for bringing business to the royal courts was enlarged. It was further extended by the invention of new actions, of which the king's courts had the monopoly. Instead of immensely long proceedings, leading ultimately to trial by battle to determine a right, an ejected party could recover possession by obtaining a writ of *novel disseisin*, which led to a swift decision by jury before a royal justice. An equivalent procedure, entitled *mort d'ancestor*, covered the question of succession. The aim in offering these remedies was not to deprive baronial or shire courts of their jurisdiction: they were concerned, to begin with, only with very recent dispossession, and anyway left open the possibility of determining the underlying question of right in the old ways. But they reached further back in time as their dates of limitation remained unchanged for long periods, and their efficiency and status as royal actions ensured their general acceptance as tests of title.

The standardizing and general availability of these and other procedures through the writ system, at a time when landholders were becoming more familiar with documents, made recourse to the Common Law easy and natural. Any man of reasonable substance could bring a case, if prudence allowed, even against his lord. It was no longer necessary to formulate a request relating to an individual instance, get it accepted by the king, and have an order drafted to cover the particular circumstances. Literacy thus made redress more readily obtainable, and at the same time tended to confine procedures within set formulas around which legal expertise developed. The text known as *Glanvill* (*c*.1188)—though Henry II's justiciar was probably not its author—arranges its account of the custom of the king's courts around the writs available to litigants there. It is the work of a practical mind grappling with a fast-growing body of knowledge, rather than that of a theorizer. Registers of writs remained central to the education of those who ran the courts. But by the 1220s and 1230s, when the other great treatise of English law (equally misleadingly called after the judge Henry Bracton who flourished two decades later) was written, we see a well-established legal system, presided over by a group of royal judges who were alert to precedent and eager to perfect the tradition within which they were aware of working.

Although honorial jurisdictions were weakened by the rise of the Common Law, its development should not be seen as occurring apart from, let alone in opposition to, the aristocracy. The advance of royal justice, like the growth of administration in the regions, incorporated and even harnessed the baronage. Aristocrats were users of the courts, just like other freeholders. The judges of the time of Henry II were not specialists; they included lay barons who turned their hand to the law as readily as to other aspects of the king's business. To some extent this remained the case in the early thirteenth century, though by then career judges were appearing. They were a varied lot; but not a few came from gentry families, where the legal knowledge needed to protect and augment property was part of the air men breathed. The whole of landed society must by 1200 have been acclimatized to the courts and their procedures. Where men had not experience as plaintiffs or defendants, they had served as jurors on the assizes or as sureties for other litigants. They were well on the way to making the law of the king's courts their own. The records of the early thirteenth-century judicial system are full of cases which appear to be serious disputes, but on inspection have all the marks of collusive affairs brought between family members or between lords and tenants, who were using the courts to sanction and register property transactions or amicable settlements. Royal justice grew, not just

because the Crown thrust it forward, but because it met the require-
ments of the landed élite in an increasingly literate age.

The expansion of English administration, from a base that was
firm to begin with, had political implications which will be considered more fully in later chapters. The monarchy constantly touched
the lives of the baronial and knightly classes; and, as the law graphically shows, they in turn had a stake in the king's government. This
contributed to a sense of political community that appeared early in
England, and went deep, as it embraced—potentially at least—groups
other than the magnates or the inhabitants of the royal towns and
estates. The growth of government was a double-edged affair. It
signified the strength of the Crown, yet tended to provoke opposition, for there were limits to what even a population habituated to
dealings with the centre could tolerate. King John's difficulties arose
from his mismanagement of baronial families in a climate soured by
military defeat. But the enmity of sections of the aristocracy chimed
with a broader resentment amongst all those affected by a grasping
and intrusive administration. Magna Carta was, among much else, an
assertion that royal government was a concern of others besides the
king.

English government in Ireland

The development of English government is highlighted by the for-
mation of a royal administration in Ireland, where the conquests and
settlements coincided almost exactly with the age of *Glanvill* and
Bracton. We know very little about government in Ireland before
John became king of England in 1199, thus bringing the Lordship
within the scope of the proliferating records of the royal chancery.
There had been a royal representative at Dublin from the time of
Henry II's visit in 1171–2. Since Henry had kept substantial areas as
demesne, and insisted upon a regular feudal relationship with the
baronage, there can be no doubt that English law and administration
had already made headway within the occupied areas before the end
of the twelfth century.

That the Lordship of Ireland should conform to English styles,
rather than developing its own hybrid institutional structures, is not
as surprising as it may appear. There was no coherent native scheme
of allegiances and government to take over; and, at a time when
English law was crystallizing and becoming the subject of treatises,

integration with the very different customs of the Irish would have been difficult in practice, and likely to be discouraged, not merely by the Crown but also by the leaders of an aristocratic society that likewise spanned the Irish Sea. By the early years of Henry III's reign the idea that the laws of England and Ireland should be identical had become a commonplace: a series of rulings between 1222 and 1246 included statements such as 'as you well know, . . . the laws of our land of Ireland and of England are and ought to be the same'.[1] Recent research has, furthermore, tended to confirm the historical basis of Henry's reiterated belief that his father had enunciated such a principle in a council held during his Irish expedition of 1210.

It may, however, be misleading to lay too much stress on deliberate royal action and formal declarations. That a theory developed is, of course, significant; it reflects the self-consciousness English government had now attained. But what John and Henry did was not so much to export English law to a dependency, as to state (and consecrate) a fact—and then to supply from year to year the refinements the legal system needed. For in essence the law was the version of feudal custom familiar to a ruling class, who had carried it to Ireland in their baggage. The justices who criss-crossed England in the time of Henry II and Richard I included men of exactly the stamp who were picking up property in Ireland: Bertram de Verdon and Gilbert Pippard, who arrived with John in 1185, and whose families became landholders in Louth, were regular justices on the English eyres of Henry's time, and also well-tried sheriffs. Almost any knight or substantial freeholder who gained Irish interests would have had experience as a litigant or juror. Robert of Wootton, a west midlands landholder associated with the Verdons, turns up as a litigant, juror, assessor of taxes, military arrayer, and justice of gaol delivery in Shropshire between the 1220s and 1240s; he was a working knight *par excellence*. He also had property in eastern Ireland; at one point we hear that he 'crossed over to Ireland for a year and more, and drew revenues [from his Shropshire lands] throughout that time'.[2] Ireland was occupied and organized by men well used to seeking and providing royal justice.

English law and administration were an artificial implantation to the extent that they were the possession of a foreign élite. But within colonial society their growth was natural. By the early 1200s it is reasonable to regard the Common Law as developing in England and Ireland at the same time; indeed the necessity to provide reference material for judges working out of Dublin, and thus spending many months at a stretch deprived of easy contact with their fellows in England, may have been an important stimulus to the growth of a legal literature, and thus to the definition of English law itself. Nor was it only magnates with Irish property who crossed the sea: from John's time onwards Ireland was part of the normal field of operations for the class of clerks and laymen who made government their career, and possibly no more distant a field than the far north of England. John's justiciars of Ireland included two of his most trusted curial clerics, John de Grey, bishop of Norwich, and Henry le Blund, archdeacon of Stafford, who became archbishop of Dublin. In the earlier thirteenth century the judges in Ireland, and the administrative commissioners sent there from time to time, included members of the emerging corps of professionals, such as Henry of Bath, Roger Huscarl, Simon of Hale, Richard Ducket, and Master Robert of Shardlow, who had been Henry III's proctor at the papal curia, as well as a justice in eyre in England.

The Common Law presupposed a governmental structure along English lines. Ireland saw the first of what were to be several reproductions of English administration within the British Isles, though for obvious reasons Irish government grew more slowly than the administrations set up in north Wales and southern Scotland by Edward I in the wake of his conquests. In Ireland central government was smaller and simpler than its English parent, but followed its terminology and organization very closely. From 1204 the justiciar had authority to issue writs originating the assizes of *novel disseisin*, *mort d'ancestor*, and other actions under his own seal. Then in 1232 the making of a great seal for Ireland was authorized, and the office of chancellor created. An exchequer emerged more quickly: an Irish pipe roll survives from 1212; like the sole pipe roll of Henry I, it is clearly one of an established series. By that time a significant regal coinage, of the same weight and fineness as its English counterpart, was being struck in the royal cities of Dublin, Waterford, and Limerick. The presence of borough, mint, exchequer, justiciar, and original writ meant that Ireland had already received key features of administrative kingship on the English style.

A structure of shires also developed. To begin with, apart perhaps from Dublin, where the king took over the area of the Norse kingdom, and had the lords of Leinster and Meath for his neighbours, the Irish counties were not closely delimited territorial units; they are better thought of as fluctuating command-districts dependent on the boroughs. In 1212 there were three sheriffs: of Dublin, of Waterford with Cork, and of Munster. By 1254 sheriffs had appeared in Louth, Kerry, and Connacht, while each of the southern counties had divided in two, to form separate shires of Waterford, Cork, Limerick, and Tipperary. That much of eastern Ireland was not shired arose from the existence of the great lordships. But Leinster and Meath were liberties on the English model, lacking the jurisdictional independence and distinctive customs claimed by the lords of the Welsh March. In 1208 King John gave them new charters which made it plain that the royal pleas of treasure-trove, rape, forstal (assault on the king's highway), and arson lay outside the lord's competence, and that aggrieved litigants could allege default of right in the liberty court, and have their cases transferred to the king's court. The pipe roll of 1212 shows the exchequer taking accounts from the sheriffs, William Marshal's seneschal of Leinster responding to Dublin in matters that belonged to the Crown, and a royal seneschal exploiting Meath, which Walter de Lacy had forfeited, on behalf of the king.

Irish local government was not, of course, strictly comparable with English in much that mattered. Above all, the counties and liberties were, and remained, territorially incomplete; they had unassimilated uplands and boglands, where their sheriffs and seneschals exercised at best a loose authority over native Irish lords. Other differences, however, seem less radical when Ireland is compared, not with lowland England (on which generalizations about shire government tend to be based), but with the north. The county of Munster, with its sizeable compact lordships (which reflected the pre-existing Irish territories known as 'cantreds'), had a good deal in common with the shires of north-west England—a point perhaps not lost on Theobald Walter, lord of Eliogarty and other Tipperary and Limerick cantreds, who also held the lordship of Amounderness and served as sheriff of Lancaster during the 1190s. Theobald in many ways epitomizes the growth of royal government. He was a member of a minor Norfolk landed family whose members, thanks in part to a connection with the Glanvill clan, made their way forward through royal service. Grants from the Crown in Ireland gave Theobald baronial status. However, he retained close links with, and dependence on, the court: his advance and that of the king's interests went hand-in-hand. He played a part in the movement of administration into two rather different outer regions in a way that bears a resemblance to the advance of royal authority in south Wales in the time of Henry I. By 1200 much of Britain and Ireland formed an arena where English law and government were developing under one ruler and through a single governing class.

Although the Lordship of Ireland had English institutions, it did not at this stage possess the fairly coherent political community that already existed in the ancient kingdom of England. The magnate society of England, it is true, spilled over into Ireland, Scotland, and north-west France; but by the early thirteenth century there was little doubt where its main centre of gravity and source of identity lay. By contrast, any list of the 'barons of Ireland' was likely to contain many men whose interests and activities were partly, and in some cases predominantly, British. In addition, the tenurial geography of Ireland, with its lordships on a cantredal and provincial scale, ensured that the horizons of the knights and freeholders were far more circumscribed by their tenurial status than was the case in most of England: the terms 'barons of Meath', 'barons of Leinster', or 'barons of Ulster' denoted relatively self-contained honorial societies. Nevertheless alongside the ties of lordship there was a pull exerted by royal government, apparent in requests for taxation and military service. Its force was to increase in the later thirteenth century.

Scottish royal government

The development of government in Scotland at this period is as striking as in England; it may even be more so, since it took place from a less advanced starting-point than the one William of Normandy inherited from the Anglo-Saxons. What happened in Scotland between the time of David I (or a little earlier) and that of Alexander III amounted to a marked assimilation of institutions north and south of the border. There is no doubt that the Scottish kings and those around them were heavily influenced by Anglo-Norman assumptions and practices, and little mystery as to why this should have been so. As Carolingian influences on Anglo-Saxon kingship and government suggest, the flow of ideas and techniques from one kingdom to another was not uncommon. In that case their passage was accomplished through diplomatic contacts between the royal houses and the movements of religious and mercantile personnel. The Anglo-Scottish relationship also had those features; but it went much deeper because of the close weave of landholding ties, including those of the royal house, that stretched across the border. English overlordship itself could promote the development of government, sometimes in unexpected ways. When Henry II occupied castles in southern Scotland under the Treaty of Falaise, his action concentrated William the Lion's itinerary and attention upon his more northerly centres, contributing to the intensification of government in the region between Perth and the Moray Firth. It seems possible, too, that the need to make several large payments to the English between 1189 and 1209 had a beneficial impact—as tributes often did—on the fiscal authority and organization of the subordinate polity.

To say all this is not to suggest that the Scottish kings had a vision of an Anglo-Norman system which they were seeking to emulate. Influences were received piecemeal and no doubt often unconsciously; patterns that seem obvious to historians were less so to contemporaries, who might also be perplexed by the state-building motives sometimes attributed to them. Nor was it the case that the development of royal rule was wholly Anglo-Norman in inspiration and style: even before 1100 the ruling house had contacts with other parts of the northern French world, and by the time of William the Lion a Capetian alliance was a familiar tactic. Above all, the influences that came into Scotland did not enter a political and institutional vacuum; their impact was shaped by existing traditions and structures.

The difficulty is that the Scottish kingdom is almost without written records before the time of David I. We can compensate in some degree for the absence of contemporary documents by detecting traces of earlier institutions in the charters of the twelfth and thirteenth centuries. But the evidence remains thin, patchy, and awkward to interpret. It is not always possible to gauge the antiquity of this or that 'pre-feudal' (or perhaps merely 'non-feudal') feature, or to assess its distribution. The evidence can often be deployed to argue with almost equal ease either for or against the unity and institutional maturity of eleventh-century Scotland; much depends on the cast of the historian's mind. Scottish scholars have mostly inclined towards a positive view of the early kingdom, and a contrary case remains to be made out: the quality of their work disallows a facile scepticism.

If royal government in late Anglo-Saxon England was precocious by the European standards, Scottish government at the same period was not. The first surviving royal charters date from the 1090s, and were issued under English influence; the first regal coins were struck by David I as late as 1136. But this does not mean that the Scottish kings, any more than the rulers in Ireland, lacked the capacity to exploit men and land. Within the royal heartlands of the south and east there were numerous royal centres to which renders were due from dependent settlements. These 'discrete' or 'multiple' estates were presided over by 'thanes' or 'grieves', who supervised the exaction of the king's rights, and were in turn supported by a share of the produce. In places the estates were termed *scirs*, as in Northumberland; but they were not administrative districts in the manner of the shires south of the Trent; they are better thought of as islands of intensive royal authority set within a sea where the king's rights to tribute and hospitality were more limited. It seems probable that the king and his entourage maintained themselves through a combination of travelling between favoured centres and consuming on the spot, and having food carted, driven, or floated to wherever they might be. No doubt buying and selling took place, and the king may have had some cash revenue. As Irish and Welsh examples testify, kingdoms without their own coinage were not necessarily devoid of coin; and the centres which received royal charters giving them burghal status in the twelfth century are likely to have had a trading function at an earlier stage.

Beyond the royal core of Scotland, organization seems to have been similar despite differences in nomenclature (in the Gaelic regions the *maer* fulfilled the role of the thane or grieve). An intensely complex political situation might be summed up by saying that elsewhere the system was geared not towards the direct support of the king but towards that of provincial lords who ran the gamut from officials with a high degree of independence, to figures who were themselves regal, but intermittently subordinate to the king of Scots (or the king of Norway). Some of the *mormaers* ('great stewards') north of the Tay may be placed in the former category, and the *reges* of Galloway or Argyll in the latter. The powerful *mormaers* of Moray, from whose line Macbeth had come, fell somewhere in between the two, while the king himself, or a member of his family, had long held the subkingdom of Strathclyde. Compared with eleventh-century England, the core of royal Scotland was much smaller in relation to the fringes; it was also less wealthy and governmentally advanced.

Although administrative growth was a feature of Scotland in the twelfth and thirteenth centuries, government never approached its English counterpart in scale, complexity, rapacity, or in the amount of parchment it generated. If its background was different, so too was its contemporary context. English administration was driven by the needs and ambitions of the Norman and Angevin rulers, and by the fact that exploitation had to continue during their frequent absences. Save for their English estates, the Scottish monarchs had a single sphere of operations, within which they were normally resident. Comparisons between the burgeoning administrative kingship south of the Tweed and the more limited, conservative, and intimate rule of the Scottish kings can illuminate both; invidious comparisons, however, seem beside the point.

From the time of King David the household of the Scottish kings was dominated by Anglo-Normans. Newly introduced families supplied them with household stewards (FitzAlan), constables (Moreville), and butlers (Soules). The ecclesiastics who staffed their chapel served them as chancellors and clerks, and familiarized Scotland with royal charters of a type almost indistinguishable from their English equivalents. The emphasis on a small number of hereditary household officers (or their deputies) seems more reminiscent of French than Anglo-Norman or Angevin kingship; but the similarity may have arisen less from a desire to copy the Capetians, than from the small administrative needs of kings who, like the French before the time of Philip Augustus, ruled a nucleated principality with which they had an ancient association. Their limited governmental ambition is also reflected in the restricted amount of writing done on their behalf. In the twelfth century the chancellor and two or three clerks seem to have sufficed. They produced perhaps two hundred charters a year, and there appears to have been little if any increase between the reigns of William the Lion and Alexander III. Nor did the Scottish chancery adopt the habit of keeping copies of the documents it issued; apart from some solemn diplomatic instruments, the charters we have were preserved by their recipients.

The lack of documentation compared to England, where writing and record-keeping mushroomed, sprang from the different structures and circumstances of the two administrations. The Scottish kings had a tiny group of officials, and there was little of the departmentalization that generated parchment and reference materials in England. Nor were they inveterate long-distance travellers whose households had to stay in touch with ministers based away from court or with lords and communities dispersed from Cork to Bayonne. The financial arrangements of the monarchy were also comparatively simple. Even in the thirteenth century there was no treasurer or central treasury. The king's funds, which were deposited in his more important castles, were managed by a chamberlain based in the household. Although there was an exchequer which checked the accounts of his local ministers, it did not have a permanent existence in a set place. The term was used of the occasions during the year when the chancellor and other members of the council met to conduct audits. Financial accounts were kept—those of 1264–5 are the earliest to survive—but there is no hint of an equivalent of the complex interlocking records that were compiled in the English exchequer at the same period.

The lack of bureaucracy at the centre was no obstacle to the spread and intensification of royal control in the localities, which was a feature of government between the early twelfth and late thirteenth centuries. This growth was associated with modest but significant changes in the economy. Whereas Malcolm Canmore took what was due to him mostly in kind, the revenues of William the Lion a century later were primarily in cash. William struck coins at Roxburgh, Berwick, Stirling, Edinburgh, and Perth, five of his main burghs. The number of royal centres with burgh status at the beginning of his brother's reign in 1153 was fifteen; it had more than doubled when William died in 1214. The creation of burghs was closely linked to the enlargement of the political and financial base of the monarchy. A prosperous burgh whose élite looked directly to the king was a source of regional influence and control, while the *fermes* (fixed rents) owed by burghs, and the customs dues (known as *cán* of ships) collected in them, formed an important part of the king's increasing cash revenue.

The burghs clustered within the established zones of royal power, and also extended and deepened them: in 1153 there were four burghs between Perth and the Moray Firth; in 1214 there were eleven, including Inverness. The growth of burghs was linked with the emergence of the sheriffdoms. In the time of David I the name 'sheriff' was applied to men, usually of Anglo-Norman origin, placed in charge of the castles in certain royal centres and the regions dependent on them. As royal control expanded and intensified, the number of sheriffs grew, and by the mid-thirteenth century all Scotland south and east of the highland line lay within the network of sheriffdoms. The spread of the king's authority in the south-west, for example, is marked by the appearance in the record of Ayrshire (1207), Dumfriesshire (1237), and Wigtownshire (1263). Some sheriffdoms grew out of the old *scirs*; but they had by the thirteenth century more in common with English shires than with the old discrete estates. Despite many differences—not least their much later development—the association of burgh and sheriffdom, each with a part to play in the raising of revenue under central supervision, resembles the means by which royal power was articulated in England.

The history of Scots law brings out the similarities and contrasts between the kingdoms, together with the extent of English influence, with special clarity. The legal system of pre-twelfth-century Scotland is obscure. There is no reliable evidence that the kings of Scots legislated; probably the law was in essence regional and customary. The *judices* who appear in later charters, usually associated with the northern provinces, seem to have been members of an ancient class of lawmen or 'dempsters' who specialized in interpreting traditional law. The king may have played some part in enforcing, and profiting from, judgments given in the courts within the areas where his authority was strong. But we know so little about his judicial role that it is difficult to estimate how far the changes of the twelfth and thirteenth centuries were of substance, and how far merely of style.

The most obvious novelties were connected with the arrival of the new aristocracy, who carried courts and the Anglo-Norman brand of feudal custom with them. Since David I, who had been a justice in King Henry's service, and his successors belonged in most respects to that same society, they assumed without discomfort the judicial functions of the feudal overlord. In Scotland as in England, royal and baronial justice advanced together, though not of course without tensions; and the customs of the Scottish and English kings' courts sprang from the same roots. The shared origins are apparent in the most famous Scottish medieval law book, *Regiam Majestatem*, which was probably compiled around 1318: in essence it is a rehandling of *Glanvill*. But that fact itself suggests important contrasts: to contemporary professional lawyers in England, *Glanvill* would have been chiefly of antiquarian interest.

Although Scots law grew alongside English Common Law, and was deeply influenced by it, the two were never identical either in content or in their administration. Up to a point the interaction is striking. The charters of William the Lion and Alexander II reveal procedures and jurisdictional rights which echo those of Angevin England. When William gave Robert de Brus a new charter for Annandale around 1178, he kept back 'the regalia belonging to my regality, that is, cases of treasure-trove, murder, premeditated assault, rape of women, arson, plunder—which cases I have reserved to myself', making provision for them to be tried before his justices within the sheriffdom of Roxburgh.[3] The charter speaks as though it is confirming arrangements dating back to the original grant of Annandale by David I *c.*1124, which is recorded in a short, unspecific charter; in fact it testifies to the growth of royal jurisdiction in the intervening period, which in turn led to a closer definition of baronial liberties. From 1245 there is evidence that the English procedure for the indictment of criminals before royal justices by neighbourhood juries was in operation in Lothian. By that time we also know that the king was issuing writs of *dissasine* and *mortancestor*, to inaugurate actions in his courts akin to those of *novel disseisin* and *mort d'ancestor*, which lay at the heart of English land law. The migration of these to Scotland was probably encouraged by a demand from below. Landholders with property or family ties in England were likely to be dissatisfied with the absence of a Scottish equivalent of such swift and popular means of redress. Their outlook may well have been similar to that of the tenants of the liberty of Durham, who felt disadvantaged by the old-fashioned remedies offered by their bishop's court, and sought permission from the Crown to introduce the possessory assizes.

Assimilation, however, had its limits. Scotland, needless to say, was different from Ireland, where English law was formally received. Most of our knowledge of Scots law before the fourteenth century has to be deduced from charters: we can glimpse procedures in operation but often have no idea of when or how they were introduced. The kings did issue assizes that changed legal practice; but, whereas in England official texts of legislation survive, either in contemporary chronicles or in the royal records themselves, Scottish legislation is preserved only in unofficial compilations that may contain a jumble of provisions, clearly from different periods but attributed retrospectively to a particular king. They have more in common with Anglo-Saxon or early Norman laws than with the legislation of the English monarchy of the thirteenth century. Scottish rulers seem to have adopted and adapted whatever features of the Common Law seemed useful, and ignored the rest. Henry III's reissues of Magna Carta were current in Ireland as well as in England, but the Charter—many of whose provisions were designed to regulate the conduct of Angevin government—passed Scotland wholly by; so too did the statutes of the later thirteenth century, which were concerned with matters particular to English law and its administration.

Like the kingdom itself, Scots law was less centralized in its administration than English. Royal writs gave those who acquired them a hearing under the king's authority according to recognized processes. But the case, unless it was before the king himself, would be heard locally, since there were no central courts or specialized judiciary. These fundamental contrasts are apparent in many ways. The writs that began actions were not returnable to the central government, which kept no judicial records. Charters issued by lords seem less concerned than their English equivalents to warrant the titles they conferred on their recipients against challenges in the king's courts—for these were a more remote eventuality in Scotland. Proceedings of *dissasine* and *mortancestor* could be brought in the sheriff's court, whereas in England and Ireland they could only be heard by royal justices.

The application of the law, much more than in England, remained in baronial hands. The king appointed magnates as justiciars in Lothian, Scotia, and Galloway. They held courts where the major criminal pleas reserved to the Crown were heard, together with the land-pleas that were the stuff of medieval litigation. The office of sheriff, which brought with it the presidency of a court which was less circumscribed in its jurisdiction than the English shire court had become, tended to be the preserve of local lords who in many cases had a hereditary grip upon it. Such a scheme of legal organization reflected accurately enough the structure of a kingdom that was far more an agglomeration of lordships than was England. A partnership between Crown and magnates was the best, indeed the only, means of getting the king's work done. That fact was also apparent in the large number of privileged baronial lordships outside Lothian. The Brus liberties at Annan were paralleled by those of Earl David and his descendants in Garioch, and by the host of northern magnates who had 'pit and gallows' jurisdiction. The baronage thus administered the same law in two guises: as royal ministers, and as possessors of franchisal rights which were by 1200 in theory at least closely defined by the Crown. Scottish royal government may have been less interventionist than its English counterpart; but even so by the time of Alexander III it had helped to create, sustain, and extend a common law that was dominant over all Scotland save for the far west and north.

The particular distribution of power in Scotland, and the resulting management of the kingdom through collaboration between a monarchy with restricted administrative needs and an aristocracy that was a blend of Anglo-Norman and native, had consequences that were to run throughout medieval Scottish history. Government touched directly a narrower spectrum of society than in England; as a result, the political community that emerged tended to remain an aristocratic affair. The kingdom of Scots was in that sense less 'modern' than England. But its inhabitants, spared the attentions of a meddlesome and rapacious central authority, may have viewed its conservatism with equanimity.

This contrast is one of many, for the styles and intensities of royal government varied greatly, not just between the English and Scottish territories, but also within them. The shape and impact of institutions depended on the physical geography of regions, their history of settlement, past patterns of political organization, the goals and decisions of contemporary rulers, and much else besides. To employ the growth of royal administration as an all-embracing theme is to flatten the contours of the past, and to risk evacuating it of the particularities that give it interest. The theme nevertheless is an important one. It may direct attention towards the lowest common denominators; yet it is no small matter that between 1100 and the mid-thirteenth century a world came to exist from Athlone to Norwich and from Inverness to Southampton that lay within the compass of royal government and law, and was marked by many similar assumptions and techniques.

5. Kings and Princes

IN 1100 the British Isles contained many and varied kings; by 1270 the rulers who had a colourable claim to royal rank had declined sharply in number, and the definition of what made a king had narrowed decisively. The kings of England and of Scots, despite the gap between them in style and wealth, were uncontestably royal; their ever more monopolistic authority had obliterated some other kingships, and was asking hard questions about the status of those that remained. They now served as a model towards which all would-be kings had to aspire. In Ireland the major native rulers who survived in the north and west had declined in power and standing to the point where their ability to compete was doubtful, though they continued to use royal titles spasmodically for another century. In Wales the princes of Gwynedd had been more successful in demoting their local competitors and absorbing some attributes of up-to-date regality. But their fate shows all too clearly the obstacles that stood in the way of anybody in Britain, save for the king of Scots, who tried to be more than an aristocratic vassal of the English Crown.

The process by which kingship was restricted was an old one. The Anglo-Saxon kingdoms of the seventh century seem to have been composed of agglomerations of sub-kingdoms, whose rulers lost their royal rank. The kingdom of England was in turn a product of the disappearance, in the face of Viking and West Saxon conquest, of the provincial kingdoms. Between the sixth and tenth centuries England passed from multiple, many-tiered kingship to a unitary kingship, albeit within a land where provincial divisions were still strong. In Scotland the descendants of Kenneth had not by 1100 established the same exclusive lien on kingly rank, but over most of the country they had smothered or outdistanced other royal dynasties. The position in Ireland and Wales was not so clear-cut. Kings remained numerous, and were superimposed on one another in unstable hierarchies. Welsh kingship has been described as 'relative',[1] while the *Song of Dermot and the Earl* remarks of the late twelfth century that 'there are as many kings in Ireland, as there are counts elsewhere'.[2]

Yet both Ireland and Wales were experiencing changes in some ways comparable to those that had already occurred in England and Scotland. In the early Middle Ages Ireland had been made up of more than a hundred *tuatha* (small territories or population groups) each with its *rí* (king). *Tuatha* had long been grouped in shifting federations presided over by greater kings. But between the tenth and twelfth centuries they were far more effectively clumped together under the domination of powerful overlords; their loss of status is reflected in the replacement of the term *rí* by *taoiseach* (chief). Around 1100 only some dozen dynasties may be regarded as having serious claims to royal status. Each ruled an area at least the size of a later county (to that extent the *Song of Dermot* spoke the literal truth). Similarly in Wales there was a tendency for a small number of kins to arrogate regality to themselves, leaving the subordinated majority to sink out of the royal ranks. There, too, the swallowing of the lesser by the greater is mirrored in changing terminology, as the title of *brenin* (king) gave way to that of *arglwydd* (lord). A discussion that begins around 1100 faces complications aplenty, but at least it can with a clear conscience set ancient petty kingship aside. The interactions that mattered were between regional overlordship of an old-fashioned sort on the one hand, and 'modern', unitary kingship on the other.

European kingship in England and Scotland

In the time of Henry I the English monarchy was, by contemporary standards, immensely strong. It had no rivals in England, and benefited from a long-established royal tradition and an unusually effective system of government which provided a foundation for the precocious development of what has come to be called 'administrative kingship'. Such characteristics place England at this stage well in advance (in the view of the historian who favours centralization) of the less coherent kingdoms of Germany and France. However, in the structure of the royal house and the outward forms of the kingly office, the Normans were in step with the Salians and Capetians: all three may be seen as exponents of a Frankish model of kingship that was becoming the European norm.

Like the aristocracy, the royal kins were organized as lineages. They had a sense of identity that persisted through the generations, associating them with the kingdoms they ruled, just as noble lineages were identified with their main lordships. Basic to this connection (which in turn sharpened the sense of a territorial kingdom) was a familial order that could carry the royal house across the chasm that opened each time a king died. The transmission of office and property was also being made more predictable by the Church's permeation of family life, which brought stricter controls over marriage and the drawing of a firm line between legitimate offspring (who could inherit) and bastards (who could not). No kingdom of the period had a formal law of succession that arranged family members in order. But certain presumptions existed. The most important was that the kingship, and by implication the kingdom, were indivisible. It was also common ground that the natural heir was the king's eldest son, or, in the absence of sons, his next brother. More awkward decisions, such as that between John and his nephew Arthur in 1199, would be resolved by the balance of political support, with or without violence. The prospects of cadets depended on what a ruler had to offer. An accretion of territory, through marriage or conquest, might enable him to provide a younger son with princely status. A more likely outcome was the creation of an endowment within the realm, perhaps through marrying him to an heiress: John had the best of both worlds, since he was granted Ireland by his father, and also gained by marriage much of the inheritance of the earls of Gloucester.

In its rites of inauguration, the English kingship possessed other qualities typical of the leading monarchies. The king was crowned in a great church by the archbishop of Canterbury, the embodiment of the ecclesiastical integrity of the kingdom. With the coronation ceremony was associated the more intimate act of anointing with holy oil, the deepest symbol of Christian kingship. The rite of unction had been used in Gaul when Pippin, the father of Charlemagne, was promoted to kingship in 751. In the tenth century it was adopted by the West Saxons, as well as by the successors of the Carolingians in Germany and France. The Normans and Angevins had every interest in preserving the established rites, which placed them among a small élite of European rulers. The God-given nature of the kingship was also displayed by the use, constant in royal documents from the 1170s onwards, of the *Dei gratia* formula in their titles.

These well-established and wealthy kings of England, who even after 1204 remained important continental princes, controlled a powerful and literate government. From the early thirteenth century the records of the royal chancery and courts, the growing literature of the law, and the (often hostile) comments of chroniclers leave evidence of theories of royal rule. Historians have not been slow to detect the presence of authoritarian ideas in the reigns of John and Henry III.

Letters issued in John's name frequently stress the royal *vis et voluntas* ('will and pleasure'), a right to command that could override custom; and this aspect of John's rule seems to accord with the tyrannical reputation that came to be attached to him. Statements and judgements made by Henry III in person during the 1240s and 1250s display a concern with royal sovereignty and a wish to assert what he regarded as his rights over magnates and churchmen alike. Henry was especially sensitive on the question of the liberty jurisdictions claimed by his subjects, and his actions at this period foreshadowed in many respects the *Quo warranto* proceedings of the 1270s and 1280s. His outlook has been thought to accord with the well-known statement in *Bracton*, that the king was subject not to man, but to God alone; and in 1258 his baronial opponents (echoing the suspicion that, in an age when the study of Roman law was reviving, foreign advisers were harbingers of oppression) told the pope that Henry's Poitevin half-brothers had encouraged him to believe that he was above the law, the *princeps legibus solutus* of the Roman maxim.

That authoritarian tones should invade English government is in no way surprising. The emergence of a class of ministers and advisers who were learned in canon, and to some extent in civil, law was a feature of the monarchies of the period. These men were skilled at defining and rationalizing royal power, which they articulated in striking language. The desire to defend the authority of kings against the claims of popes was a significant stimulus to their endeavours, and the royal chanceries had a way of taking over the ringing phrases of papal diplomatic. High views of royal authority were certainly promoted by Peter des Roches, the Poitevin bishop of Winchester who was John's justiciar from 1213 to 1215 and masterminded Henry III's ill-fated regime of 1232–4. Henry had close links with the imperial court of Frederick II, that great enemy of popes; in 1235 he entertained the imperial ambassador, Peter de Vinea, Frederick's legal draftsman, to whom he assigned an annual fee. Henry of Susa, or 'Hostiensis', the most famous canonist of the age, was a clerk in his service from about 1236 to 1244. But foreign personnel were hardly necessary to infect government with authoritarian rhetoric; not a few native judges and ministers, including Henry Bracton and William of Kilkenny (the keeper of the king's seal from 1250 to 1255), were also learned in the laws.

It is, however, one thing to discover traces of such ideas in royal circles, and quite another to conclude that kings had embarked on a conscious and consistent attempt to establish their rule upon abstract principles of a 'Roman' type. When it suited him (as it often did), King John was as likely to uphold custom as to assert his *vis et voluntas*. Henry III's personal government in the years 1234–58 was in reality marked by considerable indulgence to the baronage, not least in the matter of liberties. His utterances about his royal rights and the obligations of his subjects were scarcely extreme, and were balanced by confirmations of, and murmurs of respect for, Magna Carta. Similarly, alongside the remarks in *Bracton* about unfettered sovereignty can be set other passages in which the stress falls upon the king's duty to rule in accordance with the law, and even the possibility of a baronial bridle being placed upon a refractory monarch. Kingship in England betrays not just wide gaps between the theory and practice of government, but a range of divergent theories. Kings and their servants appear to have seized upon those that suited their immediate purposes, and to have had less trouble than some modern commentators in coping with apparent inconsistencies. Nevertheless the constant expression of high views of kingly rights was significant. As the reign of Edward I would show, familiarity with them could be an additional weapon in the hands of a ruler who (unlike John and Henry III) combined an authoritarian outlook with political competence. In the early thirteenth century, however, their appearance serves chiefly to confirm England's place amongst the wealthier and more developed monarchies of Europe—for it was in the fertile soil of ambitious, intrusive administrations that high regalian notions most readily took root.

Scotland has, with justification, been presented as an example of a different type of kingship. Royal rule there was less centralized and interventionist. Scottish kings had fewer resources, and a far smaller and simpler administration. Though they did at times quarrel with some of their greater subjects about matters of patronage or regional power, there is little sign of the tensions over the character and limits of royal government that were common in thirteenth-century England. Nor do they and those who served them appear to have been proponents of exalted theories. The loss of Scottish royal records may, of course, to some extent disguise the aggressiveness of rulers who were, after all, for much of the twelfth and thirteenth centuries busy expansionists. But everything suggests that Scottish kingship had little in common with the abrasive, meddlesome rule that existed south of the Tweed. Nevertheless the kings of Scots belonged within the family of conventional European royalty, many of whose attributes they came to share, while remaining innocent of the more assertive features of 'administrative kingship'. Alexander I, David I, and their successors were aware of standards, especially in the religious sphere, which they set out to achieve; and although they were scarcely working to some blueprint of modern monarchy, it is hard to avoid judging their success by the extent to which they moved towards conformity with the models of unitary rule, family structure, and kingly status familiar in England and France. The most profound changes arose from their involvement in Anglo-French society, and the penetration of Scotland by its influences.

As a kingdom, eleventh-century Scotland was further from completion than England. The regions in the west and north that remained to be integrated had regal traditions that the sparseness of the evidence, and the concentration of historians on the eventual victors, may lead us to underestimate. Those who ruled on the fringes cannot be arranged in neat constitutional categories; it is unhelpful to seek a simple answer to the question whether they were within, or outside, a Scottish polity. They were less powerful than the king of Scots, and might on occasion play the part of sub-kings by joining his army, as the men of Galloway and Argyll were to serve David I at the Battle of the Standard in 1138. But they retained considerable freedom of action, and could often find allies and patrons in Ireland or Norway.

Before 1100 the Scottish royal house for its part betrays distinct traces of its Gaelic origins, not least in its patterns of inheritance. On the whole sons did not succeed their fathers; the royal office was the subject of competition among the branches of the kin. The sub-kingdom of Strathclyde was used to support a designated heir, or king-in-waiting, in the fashion of an Irish *tánaiste* (lit. 'second'). Moray tended to serve as a base for rival segments of the dynasty. The subsequent territorial expansion of the kings of Scots thus went hand-in-hand with the extinction of other royalties. It was also inseparable from the triumph of the line descended from Malcolm Canmore's marriage to Margaret over older branches of the mac Alpin kin, whose challenges arose on the fringes of the kingdom and seem to have been associated with provincial hostility to the power of the centre and the acquisitive new aristocracy that embodied it. The enlargement and unification of the kingdom of Scots, and the changing structures of the royal kin, form a single story.

Galloway, which saw armed resistance to Anglo-Norman colonization in the third quarter of the twelfth century, lost its regal status only slowly. Its ruler, Fergus, who died in 1161, was frequently called *princeps*, and once *rex*; he may, like Alexander I, have married an illegitimate daughter of Henry I. His successors abandoned the royal styles while retaining some regal attributes. They had diplomatic dealings with both the Scottish and English courts, and were still referred to as *principes*—the term that was currently being applied to the more important Welsh rulers—by English chroniclers. Even in the early thirteenth century Alan son of Roland had an ease of manoeuvre and a range of contacts on either side of the Solway and the Irish Sea that marked him out as more than a baron of the king of Scots. It was only Alexander II's intervention upon his death in 1234, to exclude his bastard son and partition his lands between his daughters, that put a final end to Galloway's royal status; even then its identity survived in a distinctive law-code, whose tolerance of blood feud was offensive in the eyes of a conventional monarchy.

The integration of the far west took longer, nor were its regal traditions so conclusively buried. Somerled (d. 1164), the chief power in Argyll and the adjacent islands, was viewed as a king by Manx and Irish sources as well as by the *Chronicle of Melrose*. A vestigial royalty adhered to his descendants, who divided his lordships amongst them. Alexander III's reign saw the apparent end of the old order in the west, with the extrusion of Norway, the extinction of the Manx kingship, and the drawing of Somerled's successors, the MacDonalds, MacDougalls, and others, into the aristocratic society that focused on the Scottish court. But in the event the Anglo-Scottish wars brought a retreat of Scottish royal authority. The MacDonalds won the regional power-game that ensued; and the memory of Gaelic kingly status was part of the tradition that went into the making of their Lordship of the Isles. That, however, lay far in the future; around 1270 the day of multiple kingship in northern Britain seemed to be done. The weight of the house of Canmore was irresistible, and its brand of kingship inimitable.

By the time of Alexander III the age of segmentary rivals to the royal line was also at an end, though until 1215 the survival of its monopoly of the royal office must at times have appeared a close-run thing. In 1093 and 1094 Donald Bán had excluded his nephews, Malcolm's sons; only the backing of William Rufus had won the kingship briefly for Duncan II (the son of Malcolm's first marriage) in 1094, and for Edgar (the son of Malcolm and Margaret) in 1097. Donald's power lay in the west and north, as did that of the series of rivals who threatened David I, William the Lion, and Alexander II. In 1130 David was compelled to take military action against Angus of Moray, whose position was regal in the eyes of the *Annals of Ulster*, and whose descent from King Lulach (1058), the step-son of Macbeth, gave him a claim to the kingship. The rebels of later generations—Donald mac William (1187) and his sons Guthred (1211) and Donald (1215)—were grandson and great-grandsons of Duncan II, who had reason to see themselves as disinherited. By the time of their risings Moray had been absorbed into the royal orbit, and the centres of their movements lay in Argyll and Ross. If, as seems likely, the support they found owed much to the resentment of central authority, the recurrent crises may be viewed as a tribute to the power of the Scottish kingship, and their ending as its ultimate vindication. Indeed the fact that malcontents in most of Scotland even before 1100 clustered around claimants to the kingship shows that David and his successors started from a position of strength.

One advantage lay in their possession of a solid landed base, to which they could add, whether through the fuller integration of Strathclyde, intensified control over the coastal lowlands north of the Tay, or military expansion further afield, even at times into England. The kingdom, while limited in scope, had territorial definition. Its core, part of which was taken over from the Northumbrian kings, was fairly well organized; and in St Andrew's it had a centre of religious identity. Its location was also significant, for it gave the kings ready access to England and north-west Europe. The receipt of outside influences by a kingship that had the stability, strength, and remoteness to absorb them without being overwhelmed was a key to success.

The external orientation of the dynasty is visible in many ways apart from its English estates and political links. Queen Margaret was the sister of Edgar Atheling, the representative of the house of Wessex, and the daughter of a Magyar princess. Her own daughters were to marry Henry I and the count of Boulogne (the father-in-law of the future King Stephen). In the early 1160s Malcolm IV married his sisters to the counts of Brittany and Holland. The Scottish royal house was moving on the same stage as the princely families of northern Europe, and one closed to Welsh and Irish kings. The names of its children are also redolent of the wider world. Malcolm and Margaret named their sons after members of the Old English royal kin (Edward, Edmund, Edgar, Aethelred), the pope (Alexander), and either an Old Testament king or a Hungarian kinsman (David); the names favoured by the Alpin dynasty disappeared, rather as those associated with the House of Brunswick vanished from the family of Victoria and Albert. The dynasty also—and here the contrast with Ireland and Wales was less wide—became agents of religious modernization. Margaret brought monks from Canterbury to Dunfermline, and gained a posthumous reputation as a reformer of the morals of clergy and aristocracy alike. Her reputation was exaggerated, but reflected well enough the outlook of the churchmen who influenced her sons. David I in particular was a founder of monasteries; his tutor, John, became the first Anglo-Norman bishop of Glasgow; and St Ailred was a member of his household before taking up the monastic life at Rievaulx.

In view of this background, it is scarcely surprising that in the course of the twelfth century the dynasty acquired the attributes of a lineage. In doing so, it parted company with one aspect of its Gaelic past, and with contemporary Ireland. From 1097 to 1286 the kingship was passed down the line of Malcolm and Margaret in a disciplined way. To begin with, this probably owed much to accident. Henry I supported the three brothers of his queen, who succeeded each other without question because the two eldest left no legitimate descendants. In David's time, however, there are signs of a self-conscious order. His only son, Earl Henry, was regarded as his heir, and is described as 'king designate' in one group of charters. When Henry died, David had the 11-year-old Malcolm, his eldest grandson, escorted round the kingdom by the senior noble, the earl of Fife, to mark him out as the new heir. When Malcolm died childless, his next brother, William, succeeded without opposition. Thereafter the kingship passed from father to son until 1286; Alexander III succeeded before his eighth birthday, an event that would have been unthinkable in Gaelic Ireland. In 1281 Alexander provided for the succession by settling the kingship on his surviving son, the Lord Alexander, and any sons he might have, then on any future sons of his own, and finally on any daughters of Lord Alexander. Though the details differed, his action in making such formal provision parallels that of Edward I in England.

Other practices of the dynasty from the time of King David onwards are also revealing. David before his accession was the last member of the family to hold an apanage that amounted to a sub-kingdom. Later heirs and cadets tended to hold the family's lordships in England and limited lands in Scotland, so emphasizing the integrity of the main inheritance. The names of the males of the royal house confirm that it was operating as a lineage on the European model. The continued use of the name 'Malcolm'—which was given to David's short-lived eldest son as well as to the eldest son of Earl Henry—has been taken as a sign of respect, amidst so much that was new, for the Gaelic past. But no other old names were perpetuated; and a more likely explanation is that 'Malcolm' was chosen because the lineage derived its identity from its descent from Malcolm Canmore. Earl Henry, in harmony with contemporary practice, used 'Malcolm' for his first born, and called his second son 'William', the name favoured by the family of his Anglo-Norman wife, Ada de Warenne. The appearance of a lineage structure needs no special explanation in view of the absorption of the royal house into the feudal milieu. But the fact that from 1113 it possessed substantial lands in England, which it wished to retain and augment, must have been a further spur to dynastic orderliness as it was understood in Anglo-Norman society.

In style too the kings tended to adopt European standards: seeking knighthood, participating in tournaments, and employing the *Dei gratia* formula almost from the moment it was adopted by the English kings. But in one crucial area they failed to match their English, French, and German counterparts: not until Robert Bruce's usurpation in 1306 was a Scottish king crowned, and it was 1331 before one was anointed. The Gaelic practice was to inaugurate a new king in a secular ceremony, held in the open air at a traditional site: the Scots made their kings at Scone, near Perth, where leading nobles installed them on the stone which Edward I was later to carry off to England. Ailred of Rievaulx tells us that David I 'was so horrified by the rites that the Scottish people, after the custom of the land, offered on the occasion of the inauguration of new kings, that the bishops could scarcely persuade him to accept them'.[3] Possibly the reference is to the sacrifice of animals. If the comment truly reflects David's views, they reveal the embarrassment of a ruler, used to the company of Anglo-Norman knights and clergy, at the crudities that still hung about the Scottish kingship. The reference to the bishops suggests that, as in Ireland, native churchmen were now playing a part in the proceedings, and may have formed a bridge between old and new.

But, even if change was in the wind, the inauguration remained remote from the episcopal crowning and anointing which was the hallmark of Frankish kingship. In 1249 Alexander III's inauguration took place in a time-honoured, though perhaps expurgated, manner at Scone; it included the recital by a Gaelic bard of his genealogy back to the mythical kings of the BC era.

Ancient forms had political benefits, in stressing the link between the king and the nobility, who regarded themselves as representing the kingdom. By the thirteenth century all those involved may have been conscious of taking part in an antique mime that symbolized their solidarity. Churchmen, however, now saw the ceremony, not so much as barbarous, but as denying them the opportunity to stress the religious dimension of kingship, and as liable to raise doubts about the status of the kingdom, and hence of the Scottish church. It was this unease, which the king may have shared, that had prompted petitions to the papacy in 1221 and 1233 for permission to crown and anoint Alexander II. These were rebuffed in the face of English objections. But it is unlikely, despite their psychological importance, that possession of the more exalted signs of royal rank would have greatly improved the prospects of the Scottish kingship in its dealings with the English. That relationship was determined by more material things than formal status: crowning and anointing were among the matters that might be stressed, or ignored, depending on the state of play at any given moment. The English kings did not doubt that their Scottish cousins were fully royal. Nor were the Scots the only European monarchs without unction: the kings of Castile, who were hardly in an inferior league of rulers, also lacked it. Alexander III was well able to elide awkward distinctions: his seal shows him bearing both crown and sceptre. The cultural and political gap between him and the king of England was much smaller than that which separated him from the native rulers in Wales and Ireland; his ancestors had reached out for, and succeeded in domesticating, the advantages the surrounding world had to offer.

Irish kingship: Promise and decay

In the eleventh and twelfth centuries the greater kings in Ireland increased their capacity to exploit men and territory; they also showed signs of acquiring some of the marks of status displayed by rulers elsewhere. They were in many ways a new phenomenon, far removed

from the *rí* of the seventh-century law-tracts on whom generalizations about Gaelic kingship used often to be based. The intensity
of the quarrels of the provincial and sub-provincial rulers, which was
once seen as a deterioration from an earlier world of petty kings under
the lordship of a high king of all Ireland, is now more likely to be
interpreted as a sign of their greater mastery of resources and techniques. Moreover, as the study of early medieval kingship in general
has advanced, the gulf between kings in Ireland and those in other
parts of Europe has come to seem less impassable. Where historians
once equipped the German kings of the period 950–1050 with
administrative policies and systems, they now stress their dependence on military expansion, constant itineration, ceremonial display,
and a form of rule that relied on manipulation of the feuds of the
nobility. By comparison Irish kingship was, of course, a small affair;
but its raids, circuits, hostage-taking, plunder, and tribute look less
like antiquated barbarism. Indeed the insight that power was amassed
most readily in border districts such as Saxony and Bavaria, where
wealth and prestige could be grabbed, may have something to teach
us about the O'Briens, O'Connors, MacMurroughs, and others, who
turned much of Ireland into a military frontier.

The range and organizing capacity of the greater dynasties is
impressive. In the eleventh century the O'Briens of Munster campaigned as far afield as Ulster and Leinster, and deployed naval forces
both northwards along the Shannon and eastwards round the coast to
Dublin, Wales, and Man. They turned the Norse city of Limerick
into a royal centre, and placed a *dux* (governor) over Cork. The
twelfth-century O'Connors of Connacht are equally striking. Their
power depended on the ability to establish and maintain a presence
across the Shannon, in order to exploit the human, agricultural, and
commercial wealth of Meath and north Leinster, at a time when
possession of Dublin was becoming a touchstone of dominance over
the whole island. Turlough O'Connor (Toirrdelbach Ó Conchobhair
(1119–56)) built bridges and fortresses at the vital crossing-point of
Athlone and elsewhere, a programme that shows his ability to harness
manpower in a sustained fashion. Such undertakings suggest that
kings were becoming more interventionist. By Turlough's time the
signs of administrative development are unmistakable: rulers issued
charters; they had many stewards to exact their tributes and rents at
local level; and the Treaty of Windsor of 1175 shows that Henry II
and Rory O'Connor shared the expectation that Rory would be able

to arrange for the collection of every tenth hide (or its value) from the native areas as a render to his overlord. The growth of the major kingships was nourished by economic and social changes, which in Ireland received an important stimulus from the Scandinavian presence, whose benefits native rulers were absorbing.

The links of kings with the Church in an age of reform also helped their authority and standing to grow. Irish rituals of inauguration remained very different from the crownings and anointings that took place at Rheims or Westminster, and in the north-west may have retained associations with a pagan past in which the king symbolically married the kingdom. But there are hints of change, as rulers were 'ordained' by bishops. Kings also presided over synods, occasions that emphasized the religious aspect of their power yet were not narrowly ecclesiastical in their implications. The inspiration of churchmen lay behind the promulgation of ordinances, which signified the movement of kings into the making and enforcement of law. As early as 1040 'a law and ordinance . . . was made by Brian's son [Donnchad Ó Briain of Munster], to the effect that none should dare to steal, or do feats of arms on Sunday, or go out on Sunday carrying any load'.[4] As it had done in other parts of Europe, the Church was encouraging rulers to assume responsibility for the maintenance of peace, and for the moral condition of their subjects.

On a more mundane level, religious modernization, allied to growing prosperity, helped to give kingship greater territorial definition. In the forty years before the Anglo-Norman intervention, Irish rulers began to patronize the continental monastic orders: Cistercian houses were founded by the MacMurroughs, O'Briens, MacLochlainns of Ulster, and O'Melaghlins of Meath, among others. The appearance of major new church complexes, with royal associations and often situated close to political centres, carried an obvious message in a land where stone buildings had been few and small. Moreover one of the most successful parts of the reform programme was the mapping out, in the synods of Rathbreasil (1111) and Kells (1152), of a scheme of dioceses. The diocesan framework took note of current political boundaries. Indeed the Synod of Kells reflected the provincial divisions to such effect that it equipped Ireland with four archbishops—two more than in the entire island of Britain. Given the universal connection between royal and ecclesiastical organization, and the administrative proficiency of churchmen, the consolidation of dioceses was likely to give added firmness to secular arrangements.

The literary sources, such as the annals and *The War of the Gael with the Foreigners*, make much play with the idea of an all-Ireland kingship; and it was for the status of high king that the provincial kings competed. It is a common assumption that the arrival of the Anglo-Normans halted what would otherwise have been a progression from effective provincial and trans-provincial kingship to unitary rule. The success of the O'Connors gives this idea some plausibility. Turlough's supremacy had lasted longer than most, and in the years after 1166 his son, Rory, reconstructed it. He obtained lordship over Dublin, driving out Dermot MacMurrough; his military and diplomatic arm reached into Ulster and Munster as well as the midlands and south-east; and his court attracted attendances from most of Ireland. Yet it is not self-evident that Rory's regime was different in quality or likely staying-power from predecessors that had proved all too transient. For a decade after Turlough's death, O'Connor dominance had been replaced by that of the MacLochlainns, just as the O'Brien overlordship had crumbled in the third quarter of the eleventh century in the face of the MacMurroughs, before giving way to the O'Connors themselves in the 1110s. To pin-point one dynasty as the Irish equivalent of the West Saxons (or even the mac Alpins) demands a leap of faith that is not for the faint-hearted.

Despite the strides taken by Irish kingship, it remained weak in important respects. No provincial dynasty had succeeded in gaining permanent control of the vital region containing Dublin and the valley of the Boyne. Each province remained an unstable conglomeration of sub-kingdoms with uncertain borders; their rulers were likely to ally with outside powers should the provincial overlord falter. The decline of the O'Briens was assisted by the rise in south-west Munster of the MacCarthys, with whom the O'Connors were able to ally. Similarly, the MacGillapatricks of Ossory, on the western borders of Leinster, were always likely to escape from the clutches of MacMurrough. To speak of a kingship 'of Munster' or 'of Leinster' is to beg questions almost as difficult as those raised by the concept of a monarchy 'of Ireland'. As change took place, it worked to the potential benefit of many royal kins—a point neatly made by the response of Donal MacGillapatrick (Domnall Mac Gilla Pátraic) to

MacMurrough's employment of Anglo-Norman troops: he hired some of his own.

To its comparative lack of territorial rootedness, Irish kingship added another, and in the event crippling, limitation. There is scant trace of the shifts in family structure associated with the entrenchment of European monarchies, including the Scottish. *Bouleversements* of startling rapidity took place when successful kings, such as Murchertach O'Brien or Turlough O'Connor, sickened and died. The control they had asserted over their extensive kins tended to collapse into a welter of segmentary competition which was of value to their rivals. A neighbour looking in saw, not a regnal unit, but a collection of dynastic branches and vassal-kings out of which a favourable coalition might be fashioned. All the males of the royal kin were potential rulers, though in practice the choice was likely to rest between the handful who were best placed, whether through the favour of the former king or possession of a springboard of wealth and alliances, to mount a challenge. In theory it should not have been so: the custom of 'tanistry', by which a *tánaiste* was chosen and given land for his support at the time of the king's inauguration, decided the succession in advance. The *tánaiste*, however, was rarely the king's son; indeed he might well be the head of a branch of the kin that the new king was eager to buy off. The longer a reign lasted, the more likely he was to have died, or to have been elbowed aside by the ruler's sons, who in practice were the most probable inheritors. Kingship could, of course, pass lineally, especially if an able ruler lived long enough to prepare the way for an able son. But wars were frequent, and partitions presided over by outside powers not uncommon.

Irish custom gave intra-dynastic rivalries a special edge. The upper classes, aided by an ease of divorce that scandalized reforming clergy, practised what amounted to serial monogamy. The Church failed to capture the institution of marriage, or to impose its harsh distinctions between legitimate sons and bastards. Virile, long-lived kings left behind them a galaxy of sons, born of women of varying origins and status. Links with the mother's family, together with the practice of fosterage (a version of the European custom by which young nobles were educated not in their father's house but in those of other aristocrats or kings), and the frequency with which royal boys served as hostages, gave brothers and half-brothers varying sets of associations among sub-kings and neighbours; this ensured that their conflicts would sprawl across and beyond regional society. Though brothers and their families could, of course, compete eagerly in the feudal world, in Ireland, as in Wales, fraternal conflict was built most effectively into the family structure; often it resulted in blinding, castration, or death. Rory O'Connor himself lost the ability to discipline his kinsmen in his later years; after his withdrawal from the kingship of Connacht in 1183, the dynasty suffered nearly two decades of turmoil as his sons, grandson, and brothers competed for the kingship. The segmentary flames were fanned, it is true, by magnates such as the Burghs and the Lacys, for the greater predictability of Anglo-Norman inheritance turned settler lords into stable points around which the more fluid native polity arranged itself. But the record of Irish dynasties suggests that difficulties might well have attended the O'Connor succession even without new complications.

The establishment of the Anglo-Norman regime also had effects of a more brutally straightforward sort. Its presence ended any trend there had been towards a unitary kingship and, at varying speeds in different provinces, undid or set back the consolidation of the major kingships. The seizure of Dublin and Meath by the Crown and the Lacys deprived the O'Connors, and any possible competitors, of the wealth and control of communications that made domination of the island possible. The truncated overlordship conceded to Rory in 1175, bereft of an adequate centre, was unsustainable. Within the entire south-eastern quarter of Ireland the density of foreign occupation reduced the native kings for more than a century to the level of impoverished lords of the uplands and bogs. At the other extreme, the failure of the Anglo-Normans to penetrate in depth into the north-west left a zone where the O'Donnells of Tyrconnell and the O'Neills of Tyrone could maintain a viable, though cramped, regality. The fate of the native rulers elsewhere is well illustrated by the case of the O'Briens. By 1200 they had irretrievably lost the city of Limerick which had been a cornerstone of their advancing power in the eleventh century. During the thirty years after 1185 the rich lands south of the Shannon were absorbed by Anglo-Norman lords. The process of colonization encountered little steady opposition from the O'Briens. After the death of King Donal Mór in 1194, they were plagued by internal disputes; the parties were caught up in alliances with the foreigners, and may have consoled themselves that the main losers, in the short term, were vassals who were anyway out of control. But the result was to confine the O'Briens to a rump of their former overlordship, across the Shannon in Clare. The

MacCarthys, who were ejected from Cork city and restricted to the far west of the county, suffered a similar fate. So too, through time, did the O'Connors, whose loss of Athlone and easy access to the midlands was followed from the 1220s by the occupation of key centres in Connacht by the Burghs and their allies. The incomers were seizing the best of the resources on which kings had fed, standing in the way of the military expansion that fuelled royal reputations, and beginning to fill the part of provincial overlords.

Such straitened conditions did not favour the maintenance of regal status, though the decay of kingship was slow, and never complete. In the early thirteenth century the Crown and the papacy both accorded the major rulers the dignity of a royal title. John and Henry III dealt with them alongside the baronage, and at times saw advantages in shoring up the native political order. The O'Connors and the O'Briens in particular tried to accommodate themselves to changed circumstances. Their actions show awareness of the problems territorial vagueness and unpredictable succession posed in their relations with the English. Kings of both dynasties were anxious to acquire charters from the king granting them portions of their former lands, and for Cathal O'Connor (Cathal Crobderg Ó Conchobhair (d. 1224)) this desire was connected with an attempt to pass his position on to his son. But everything was against the belated emergence of a conventional lineage-structure. The main potential losers from such a development were the other dynastic segments, for whom it would represent, not the 'advance' beloved of the historian, but the permanent loss of their birthright. (Cathal himself, by a nice irony, was a brother of Rory O'Connor who had shut out Rory's own line.) The settler lords were there to offer help to the discontented. The king was too remote, and often too identified with aristocratic interests, to make and adhere to favourable bargains. And so the erosion of the territorial base of the surviving kingships continued.

By the middle of the century the royal and papal chanceries seem to have accorded kingly titles to the Irish rulers less readily: their declining power, together with the fading of the remnants of Celtic kingship in Britain, probably made such styles appear increasingly anomalous. Within Ireland the Church, which in the interests of reform had given its blessing to Henry II's lordship, drew back from the alliance it had been forging with native kingship in the eleventh and early twelfth centuries. There were often close practical ties between Irish bishops and native rulers; but royal inaugurations reverted to wholly secular forms, with strong echoes of the pre-Christian past. Even in 1170 Irish kingship had been too distant from European models and, despite some nucleation of power, too splintered to harness foreign influences as successfully as the kings of Scots had done. The tragedy was that rulers who were left with only the shell of their royal rank were unable to find an alternative niche as members of an aristocratic community.

Welsh princes between two worlds

By the middle of the thirteenth century the kings of Scots had established unitary rule of an unquestionably royal sort. Ireland by contrast had not thrown up one dominant dynasty, and the native kings were on the point of sinking below the regal horizon. Wales lay between these poles. The authority of the Welsh princes was an intriguing mixture of old and new. Disagreement existed about where they lay in the spectrum that stretched from the merely noble to the clearly royal, and about the nature of the relationship between the dominant princes of Gwynedd and the other Welsh lords. For these reasons, and because of the survival of a good range of evidence that has been minutely analysed by modern scholars, their history is specially illuminating.

At Montgomery in 1267 Llywelyn ap Gruffydd, a descendant of the kings of Gwynedd, was recognized by Henry III as 'prince of Wales'. Over the previous twelve years Llywelyn had reintegrated Gwynedd and expanded its frontiers after a decade of dynastic strife and territorial retreat. His grandfather, Llywelyn the Great, had dominated native Wales for more than three decades before his death in 1240. But the settlement of 1267 was the first occasion that the Crown had formally accepted that the authority of a single Welsh ruler stood between it and the rest of the Welsh lords.

That Wales should appear capable of sustaining a prince, when Ireland could not, may seem odd. Wales was smaller and poorer, with a physical geography equally inimical to centralized rule; it had been deeply penetrated by the Normans at an earlier stage than Ireland; and its proximity to England made any concentration of hostile strength more likely to provoke retaliation by the Crown. But it was precisely the interaction of geography and politics, within a particular chronological framework, that accounted for the possibilities open to both Llywelyns. In the east and south, Wales was vulnerable to

3. The house of Gwynedd and some of its connections

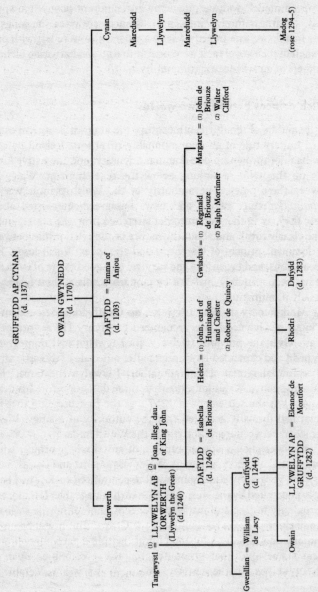

encroachment from England, and provided only limited space for native kings to construct power-bases. Gwynedd, on the other hand, had its almost impregnable core of Snowdonia, which contained enough cultivable land to form a workable lordship even when times were hard. Traditions of supremacy had long been associated with its ancient royal centre at Aberffraw on Anglesey. From this inner redoubt, its rulers could expand along the coastal lowlands east of the Conwy, and also into Merioneth and northern Powys; when circumstances aided them, they could gather allegiances and tribute further south. Nor did the comparatively intensive relations between Welsh and English rulers necessarily work against the interests of the former. The Crown's desire for stability and convenience, and also at times for a counterweight to marcher lords, led it to confirm and build up native overlords, as was the case in Henry II's dealings with Rhys ap Gruffydd of Deheubarth (the Lord Rhys) in the 1170s. Dafydd ab Owain Gwynedd, Rhys's northern contemporary, was given Henry's illegitimate half-sister, Emma of Anjou, in marriage, together with Ellesmere in Shropshire. Dafydd, an English chronicler relates, welcomed the match because he could 'strike terror into the other Welsh through this new relationship'.[5] By the 1170s the history of dealings between Welsh and Anglo-Normans was already more than a century old; the decades of ebb and flow had given Welsh kings greater opportunities to adjust than were allowed to their Irish equivalents, who were faced between 1170 and 1240 by an almost unbroken advance by an alliance of aristocracy and Crown, at a time, moreover, when the barriers between peoples were becoming more difficult to cross. The Welsh had long since begun to come to terms with the newcomers; as in Scotland, adaptation might take the form of emulation.

The changes in Welsh society in the twelfth century, which were exploited by the leading dynasties, were not wholly the product of foreign intrusion; but there can be little doubt that they were accelerated by the interplay between native and Norman. Wales shared in the trend of rising population, and commercial exchange and familiarity with coins may have been increasing even in the eleventh century. But the economic advance cannot be separated from the arrival of colonists from England, and the enterprise of new lords who founded boroughs throughout south Wales and the marches, so drawing the Welsh hinterlands into a broader trading nexus. As the power of the Lord Rhys spread in the 1160s, he benefited from the wealth and manpower of the districts he took over. Welsh kings had long since passed from demolishing to occupying Norman castles; by the 1110s they were already constructing castles of their own. Rhys did not destroy a captured centre such as Cardigan: he rebuilt and used it. Similarly, the updating of the Church did not depend solely on Norman influences. The territorial dioceses, which were taking shape in the eleventh century, reflected the major kingships; and in the twelfth century the native rulers, like their Irish contemporaries, became patrons of the new religious orders. But episcopal government grew most rapidly in the dioceses of St David's and Llandaff, which were deeply affected by conquest and settlement. Monastic foundation likewise received its chief impetus within the colonized areas. One of the greatest of the Welsh Cistercian houses, Strata Florida in Ceredigion, which was to serve as a venue for political assemblies in the time of Llywelyn the Great, was founded by Robert fitz Stephen in 1164, and taken over by Rhys ap Gruffydd two years later. The transformations in Welsh politics were perhaps less dramatic than those in Ireland, but also more durable. Kings did not lord it over major urban centres such as Dublin, Limerick, or Cork, for there were none in Wales: but by the same token they did not abruptly lose them. Nor did they preside over great reforming synods in 1100, only to see the Church's endorsement of their kingship falter a century later.

The development of the capacities of native lordship in Wales continued in the thirteenth century, but with the difference that now only Gwynedd had an effective princely regime. Deheubarth in the days of the Lord Rhys was the more advanced, but also the more vulnerable, area. Upon his death in 1197 the dynasty underwent a prolonged spell of segmentary competition, which coincided with the rise of Llywelyn the Great in the north. Llywelyn seized the chance of the turmoil that marked the end of John's reign and the minority of Henry III to extend his lordship far to the south. He was so successful that he was left in control of the royal castles of Cardigan and Carmarthen until 1223. The reputation and resources that expansion generated were the best possible cement of his position within north Wales. The heirs of Rhys, who accepted a partition arranged by Llywelyn at Aberdyfi in 1216, remained squeezed between Gwynedd, the marchers, and the Crown, and were never able to regain the position he had held. So the northern dynasty alone was able to build upon the changes of the previous century. It laid an exclusive claim to princely status which it proved unable, despite 1267, to vindicate as the kings of Scots had done. The careers of the princes were fraught with unresolved tensions: between multiple and unitary rule, between custom and innovation, and between splendid titles and slender substance.

The development of princely government within Gwynedd by the time of Llywelyn ap Gruffydd is impressive. The princes built and maintained castles which formed an integrated system, with inner and outer rings, designed to dominate communications, protect their heartland, and consolidate the power they were exercising beyond it. They were able to create support-systems to provide for fortresses erected away from old royal centres: Dolwyddelan in Merioneth had twelve vaccaries (cattle-ranches) in its vicinity. This management of resources is typical of a regime alert to economic opportunity and fiscally innovative. Although the princes are not known to have struck coins, the economy of north Wales was increasingly monetized. They took tolls from trade and raised revenue from ferry charges, a significant item in a dominion that contained Anglesey and had a heavily indented coastline. Like other kings and lords, they promoted the development of boroughs; these included Conwy, and the important centre of Llan-faes on Anglesey, which was to be uprooted by Edward I when he built his castle of Beaumaris. There are also signs that, as well as taking the renders to which custom entitled them, the princes introduced periodic general taxation, assessed on the cattle which were the chief item in the rural economy.

These developments were accompanied by an extension of the princely role in the legal area. Welsh law, in common with other early medieval systems, was customary, and its interpretation the preserve of an ancient class of experts. The princes, like rulers elsewhere at an earlier period, gradually took a larger part in the definition and enforcement of law. This is particularly clear in their attitude to *galanas* (the term applied both to the feud by which Welsh kins pursued their disputes and to the compensation payment made when feuds were reconciled). Dafydd (1240–6), the son of Llywelyn the Great and Joan, illegitimate daughter of King John, is said to have abolished *galanas* in the principality. Normally, however, the princes contented themselves with drawing the process of reconciliation into their courts and taking one-third of *galanas* payments in return—a classic example of the early stages of the intrusion by public authority into a legal system based upon self-help regulated by custom. The guardians of Welsh law had already been placed on the defensive in the twelfth century by the hostility of reforming clergy to aspects of traditional custom, notably where it conflicted with their notions of sexual propriety. Now they felt threatened by the expansion of the authority of rulers who were influenced by alternative legal models and not slow to set custom aside. Partly in an attempt to retain the support of the princes, they were at pains to emphasize the royal quality of Welsh law—stressing its attribution to Hywel Dda (the tenth-century king who may indeed have been a patron of legal codification), and in the northern versions making much of the claims of Aberffraw to be the chief royal seat.

The small size of Gwynedd, together with its nucleated character, meant that there was no need for a large, let alone departmentalized, bureaucracy; indeed the running of the vast and scattered Marshal lands, with their quasi-regal jurisdictions in Pembroke and Leinster, must have been a far more complex business. None the less the growth of government in the military, fiscal, legal, and other fields was reflected in the emergence of tiny but significant ministerial groups. Ednyfed Fychan (d. 1246), who held the office of *distain* (omnicompetent steward or justiciar) to Llywelyn the Great and Dafydd, founded an administrative dynasty whose members served in that and other offices, filled the profitable post of *rhaglaw* (roughly equivalent to a hundred bailiff) in the commotes, and picked up estates and revenues throughout Gwynedd. Members of the chapter of Bangor cathedral and of the Cistercian houses of Conwy and Cymer staffed the secretariat, and played other parts, such as that of envoy. The princes also employed constables of castles and serjeants of the peace, with powers of arrest and rights of billeting, as well as huntsmen and estate officials. The growth of administration in north Wales produced a class of men with a stake in its continuance, and in the promotion of princely jurisdiction.

From this limited but secure base the princes moved outwards during periods when the power of the marchers and the Crown was insufficient to pen them within it. The two Llywelyns led expeditions into Powys, mid-Wales, and the south. They raided and sometimes drove out those—such as Gwenwynwyn, lord of southern Powys (d. 1216), and his son Gruffydd (d. 1286)—who had the temerity to oppose them; the less obstinate might find themselves swept up into the advancing army, and perhaps rewarded with princely backing in their own dynastic quarrels. This extended power, which was at its height between 1212 and 1238 and again from 1257 to 1276, is visible also in the ability of the princes to attract widespread attendances at their assemblies, and to judge native lords from beyond Gwynedd. In 1238 Llywelyn the Great obtained support for the succession of Dafydd at a council held at Strata Florida; and in 1259 his grandson dispossessed Maredudd ap Rhys, the most powerful of the heirs of the Lord Rhys, by a judgment of his court. Llywelyn ap Gruffydd took care to define his authority in written bonds into which other Welsh lords were brought to enter: when Maredudd recovered his favour in 1261, the terms of the submission made it clear that he owed military service, and that he was subject to Llywelyn's justice in the event of a further offence. Such documents suggest a deliberate effort to unify native Wales in a single political hierarchy.

The spread of princely control within Welsh Wales was mirrored in other ways. Until 1230 the first Llywelyn contented himself with the style 'Prince of North Wales', which had been borne by twelfth-century rulers of Gwynedd. Afterwards, although he never seems to have used the title 'Prince of Wales', he did employ the style 'Prince of Aberffraw and Lord of Snowdon', which might be taken to imply a claim to pre-eminence throughout Wales. His grandson used the title 'Prince of Wales' on occasion from 1258, and regularly from 1262, until it was finally sanctioned by the Crown five years later. At the same time the growing habit of describing the other Welsh lords as 'barons of Wales' signified their incorporation within the princely structure; like the barons of Chester, or the barons of England, they were being presented as members of a feudal community. The princes' ability to move on a wider stage is also striking. Llywelyn the Great married one daughter to John of Scotland, earl of Huntingdon, who was also nephew and heir of the earl of Chester, and others into leading marcher families. Llywelyn ap Gruffydd himself married Eleanor de Montfort, a daughter of Earl Simon and his royal wife, Eleanor the sister of Henry III. Diplomatic contacts, not just with the English and papal courts, but also (in 1212) with France and (in 1258) with a group of Scottish barons, also fed the sense of special status. As early as 1224 Llywelyn the Great claimed that, like the king of Scots and unlike mere English magnates, he was free to receive those who had been outlawed in the English courts. Llywelyn ap Gruffydd was to show an even greater inclination to make what he saw as telling comparisons.

Thus described, the activities of the princes seem to amount to a promising piece of state-building. They had exploited the nucleus of their principality, expanded their frontiers, drawn other Welsh lords willy-nilly within their system of allegiances, portrayed themselves as the embodiment of the political identity of which Welsh law and literature spoke, and gained a measure of external acceptance. They might appear to be following the same path as the kings of Scots. But the analogy is in crucial respects a false one. There was, needless to say, a much greater disparity of power between the Welsh princes and the English Crown (whose barons held much of the best land in Wales) than between the English and Scottish kings. The periods of Gwynedd's widest expansion, and hence greatest internal cohesion, coincided with times when John and Henry III were weakened by political tensions and civil war or its aftermath. Its rulers were taking off from a point too far back from the fence that had to be cleared if they were to validate their status as holders of a unitary, privileged principality under the Crown.

Not only was the heartland of Gwynedd small and poor; the effort to organize and exploit it created political strains. The ministerial group on which the princes' rule came to depend created a pressure for rewards that they were unable to satisfy, while conflicts with the Church seem to have arisen because prince and churchmen were competing for the same scarce resources. The very achievement of Llywelyn's ambitions in 1267 exposed the weakness of his position. Henry III granted the princely title in return for 25,000 marks, towards which Llywelyn paid 3,000 marks annually between 1267 and 1272. Whereas the kings of Scots could meet English demands, and possibly even benefit from the excuse they gave to tax their own people, within the tiny principality the quest for revenue aggravated tensions. Payments fell into arrears, yet at the same time Llywelyn's government was viewed as oppressive. Nor were the princes so able as the Scottish rulers to control the political impact of change. The clergy who did their work had in many cases been educated outside Wales, and had wide contacts and divided loyalties. Their lay ministers belonged to a type who were also serving other Welsh lords, marcher barons, and indeed the Crown. As Llywelyn ap Gruffydd's rule generated increasing friction, and as royal power in the time of Edward I infringed more and more on the principality, Gwynedd's 'new men' had no difficulty in making alternative arrangements in a wider world with which they were perfectly familiar. The modernizing of a small society with scant resources had made it more porous.

The dominance exercised beyond Gwynedd was far from continuous, and often superficial; effective as the princes' leadership and capacity to impose discipline sometimes were, they did not achieve the consistency and regularity to be termed government. The 'barons of Wales' included men who were themselves heirs to regal traditions, one mark of which was the habit of dealing directly with the English Crown. Their acceptance of a subordinate place in a single polity was not whole-hearted, and the principality remained an unstable federation. Even in northern Powys, which was adjacent to Gwynedd and split between several dynastic branches, the control of the princes depended on constant diplomacy among the local élite. Larger figures, such as Gruffydd ap Gwenwynwyn or Maredudd ap Rhys, manœuvred between the various external powers, whether Welsh or English, that beset them. Amidst his vigorous claims to lordship, Llywelyn ap Gruffydd himself seems to have been aware of the delicate ground on which he was treading, and of the need to show formal respect for the ancient equality of Welsh leaders. Some of his charters speak of 'friendship' and 'alliance', and avoid the provocative language of domination.

If in these and other respects the principality of Wales lagged behind the kingdom of Scotland, in one crucial area it scarcely began to compete: the dynasty itself, like the Irish royal kins, failed to develop a succession system capable of passing power intact down the generations. The dynastic patterns of the old Welsh kingships had much in common with those of Gaelic Ireland. In theory the royal office passed to a single heir designated during the king's lifetime. But sons, brothers, and other kinsmen had expectations of power; and in such small worlds it was a short step from the creation of a subordinate lordship for a vigorous cadet, to the splintering of regality itself. Kingdoms were too incoherent and territorially fluid to be readily transmissible. In practice kingship tended to be treated as partible in the same manner as ordinary landed inheritances, a point not lost on manipulative overlords, including the kings of England.

In the thirteenth century Gwynedd was, of course, acquiring firmer contours, and Llywelyn the Great was fully aware of the importance of orderly succession. His attempts to arrange it reveal more clearly than anything else the extent to which the princes were caught between conflicting pressures and conventions. In a settlement made with King John in 1211, the king had insisted that, on

Llywelyn's death, Gwynedd should pass to his heirs by his present wife, John's illegitimate daughter, Joan; failing those it would fall to the Crown. Though this threatening charter was later cancelled, Llywelyn himself spent the 1220s building up Dafydd, his son by Joan, as his heir. Gruffydd, an older son born of a Welsh mother and now stigmatized as a bastard, was set aside, but compensated with lands in Merioneth and northern Powys, outside the core of the principality, an arrangement which he was bound to regard as a reversal of the proper order of things. Like other able sons of kings, Gruffydd had a body of clients and allies; and once Llywelyn's health failed in 1238, a predictable conflict arose between Gruffydd's party and Dafydd's. At this point the full irony of the situation appeared. Dafydd's very closeness to the English royal house may have made him appear specially dangerous to Henry III. Henry proceeded to make a mockery of Llywelyn's strategy by extending favour to Gruffydd. From the 1240s onwards the English, to whose standards Llywelyn had tried to accommodate himself, were frequently to be found in alliance with the more conservative elements in native Wales—posing as defenders of the custom of partibility and offering shelter to the princes' dynastic rivals and the lords who would not accept their reduced status as barons of Wales.

Lack of resources, segmentary strife, the opposition of other Welsh lords, together with the capacity of Crown and marchers to exploit these and other weaknesses, made an inadequate base upon which to build a princely structure. The princes were never sufficiently secure to resolve the tensions between old and new in Welsh political society, as the house of Canmore had done in Scotland. The status of their regime remained as uncertain as its boundaries. It is somehow appropriate that the first use of the title 'Prince of Wales' should have occurred, not in the heady days of Llywelyn the Great's expansion, but in 1244–5, when Dafydd had been undermined by Henry III, and reacted by briefly gaining acceptance of his princely rank from the pope. Rather than forming the coping-stone of a stable realm, the title covered a deep vulnerability. In a world that increasingly left room for only one type of royal rule, exercised by the God-given big battalions, the princes of Gwynedd could not compete except at those moments when circumstances within and outside Wales specially favoured them.

By the time of Edward I's accession in 1272 royal status in the British

Isles was much less widespread than it had been in 1100. The vestigial kingships of the Scottish fringes had disappeared, as had the kings of Man and the Isles. Native kingship in Ireland had declined drastically in power, status, and confidence. In Wales only the princes based in Gwynedd preserved, in fresh but fragile forms, the traditions of Welsh kingliness. The Scottish royal house had alone managed not just to retain its kingship, but to amplify it convincingly in a region of Europe dominated by a rich, centralized, and assertive monarchy. The Scottish kings, with the help of a national church and a developed aristocratic community, would continue to show that medium-sized, unbureaucratic regnal units were viable. By contrast, the work of the Welsh princes, in giving solidity to a tiny lordship, would serve only to provoke and assist its seizure by the irresistible might of the English Crown.

PART TWO

Incorporations and Divisions, 1270–1400

6. The British Isles in an Age of War

PROMINENT among the themes of the first part of this book were the growth of English government and the enlarged authority of kings who during the two centuries after the Norman Conquest built a superiority that came close to making real the claims to lordship over the British sphere that had once decorated Anglo-Saxon charters. The advance of royal power in England was not an isolated phenomenon. The twelfth and thirteenth centuries were a time when the administrative and fiscal capacities of European monarchies were increasing, nourished by rising population and cash revenues, and by the expansion of the class of clerks and literate laymen who made careers in royal service. Since leadership in war remained a prime function of kingship, developments in government are visible above all in the military field. It is thus appropriate to begin a discussion of politics and government in the British Isles during the late thirteenth and fourteenth centuries by stressing war and its implications: for this was to be an age of constant military activity. From the time of Edward I (1272–1307) and Philip IV of France (1285–1314) northwest Europe, which had known few large wars since the defeat of King John's coalition by Philip Augustus at Bouvines in 1214, saw a series of conflicts which often overlapped. The British Isles were increasingly locked into alliances and wars that sprawled from Ireland and the Hebrides to the Rhineland and Iberia. The consequences were both profound and many-sided.

Intensive war, with important political repercussions, was not of course a novelty. Richard I and John had fought a long and bitter war to defend their continental lands against Philip Augustus. Richard's campaigns had succeeded partly because of his reputation and gifts of leadership. But their outcome also reflected the ability of the Angevin government to gather the wealth needed to pay troops from within and without his dominions—for the sustained warfare of the time could not rely solely on unpaid service, feudal or otherwise. Similarly, Philip's war effort was sustained by the growing resources of the Capetian lands and the skill with which he used them; his reign saw an increase in financial record-keeping, and his armies drew upon the manpower of the rich towns of the royal demesne. A disaster on the scale of John's loss of Normandy and Anjou in 1203–4 would have been politically damaging to a ruler in any age. But the nature and results of John's response to his failure are characteristic of the period. His anxiety to recover his position in France led to a furious quest for resources, in which his administration bore down heavily upon his subjects in Britain and Ireland. The decade 1204–14 saw, besides capricious manipulation of royal rights of patronage and jurisdiction, the repeated imposition of taxes, including general aids which prefigured the regular subsidies of the later Middle Ages. The crisis that broke in 1215 arose from the collapse of relations between the king and leading barons. But integral to it, as many clauses of Magna Carta show, were arguments about the financial demands of the Crown. War revealed both the strength and the weakness of kingship; in an age of fiscal inventiveness and bigger administrations it remained as central as it had been when simpler warrior-kings, who had fewer predictable resources and less capacity to institutionalize their power over wide areas, led their men into battle.

It is therefore important to approach the later Middle Ages with a sense both of the sheer persistence of warfare and of the links between conflicts in widely dispersed theatres. In retrospect Edward I's Welsh campaign of 1282, together with the castle-building that accompanied and followed it, may seem to open the new age of intensive, large-scale hostilities. But it was in the next decade that familiar patterns were laid down. By the Treaty of Paris (1259) Henry III and Louis IX had appeared to end the ancient quarrel between the Angevins and Capetians. Henry gave up all claim to Normandy, Anjou, and Poitou; in return Louis confirmed his status as duke of Gascony. But the settlement left areas of likely difficulty. Above all Henry's acceptance that he held Gascony, not allodially as his ancestors had claimed, but as a fief of the French Crown, meant that each new king of England was bound to do liege homage to each new king of France—a requirement that might be thought to raise questions about the English monarch's status (the French kings had long upheld the doctrine that they themselves did homage to no man). For nearly forty years the wish of both royal houses for stability was enough to stop recurrent frictions from leading to war. But in 1293 a clash between English and Norman sailors was taken up by Philip IV, who insisted on asserting what he saw as his rights of jurisdiction over Edward I, whom he eventually adjudged to have forfeited Gascony. The Anglo-French dispute became entangled with other conflicts. Edward supported the Flemings against Philip, and sought to build a system of alliances on France's northern and eastern borders. At the same time Edward himself was engaged in a dispute with John Balliol, who had done homage to him upon becoming king of Scots in 1292. Late in 1295 the French sealed an alliance with the Scots, and in 1296 the first Anglo-Scottish war since 1217 began. The fourteenth century was to show that it was far easier to adopt warlike postures than to abandon them.

Though the Anglo-French conflict fizzled out by 1298, the war with the Scots was more enduring. Especially during the reign of Edward II, it had a deep impact on the British Isles as a whole. Edward's failure to counter Robert Bruce, who had seized the Scottish kingship in 1306, left northern England open to devastating raids, forcing its communities to pay blackmail to the Scots. After Bruce's victory at Bannockburn in 1314, Scottish forces, led by his brother Edward, also entered Ireland. Edward Bruce was inaugurated as king of Ireland by his Gaelic Irish supporters soon after his landing, occupied Ulster from 1315 to 1318, and conducted destructive expeditions into the southern provinces. Robert joined him early in 1317, and for a moment it looked as though Dublin itself would fall to the Scots; had it done so, the Bruces might well have carried the war into Wales, where they had been diplomatically active. Even after Edward Bruce was cornered and killed by the English of Ireland in 1318, Robert's influence in the region remained strong. After the deposition of Edward II in 1327, he was able to intervene in Ulster as well as in northern England, so magnifying the pressure on Queen Isabella and Roger Mortimer, who were ruling in the name of the young Edward III. The outcome was the Treaty of Edinburgh (1328), in which the English at last recognized the Bruce monarchy.

The treaty proved short-lived. Robert Bruce died in 1329 and was succeeded by his five-year-old son, David II. In 1333 Edward III collaborated with a group of exiled lords who had claims to Scottish lands, and reopened the war. The leader of the 'disinherited' was Edward Balliol, son of the former king, whom Edward now recognized as king of Scots. The price paid by Balliol included not only homage but also, in 1334, the cession of much of southern Scotland to the English. This action led to the forfeiture of many lowland landholders and the intrusion of English grantees who were to retain a vested interest in obstructing any peace that involved the return of the southern counties to the Scots.

For a time in the mid-1330s it seemed as though Edward III and Balliol would destroy the adherents of David Bruce. That they failed to do so owed much to the fact that the Anglo-Scottish war did not remain self-contained, but almost at once became caught up in the latest round of Anglo-French disputes. Upon the death in 1328 of Charles IV, the last of three sons of Philip IV to occupy the throne, the Crown had passed to the nearest heir in the male line, Charles's cousin, Philip of Valois, who became Philip VI. English lawyers had put in a claim on behalf of Edward III, whose mother, Isabella, was Charles's sister. They argued that, while a woman could not inherit the Crown, she could transmit it to her male descendants. The case was not negligible, but it raised the spectre of endless strife when the daughters of Charles and his two elder brothers were old enough to bear sons; and anyway Edward was in no practical position to challenge for the Crown. He did homage to Philip in 1329, and confirmed it in 1331 when he was of age.

During the 1330s Philip was eager to establish his line through diplomatic and military successes. Above all he wished to emulate his ancestor, St Louis, by drawing western Europe into a crusade under his leadership. Edward III's co-operation was crucial to his plans, which were grievously set back by the Anglo-Scottish war. So, when David Bruce fled into exile in 1334, Philip welcomed him, used him to put pressure on the English, and played the part of an officious mediator. Between 1334 and 1337 events gained a momentum reminiscent of the 1290s, as the princes of north-west Europe were swept up into rival alliance systems, and the French again seized Gascony. When in 1338 Edward III crossed the Channel at the head of an army, confident in the support of a bevy of princes of the Low Countries and the Rhineland whom he had purchased at enormous expense, he set in train what future historians were to know as the Hundred Years War.

The Hundred Years War was an episodic affair punctuated by truces and periods of inactivity. But it was pursued with some vigour from 1338 until the Treaty of Brétigny in 1360, and again from 1369 to 1389. On the whole the English were in the ascendant in the years 1346–60, which saw famous victories at Crécy (1346) and Poitiers (1356), while the French had the better of the later phase. The wider conflict helped to keep the Anglo-Scottish war alive. After 1337 Edward was unable to concentrate his resources on Scotland, and contented himself for the most part with funding the northern lords and garrisoning his castles in southern Scotland. The Scots for their part more than once acted in concert with the French. In 1346 David II invaded England while Edward was overseas, only to be defeated and captured by the northerners at Neville's Cross, near Durham. Though David remained a prisoner for eleven years, the Scots were not subdued. In 1356 they were able to attack Berwick and disrupt Edward's plan to take part in the continental campaign that was to result in the Black Prince's triumph at Poitiers, where John II of France was captured. The victory left Edward free to dictate terms to the Scots as well as to the French. David was released in return for the promise of a large ransom, and from 1357 to 1384 formal hostilities between the two kingdoms ended. By now, however, the militarization of the north and the rival territorial claims of English and Scottish lords meant that border war had acquired an impetus of its own: indeed much of the land ceded to Edward III in 1334 was regained by the Scots during a fourteen-year truce negotiated in 1370, largely because the truce coincided with costly English setbacks in France. In the mid-1380s, when the French threat to English interests on land and sea was very real, the Franco-Scottish alliance revived. In 1388 the failure of English arms on the Continent was matched by the victory of the Scots at Otterburn.

The inability of the main parties in the Hundred Years War to reach a firm settlement, even when they might seem to have had strong motives for wishing to do so, appears puzzling. But there were many reasons for it. The very range and complexity of alliances—which sucked other disputes, from Scotland to Germany and Spain, into its vortex—made peace elusive. Furthermore, the question of the French succession distinguished this war from former bouts of Anglo-French hostility, and made the central conflict itself harder to resolve. In 1337 Edward III had ceased to address Philip VI as king of France; in 1340, after some hesitation, he himself assumed the title. The claim to the Crown had the effect of raising the stakes: Edward or a successor might choose to give it up, but he could do so without loss of face only in return for substantial, and visible, compensation. The minimum terms acceptable to the English in Edward's time always included Gascony, with its frontiers generously drawn, and held in full sovereignty, free of homage to the French king. Such an arrangement,

4. The Plantagenet kings, 1272–1399, and the French succession

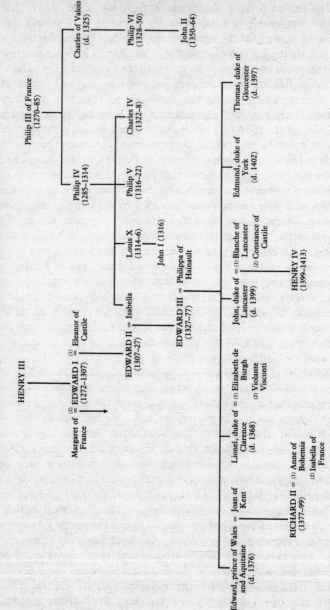

even without the extra territorial gains that Edward hoped for, amounted to the dismemberment of the Crown of France, something the French could not accept. Though they were brought to concede as much at Brétigny, they never put the settlement fully into effect, while Edward for his part omitted to make a final renunciation of his claim to the throne. When the war turned against England, an alternative solution was mooted: that Gascony might be held by a Plantagenet cadet. But this too had drawbacks. It laid Richard II open to the charge of giving away dominions belonging to the Crown of England, and also faced opposition from Gascons, to whom the English connection seemed to guarantee their customs, property, and commercial prosperity.

The case of Gascony suggests that the propensity of the kings of the period to become the prisoners of claims that they could neither vindicate nor abandon was connected with the growth of the late medieval state itself. The duchy was not merely a Plantagenet family possession over which Plantagenet and Valois could strike a deal at whim: it symbolized on the one hand the sovereignty of the French king within his kingdom, and on the other the integrity of the lands regarded as appurtenant to the English Crown. The development of the state was also apparent on a less theoretical level. The costs of warfare were such that kings drew heavily upon the resources and goodwill of their subjects, who had to be persuaded to share their rulers' goals. In England Edward III's military success and propaganda skills led to a widespread popular identification with his aims. Any lowering of the royal sights was thus a matter of consequence for the political nation as a whole. It was not just that moves towards peace were likely to be opposed by royal princes and other nobles who hoped to do well out of the war: such men could rely upon a wider feeling that concessions meant loss of face for the kingdom as well as for the king.

Above all, the durability of the Anglo-French war and the conflicts associated with it sprang from the capacity of later medieval rulers to sustain military and diplomatic activity on a large scale. The cash, supplies, and manpower required were vast by the standards of the time, and war tended to expose the limitations of the organization, and even more the financial and political credit, of the major kingdoms. In England political crises, such as those that faced Edward I in 1297–8 and Edward III in 1340–1, sprang directly from their inability to keep their goals in due relation to their means of achieving them. Great Italian financial houses, like the Riccardi of Lucca in the time of Edward I, were bankrupted in their service. Furthermore, the constant need to have recourse to general taxation, which could not be raised unless it was justified in public and consent obtained, exposed the Crown to scrutiny and dragged it into forms of debate that would have been unthinkable in the time of Henry II or John. But when all is said, rulers surmounted the dangers, and in doing so broadened and deepened their authority.

Although after 1294 Edward I may appear to have stumbled from one crisis to another, his success in tapping the wealth of his dominions was remarkable. In 1284 an estimate put the ordinary annual revenue of the Crown, including customs duties, at £26,828. Yet Edward was able to spend at least £120,000 on the Welsh campaign of 1282-3, and gained subsidies assessed at £56,000 from the English clergy and laity in the latter year towards that expenditure. Between 1294 and 1298 he spent a staggering £750,000 on the French and Scottish wars and the suppression of a Welsh rising. In 1294-5 alone he may have gathered into his coffers—from regular revenues, taxation, and loans—one-quarter of the coined money in the realm (estimated at about £1,000,000). The ability to find money was matched by that to mobilize men: some of the forces Edward raised against the Scots—notably the 3,000 cavalry and 25,700 infantry mustered for the Falkirk campaign of 1298—were larger, save for Edward III's forces at the siege of Calais in 1346-7, than any English army before the seventeenth century. Supplies too were levied on a vast scale. Purveyance—the right, originally designed for the support of the royal household, to take goods on the promise of future payment—was extended in order to supply armies and garrisons, and threatened to become a form of disguised taxation. The war effort is, moreover, a testimony to English power throughout and beyond the British Isles. Ireland and Gascony contributed to the supplying of the 1282-3 campaign in Wales. Later, Welsh and Irish troops served against the Scots. Indeed during the period 1296-1314 the shipping of supplies to Cumbria, the funnelling of treasure to the king's war chest, and (in 1296, 1301-2, and 1303-4) the transporting of Irish expeditionary forces to Scotland became an overriding preoccupation of the Dublin government.

The early years of Edward III's rule saw equally intensive and widespread efforts. His Scottish expedition of 1335, for instance, depended upon synchronized campaigns in the east and west, the latter involving an attack on Bruce and Stewart interests around the Clyde by an army raised in Ireland, where a land-tax was granted to support the operation. The successes of the first campaigns in Scotland left the English in control of Roxburgh, Stirling, Edinburgh, and even, for a time, Perth: by 1337 these garrisons were costing some £10,000 a year. But all this was small beer compared to the initial campaigns of the Hundred Years War. Edward's diplomacy left him with an array of continental pensioners and a commitment to land an army in the Netherlands. In 1337 the English parliament granted three subsidies, to be levied between 1337 and 1340. Despite this, and the king's attempts to exploit the wool market by creating a royal monopoly through a merchant cartel, by October 1339 Edward was in debt to the tune of £300,000. In an attempt to rescue him, the Commons in 1340 made an unprecedented (and in the event abortive) grant of one-ninth of fleeces and crops. The combination of heavy taxation, purveyance, disruption of the wool trade, and shortage of coin left no one in England unaware of the crushing burdens the king's ambitions entailed.

Edward was clearly shaken by the disintegration of his plans, and by the extent of the opposition aroused when he tried to make his ministers the scapegoats for his failure, and to impose a programme of retrenchment in England and Ireland in 1340–1. Henceforward he was more careful to cut his coat according to his cloth, abandoning the attempt to construct costly coalitions, and instead seizing every chance to harass the French from Gascony and to exploit discontent in Brittany, Flanders, or Normandy. The successes of the decade after 1346 made the war popular; and from 1356–7 ransom payments from David II, John II, and various French nobles played an important part in keeping him afloat financially. Even so the costs of war were steep, for success too had its price. Garrisons had to be funded from Calais to Brest, Bordeaux, and Bayonne. Between 1348 and 1361 more than half the expenditure in Gascony came from English sources. Then in 1361, at a moment of peace and liquidity, the English exchequer for the first time became involved in shoring up the Dublin government, which faced increasing border war and sharply reduced local revenues. From 1361 to 1376 no less than £71,000 passed from England to a dominion which a generation or two earlier had been a source of regular profit. By the latter date the French war was again imposing immense strains on English resources, as it was to continue to do until the 1390s. Yet recurrent crises over finance and criticism of royal ministers in parliament cannot hide the fact that kings were raising taxes far more frequently than in the past, and had also to some extent succeeded in loosening the ties that bound taxation to immediate military emergencies. Their position was one that Henry III, who managed to levy only four general taxes in fifty-six years, would have envied.

The impact of the enlarged ambitions and activity of the English monarchy is visible in many ways. In the later thirteenth century the sheer reach of Edward I's government is striking: Westminster had become the hub of a remarkably coherent administrative system which embraced England, Ireland, the principality of Wales, much of southern Scotland, the Channel Islands, Ponthieu, and Gascony. At the height of Edward III's power, governmental incorporation was accompanied by the aggrandizement of the Plantagenet family. Edward was the first king since Henry II to have a quiverful of healthy sons, and he sought to use them to consolidate and expand his power within and beyond the British Isles. His eldest son, Edward, the Black Prince (1330–76), was an active, not to say abrasive, prince of Wales, earl of Chester, and duke of Cornwall; his rule had the effect of associating Wales and Chester, which were major recruiting grounds, firmly with the war effort. In 1362 English sovereignty in Gascony was reinforced by giving him the title of prince of Aquitaine. As early as 1342 Lionel of Antwerp (1338–68) was betrothed to the heiress of the last Burgh earl of Ulster, who was in addition lord of Connacht and of extensive lands in Munster. Upon her grandmother's death in 1360, Lionel's wife also succeeded to one-third of the vast Gloucester inheritance, putting him in possession of another assemblage of lordships, stretching from East Anglia to Usk and Kilkenny. Although Edward from the start would have had his eye on the Gloucester lands, the firmer binding of Ireland to the Crown was also in his mind; and Lionel served as his lieutenant there from 1361 to 1366. John of Gaunt (1340–99) married the heiress of Edward's kinsman, the duke of Lancaster (d. 1361), making him the greatest noble in the north of England. During the 1360s, when Edward was engaged in negotiations with the childless David II, Gaunt seems to have been the favoured candidate for the Scottish succession. Afterwards he was taken overseas by a second marriage, to the heiress of Castile, whose claims he pursued against her usurping uncle. In the 1360s Edmund of Langley (1341–1402) also seemed destined for a marriage of prime significance in the context of the Hundred Years War, to the heiress of Flanders, though in the event the prize went to a son of the French king. These and other coups and plans chime with evidence that Edward was conscious of the Angevin past: in the 1350s and 1360s the British Isles seemed on the point of forming part of a restored and reshaped European *imperium*, bound together by a clutch of Plantagenet princes. Such a vision was grandiose; but the history of the Valois and Habsburg dynasties in the late Middle Ages should make us pause before dismissing it as hopelessly anachronistic.

Edward's schemes were undone by a combination of military retreat during the 1370s and 1380s, and illness and death within his family. Yet Richard II's reign, though it marked a conscious withdrawal from French and Scottish adventures, shows the impact of what had gone before. Richard was more fully engaged with the British fringes of his realm than his predecessors. For several decades members of the royal family had played a prominent part on the outskirts of England and in Ireland. Richard had neither sons nor brothers, and was often on bad terms with his uncles and cousins. The cessation of foreign war after 1389, moreover, created the opportunity (and perhaps also psychological pressure) for heightened royal activity within the English lands. During his reign he held the lordships that had belonged to his father, the Black Prince. Chester supplied him with administrators and a large bodyguard of archers (which a more secure king might not have needed); it was elevated from an earldom to a principality in 1397. The king led expeditions to Ireland in 1394–5 and 1399. Like Wales, Chester, and the Isle of Man, Ireland was tightly controlled by Richard's supporters, and lands and offices there were granted to members of the group of younger nobles that surrounded him. In the later 1390s, too, the tentacles of the court were reaching into the far north of England, challenging the dominance of the regional magnates. The king's denial of the Lancastrian inheritance to his cousin, Henry Bolingbroke, upon the death of John of Gaunt early in 1399, prefigured further expansion of the curial group into the northern provinces. Richard's actions may have reflected his high view of the kingly office. More mundanely, the story of the reign has much to do with his attempt to exploit for himself and his faction the position in the areas beyond the southern English heartland that had been developed by the royal house in more relaxed and confident days. The resentment by members of the higher nobility of his grasping and narrowly based regime was one reason for the success of Boling-broke's usurpation.

A contrasting testimony to the impact of English power is the way in which its opponents in Scotland, Wales, and Ireland could assume that there was a shared feeling of oppression that might be exploited. A sense of common cause, mingled with admiration, comes through in a Gaelic Irish obituary of Edward I. Edward was

a knight most prudent, most violent and most valiant. It was by him the greatest number of people fell in his time . . . for by him fell Llywelyn, king of Wales, and his brother David. And by him the Welsh were subdued, and are in servitude since, having no king of their own. By him also great oppression was inflicted on the Scots, after he had banished their king, for according to report, he slew fifty thousand of them in one day, and also a countless number on all sides on another occasion.[1]

With the resurgence of the Scots under Robert Bruce after 1307, anti-English feelings were played upon both within and outside Scotland. In 1307, when Edward I lay dying, a panicky letter from an English partisan north of the border reported that preachers who supported the Bruce cause were claiming to have discovered a prophecy of Merlin, telling how 'after the death of *le Roy Covetous* the people of Scotland and the Britons (that is to say, the Welsh) shall league together, and have the sovereign hand and their will, and shall live together in accord to the end of the world'.[2] Edward Bruce's expedition to Ireland was backed by propaganda stressing that the common ethnic roots of the Irish and Scottish peoples made it fitting that they should unite in the search for freedom. When Edward sent messages from Ireland in the hope of extending the war into Wales, he spoke in similar terms, and his words were echoed in a reply from Gruffydd Llwyd, one of the main leaders of the northern Welsh:

and I declare that, since your name is celebrated wherever it is known, just as the Saxons were expelled from Scotland by the illustrious king your brother, and more lately from Ireland by you, so in Wales you and we together shall restore the ancient state of the land which was conquered by Brutus. And when the Saxons have been trampled under foot, overthrown, and scattered, Britain shall in future be shared . . . by the Britons and the Scots.[3]

In 1363–4, when Edward III and David II were discussing the Scottish succession, the Scottish parliament showed itself hostile to the idea of an English king. An opinion was sought from somebody learned in canon law. Among the arguments he put forward against the proposal was the fate of the Welsh and Irish under English rule, pointing out that St David's had lost its metropolitan status and was subject to Canterbury, and accusing the English of destroying the Welsh 'name and nobility', and also the Irish 'so far as they could'.[4]

Such documents tell us a good deal about attitudes, but very little about political possibilities, for in practice Celtic solidarity was even more of a chimera than Edward III's plans for family aggrandizement across the face of western Europe or Richard II's effort to entrench his authority from London to the Shannon. Indeed unified native opposition even within either Wales or Ireland remained well out of reach. But the power of the English state was practical enough, manifesting itself above all in war and the capacity to assemble the resources for war. Each region of the British Isles was in its own way shaped by its encounter with, and response to, that gross material fact: many of the results of the experience, whether of subordination or of resistance, will figure largely in the chapters that follow. In England itself, and also to some extent in English Ireland, the demands of the Crown sharpened political identities and reinforced the habit of collective action. The exploitation of Irish resources by Edward I may have lessened the ability of his ministers to counter the local problems royal authority faced. Wales was more firmly integrated with England than ever before, both through the spread of royal administration into Snowdonia in the wake of Edward I's conquests, and through the bringing of the Four Cantrefs east of the River Conwy within the zone of marcher lordship. The Welsh lords who remained found it impossible to maintain a serious claim to aristocratic status in the post-conquest world. The greater size of Scotland, and the different character of its ruling groups, meant that it was unlikely to be so completely overwhelmed. But between 1296 and 1307, and again from 1333 to 1336, it seemed to be threatened with incorporation or at best survival as a maimed satellite. It was the experience of meeting that challenge, through military resistance and by cultivating the French alliance, that ultimately gave Scotland greater solidarity. In manifold ways war both reflected and promoted the development of political structures.

7. Jurisdiction and Conquest: The Reign of Edward I

THE reign of Edward I saw basic shifts in the political make-up of the British Isles. At the time of his accession in 1272 English ascendancy was already real, but sufficiently loose to be compatible with the existence of other princely regimes and with some variety of custom. By the early fourteenth century the scene looked different. The house of Gwynedd had been uprooted and destroyed, and north Wales was the seat of an English government. The Scottish kingship had lapsed after 1296; Edward regarded the kingdom merely as one of the 'lands' within his power, and had subjected much of Scotland south of the Forth to his direct administration. In 1305, on the eve of Robert Bruce's rising, the British Isles seemed to lie within the grip of an irresistible organizing force. The English exchequer audited accounts from outposts at Caernarfon and Berwick as well as Dublin. The English parliament heard petitions from the king's subjects in Ireland, Wales, and Scotland, as well as in England, the Channel Islands, and Gascony. Edward was, moreover, continuing to show an eagerness to reform the laws of other nations. In the course of the administrative settlement that followed his successful Scottish campaign of 1303–4 he accepted the customs of the kingdom (described as 'the laws of King David'), but set his face against 'the laws of the Scots and the Brets', by which he meant the systems of feud and compensation that survived in the west and north.[1] This echoed the 1284 Statute of Wales, which had incorporated much of Welsh land law while rejecting the criminal codes. It was also in line with his response in 1277 to the request of the archbishop of Cashel and other Irish clergy that English law should be extended to the Gaelic population, when he declared that 'the laws the Irish use are detestable to God and so contrary to all law that they ought not to be deemed law'.[2] We seem, in short, to have entered a less flexible age, where assimilation took the form of administrative incorporation and went hand-in-hand with pressure towards uniformity.

Edward's behaviour, moreover, presents a triumphalist face. He marked the end of the native principality in Wales by carrying off relics, which were ceremonially received in Westminster

Abbey, and by impaling the head of Dafydd, the brother of Llywelyn ap Gruffydd who had been executed after a state trial in 1283, at the Tower. He built into the walls of Caernarfon castle bands of stone of contrasting colours in imitation of the walls of Constantinople and placed imperial eagles over the main gateway. He publicly stripped John Balliol of his kingship, and carried the Scottish regalia, royal records, and Stone of Destiny into England. When he died in 1307, the Gaelic *Annals of Connacht* described him as 'king of England, Wales and Scotland, duke of Gascony and lord of Ireland';[3] the Irish annalist was making the same point as the English chronicler Peter Langtoft, who had said 'there is neither king nor prince of all the countries, except King Edward who has united them'.[4]

Yet there is little to suggest that Edward himself was dominated by imperial dreams, devoted to the construction of a unitary monarchy of the British Isles, or even irredeemably hostile to regional custom. His attitude to law probably differed little from that of Alexander III, and had something in common with that of Dafydd ap Llywelyn, the abolisher of *galanas*; his denunciation of the laws of the Irish may have been taken over *verbatim* from the petitions of the Irish prelates themselves. The absorption of the fringes by English administrative systems was not new, but the quickening of a trend discernible as early as the time of Henry I. Its dramatic advance in the late thirteenth century was, in large measure, the product of particular circumstances and Edward's vigorous and increasingly confrontational response to them. At the time of his first Welsh war in 1277 he showed no sign of wishing to step outside the established conventions of Anglo-Welsh relations; it was only after five further years of friction that conquest gained a place on his agenda. His dealings with Scotland were mostly amicable until the death of Alexander III in 1286, and restrained until 1292. The Anglo-Scottish *imbroglio* arose out of an unforeseeable dynastic catastrophe that would have had explosive consequences whenever it occurred.

Nor, despite the words of the Connacht annalist, did the subjection of Wales and Scotland lead Edward to assume additional titles: at the end as at the beginning he was 'king of England, lord of Ireland, and duke of Aquitaine'. This confirms that throughout the tumultuous events of his reign he did no more in his own view than employ his existing rights; nothing was further from his mind than the creation of novel forms of rule. The princes of Wales and the king of Scots were treated as rebellious vassals whose fiefs had come into his hands as overlord, to be administered along with his other lands if he so chose. When in 1254 Henry III had granted Edward an apanage made up of Gascony, Ireland, the royal territories in Wales, and some recently acquired English lands, he had stated that all these belonged to the Crown of England, from which they were not to be alienated. In English eyes, the homages of the Welsh and (certainly after 1292) the Scots were also appurtenances of the Crown. In 1282-3 and 1296 Edward saw himself merely as resuming into his direct control as king of England rights that had been exercised conditionally by subordinate rulers.

But if it is wrong to represent Edward I as the embodiment of some new *zeitgeist* of imperial conquest and metropolitan uniformity, it is equally misleading to ignore the deeper changes that helped to shape his actions and those of his opponents. One important influence was of course the growth in the administrative and fiscal capacity of the state; this carried with it the ability to pursue large military aims in a sustained way—which further stimulated the development of government. These transformations were accompanied by the sharpening of concepts of royal authority, leading to the more stringent definition and exaction of jurisdictional rights, such as those claimed by the English Crown over its dependencies. Like that of other monarchies of the time, the tone of English royal government was increasingly affected by Roman law, which helped kings and their servants to formulate high notions of royal power and to articulate them through tags that stressed the overriding jurisdiction of the sovereign prince. It is no accident that the period which saw Edward I asserting his lordship in Wales and Scotland also found him guarding his position in Gascony against Philip IV and his lawyers, and both kings in their turn resisting the demands of the papal monarchy of Boniface VIII. In a world of competing jurisdictions, the greater were becoming ever more effective at putting the lesser on the defensive.

Edwardian rule in England and Ireland

The position of the English monarchy in the British Isles at this time may best be understood from the perspective of royal rule within the English lands, for Edward I's dealings with the Welsh and Scots betray themes that were familiar to his subjects in England and Ireland. Of these the chief were a pervasive concern to discover and insist upon the rights of the Crown, and a habit of central intervention in the details of law and government. Such features should not be seen in isolation. The running of aristocratic estates in England was becoming an increasingly professional business, around which an instructional literature developed. On a grander level, the French kings expanded the activities of their officials, whose circuits were solidifying into administrative districts, and issued legislation that applied throughout their loose-woven realm. But the more unitary traditions of the English kingdom provided royal government with an advantageous base on which to build.

This is not to suggest that Edward's rule was merely authoritarian: far from it. Magna Carta was part of the custom of the realm, and the king could not ride roughshod over the rights of his subjects. Legal and administrative reform had been at the forefront of the baronial programme in 1258–9, and the 1267 Statute of Marlborough had accepted many of the reformers' demands, rather as the minority government of Henry III had reissued the Great Charter. When Edward returned from crusade in 1274, he set in train countrywide inquisitions, using juries of the hundreds, boroughs, and larger manors and vills. The resulting Hundred Rolls, together with rolls surviving from further visitations in 1279, form the fullest record made of medieval England since Domesday Book. Both inquiries were preceded by the clearing-out of many existing sheriffs; and the stress laid in 1274–5 upon uncovering official misconduct suggests that Edward was well aware of the importance of cultivating ground that the monarchy and its critics shared. Royal actions were hedged by practical limits and had to be decked out with justifications that often smack of sententiousness verging on humbug.

Government was not, however, primarily designed to gratify the king's subjects. The maturity of landed society and the Common Law might rule out the inarticulate violence and greed of a William Rufus, or even the emphasis that Henry II and his sons had placed on the primacy of the royal will. But Edward's inquisitiveness was closely connected with a desire to pin-point, exercise, and, where necessary, recover royal rights. Both in 1274–5 and in 1279 the extent of the king's lands and jurisdiction, and instances of their usurpation, were of prime concern. Edward was continuing a policy evident in royal circles since the 1240s; he was to take it much further largely because his drive and political skill were greater than those of his father. From the Crown's point of view, insistence on its rights could not threaten those of its subjects; indeed only by identifying what was owing to the king could the rights of others be made clear, and hence guaranteed. The outcome would be the restoration of the proper order of things: when all held in peace what was due to them (and no more), the kingdom itself would be pleasing to God. This vision of the world had its own coherence. In practice of course it was fraught with problems. The Crown's interpretation of its rights was a partisan affair, likely to provoke those it challenged, and to be established, if at all, with difficulty and at the price of much rancour. There was an area of special awkwardness, which draws attention to a barrier between Edward's mentality and our own. Royal rights were believed to be inherent and immutable; there was scant sense that they had grown and changed over time. Anything, however well established, that seemed to deny or obstruct the Crown's authority as understood in contemporary royal circles was liable to be stigmatized as an abuse. Edwardian rule was marked by a combination of high-mindedness and grasping interference.

The Crown's outlook is nowhere more apparent than in the *Quo warranto* inquisitions concerning liberties, which proceeded in a desultory way from 1278 to 1294. Liberties ranged widely in character. At the top, the bishop of Durham claimed to have royal jurisdiction virtually in its entirety within the land of St Cuthbert (that is, the later County Durham together with some outliers). Below that level, a number of lay and ecclesiastical lords claimed 'return of writs', or the right to execute royal writs through their own officers, receiving them from and returning them to the sheriff of the shire, who was excluded from the liberty except in the event of default by its holder. Below that again were the numerous 'private hundreds'—estimated at more than half of the 628 hundreds in England in Edward I's time—where the lord appointed the bailiff and took what would otherwise have been the king's share of the proceeds of the minor justice administered in the hundred court. Such liberties had emerged messily over the centuries as certain ecclesiastical and lay proprietors had remained outside the scope of this or that aspect of royal government as it developed. Sometimes kings had given explicit grants of exemption, but often these amounted merely to recognition of an established fact. Frequently, too, a vague tradition of privileged status had silently expanded to take in areas of governmental activity unknown when the liberty had first emerged.

In the 1240s and 1250s Henry III had begun to ask hard questions about the scope and justification of liberties; Edward I was to pose them more insistently and systematically. Neither was hostile to liberties as such. But privileges which, like Topsy, had 'just growed' were unacceptable: titles must be authenticated, and vagueness replaced by precision. Basic to Edward's approach was the assumption that his jurisdiction was supreme; all other jurisdictions were regarded as deriving from it, and were held on condition that they were exercised effectively and within their proper limits. Where they were held illegitimately, abused, or neglected, they automatically lapsed to the Crown.

The form of *Quo warranto* inquisitions illustrates the exacting face of contemporary government. Proceedings began with an order that all those who were identified by local juries as holding liberties should put in their claims before the king's justices. They were asked to show by what authority they held them. This in effect put men on trial without a specific accusation being laid against them: the implication was that all jurisdiction belonged to the Crown unless the contrary could be demonstrated. The best proof that a liberty was justly held was a royal charter granting the recipient the rights he or his heir now claimed; this would satisfy the royal theory that franchises were in no sense private property, but public rights devolved into private hands. The attorneys who pleaded for the king often pressed such theories to conclusions that were logical, but in practice difficult to sustain. They denied that proof of long use, in the absence of a charter, was an adequate warrant, and might even regard such proof as evidence against the claimant, since it amounted to an admission that an illegal liberty had been persistently exercised. They also denounced charters that were couched—as old charters frequently were—in general words, or that contained antique formulas difficult to reconcile with royal rights as they were understood in the late thirteenth century. The outcome by 1290 was a mass of unresolved cases, many of them against important figures in the kingdom.

The assertion of royal rights was not limited to England. Although *Quo warranto* inquisitions were not extended to Ireland or to the Welsh March, both areas were affected by the Crown's outlook. The greater part of south-east Ireland was held by the successors of the Marshal lords of Leinster and the Lacy lords of Meath, all of whom claimed the extensive franchisal rights of their predecessors. From the 1270s onwards there is clear evidence that royal ministers at

Dublin found the number of privileged jurisdictions on their door-step frustrating. By the end of the century the area of enfranchised land had been markedly reduced by the denial to the Verdon half of Meath of the liberties once held by Walter de Lacy, and by the acquisition for the king of the lordship of Kildare, the Leinster liberty that lay closest to Dublin, as part of a deal with its English lord, William de Vescy. Almost more telling is the experience of Geoffrey de Geneville, a curial magnate of Savoyard origins, who had married the other Lacy heiress. Despite a long career in royal service in Ireland, in Britain, on the Continent, and in the Holy Land, Geoffrey had to devote a fair part of his energies between 1252 and 1307 to defending the liberty of Trim against the king's ministers, as acres of parchment still surviving on both sides of the Irish Sea confirm. Marcher lords for their part had felt the need to defend their peculiar jurisdictional independence in the middle years of Henry III, as royal government operated ever more insistently from Chester, Montgomery, or Carmarthen. In Edward's time the pressure continued: judicial commissions, designed among other things to clarify the zones of Welsh and marcher custom, were a feature of 1277–81. In 1290 the king displayed his power after a series of armed clashes between the men of the earl of Gloucester, who was lord of Glamorgan, and the earl of Hereford, the lord of Brecon. The earls claimed the right to settle disputes by negotiation and, failing that, by private war by virtue of the custom of the March. Edward did not mount a frontal assault on March law, but he insisted that his order to cease hostilities overrode it; when Gloucester and Hereford would not come to heel, he imprisoned them.

It would be wrong to assume that the assault on liberties was a coherent programme relentlessly urged forward by the king. At the start of his reign Edward believed, in some cases accurately enough, that magnates in England had exceeded and abused their rights during the period of political instability that had begun in 1258. He was aware of the oppressive capacity of liberties, and knew that an attempt to curb them would not be unpopular with the lesser landholders whose dislike of bailiffs of all sorts had been evident in 1258–9; it might spread more widely, and thus help to dissipate, the odium that attached to his own sheriffs and hundred bailiffs. But he had little interest in pursuing the regalian theories expressed by his keener servants to the point where they brought him into collision with leading nobles. Cases were endlessly postponed rather than rushed to unwelcome conclusions; and in 1290 he was willing to sanction a compromise by accepting, in the Statute of *Quo warranto*, that evidence of long user going back to 1189 could be considered to establish a case for the issuing of new royal charters where acceptable charters were not forthcoming. Serious friction, save where it sprang from personal clashes with individual lords, seems to have arisen chiefly from the assiduity of officials and the delays characteristic of an over-burdened judicial system. Yet that in itself is significant. The men who served kings possessed an in-built aggressiveness, visible also in the manner in which the agents of Philip IV chipped away at Edward's jurisdiction in Gascony. The pervasive concern with rights in an age when government continued to grow more elaborate and specialized had the effect of clawing business to the centre, a trend of which the clogging of the courts was but one symptom.

English government had always involved a high degree of inter-action between the centre and the localities. In the late twelfth and early thirteenth centuries this had been symbolized above all by the general judicial eyres which brought the royal court into contact with the local communities of knights and freemen. This form of contact continued in Edward I's time, though the broad-based eyre tended to be replaced by numerous, more specialized commissions. One reason for this change was the sheer volume of business reaching the courts; it was swollen not least through the emergence of procedure by *querela* or 'plaint', which did not involve the litigant in the trouble and expense of purchasing a royal writ. The plaint, which could among other things be used to make accusations against royal and baronial officials in the localities, had been a feature of the inquiries made by the reformers of 1258–9. Edward seems to have encouraged its use during the 1270s. He also observed the spirit of the reform period by summoning regular parliaments and establishing the habit of dealing with plaints and petitions of all sorts in them. Parlia-mentary sessions tended to be followed by the appointment of judi-cial commissions to hear and decide particular cases. In all these ways the king played a larger part in redressing the grievances of his subjects.

There was a clear link between the habit of inquiry and receipt of grievances, and the series of statutes that marked the first twenty years of Edward's reign. Edwardian legislation shows in equal mea-sure the familiar concern for royal rights and a desire to reform the law in order to make it more responsive to the needs of the landholders who were its chief users. If the promulgation of statutes in well-attended parliaments (several hundred knights and burgesses, as well as magnates and officials, may have been present at the 1275 parliament, where the Statute of Westminster I was promulgated) helped to ensure that they would be observed, it also gave publicity to the king's anxiety for the welfare of his people. In such a climate of apparent openness—very different from that of the court cliques in which his father's policies had been formulated—it was easier for Edward to use parliaments as occasions for getting taxation.

Ireland provides excellent illustrations of the centralizing trend, at two levels: there was greater interaction between the central authority at Dublin and the king's subjects, while the Lordship itself was more firmly bound to England by administrative structures. The first certain reference to an Irish parliament dates from 1264; it was not until the reign of Edward I that parliaments seem to have been assembled with any frequency. The scant surviving records of the earliest ones suggest that their role was similar to that of their English equivalents. Legislation was published in the parliament of 1278; like later Irish enactments, it was concerned less with making changes in the substance of the law (for in general those were received from England), than with regulating matters of peculiarly Irish import, such as the keeping of the peace in the borderlands and the regulation of relations between the colonial and native populations. None the less it is striking that the first known set of Irish ordinances should coincide so closely with the king's use of the English parliament to publicize his legislation. Occasional records of pleas from 1279 and later show that the Irish justiciar and council received petitions and heard cases in parliament just as the king and council were doing in England. The importance of the part played by central authority is shown clearly by the parliament that met at Kilkenny in 1297. It was attended not just by the leading royal officials and magnates, but also by the sheriffs of counties and the seneschals of liberties, together with knights representing the shire communities. The session saw the publication of measures which, among other things, enlarged the number of sheriffs in the wake of the extinction of the Verdon and Vescy franchises, and imposed a series of peace-keeping obligations on local communities. Other parliaments in the last decade of Edward I's reign brought in representatives of the boroughs as well as of the counties, and saw negotiations about taxation, together with the publication of ordinances concerned with the currency and other economic matters.

The later thirteenth century brought a more thorough and regular supervision of the Dublin administration from Westminster. The fact that Ireland had its own courts and parliaments did not hamper the flow of business to England. Under Edward I the rolls of the King's Bench contain more Irish cases than at any earlier or later period. Major Irish matters—such as a quarrel that arose in the early 1290s between William de Vescy, who had been appointed justiciar, and Thomas fitz Maurice, lord of Desmond, over the handling of the MacCarthys in distant west Cork—were considered in English parliaments. Finance was another area of administrative integration. Complaints about treasurers of Ireland were investigated in England, and the Irish exchequer was subjected to more detailed controls. For almost a century after 1293 it was rare for more than two or three years to go by without an audit, which brought not only the treasurer and his rolls, but also one of the chamberlains of the Dublin exchequer, to face scrutiny by the English exchequer. Just as the buoyant Irish revenues, which supported the Welsh and Scottish wars, were a testimony to the penetrative quality of royal government in the Lordship, so the regular audits symbolized the fact that Ireland was caught within wider administrative structures of a demanding sort.

The conquest of north Wales

The quality of contemporary English government is one part of the background against which we must view the extinction of the Welsh principality centred in Gwynedd and the inheritance of parts of its structure by the Crown. Although the principality was a recent creation, its disappearance may still be regarded as momentous. The thirteenth-century princes had reshaped and built upon what remained of Welsh kingship after the Anglo-Norman invasions, so that the destruction of Llywelyn ap Gruffydd in 1282 marked the end—bar a few whimpers—of a British political order that went back to, and even beyond, the Roman period.

Llywelyn's downfall raises innumerable questions of fact and interpretation that cannot possibly be discussed here. But two general points seem particularly important. The first is that the consolidation of his power within north Wales and his expansion outside it, like his grandfather's successes half a century earlier, coincided with a period of political turmoil in England. To that extent the position he reached in the 1267 Treaty of Montgomery was unnatural. He kept gains made at the expense not only of the Crown but also of marcher lords such as the earl of Gloucester and Roger Mortimer, a circumstance at odds with the general settlement after the Barons' War of 1263–5, in which the king's supporters benefited and his opponents lost. The second relates to Llywelyn's position within Gwynedd and the wider Welsh polity. His route to supremacy had involved trampling on the reasonable expectations of his brothers, of whom Dafydd was specially dangerous. Furthermore the Montgomery settlement required him to pay 3,000 marks a year to the Crown, an obligation that was likely to impose strains on a principality for which further military expansion was no longer an option. And although some native lords beyond Gwynedd had done well through their association with him, others, such as Gruffydd ap Gwenwynwyn of southern Powys and Rhys ap Maredudd of Deheubarth, had collaborated with him only under duress. After 1267 Llywelyn was faced by the challenge of maintaining his extended power at a time when the English monarchy and aristocracy were regaining their equilibrium, and when he had enemies within Welsh Wales who were likely to make common cause with them. The situation would have presented difficulties to wealthier and more stable regimes than his.

From 1267 to the death of Henry III in November 1272 Llywelyn kept the peace and paid most of what he owed under the treaty. But upon Edward's accession he failed to do fealty to his representatives, allowed the payments to fall into arrears, and then kept up this truculent stance even after the king's return to England from crusade, repeatedly evading summonses to attend courts and parleys. He may appear to have brought upon himself the retribution that came in the form of Edward's Welsh campaign of 1277. His behaviour has long puzzled historians. To some extent he may simply have mistaken his opponent: it is easy to forget that in 1274 the achievements that shape our view of Edward I still lay in the future. It is also likely that the financial and political price of the treaty was becoming clear. The princes of Gwynedd had thriven on the repute and resources expansion provided; Llywelyn now stood on the defensive, and could maintain himself only by pressing upon his own subjects. In 1274 Dafydd and Gruffydd ap Gwenwynwyn both fled to Edward I. A letter sent to the king by the bishop of St Asaph in the following year suggests the febrile atmosphere that now attended Llywelyn's rule. According to Bishop Anian, the prince, having failed to keep an appointment with Edward, had none the less proclaimed to his own subjects that a settlement had been reached, and had gone on to impose a levy of threepence on each head of cattle to enable him to resume his payments to the English king.

As holder after 1254 of the Welsh interests of the Crown, Edward cannot have welcomed the Treaty of Montgomery. But there is little to suggest that in his first years as king he sought a conflict in Wales; on the contrary, between 1274 and 1276, when he was taken up with the reform of English government, he remained patient. Yet it would be misleading to conclude that the difficulties arose merely from coat-trailing by Llywelyn and the unstable character of his principality. The treaty left not only unresolved claims between Llywelyn and the marchers but also deeper questions about his status. By conceding the title 'prince' and superiority over the other Welsh lords, the Crown had admitted that he was more than a normal aristocratic vassal of the king. But how much more? Before Edward's return to England, both problems had become acute. Llywelyn was arguing that he would resume payment of his instalments only if the king would make the earls of Gloucester and Hereford return lands they had taken from him. He was also protesting against the government's decision to forbid him to build a castle and found a market (actions for which an English baron would have needed royal permission) at Dolforwyn in southern Powys: he accepted that he held his principality under the king's power, but claimed that its rights were 'wholly separate from the rights of your realm'.[5] The hard truth was that, once peace was restored, the assertiveness of royal jurisdiction, which had been responsible for so much friction in Wales during the 1250s, was bound to recover. The absence of the king did not help matters: just as his representatives were unable to check the marcher lords, so they lacked the independence to desist from pressing royal rights to the full. The dispute over Dolforwyn reveals the explosive mixture of practical and theoretical tensions. A new Welsh castle within ten miles of the royal centre at Montgomery was bound to alarm the king's ministers; and the increasing firmness of princely rule that Dolforwyn symbolized led in its turn to an urgent need to define the proper relationship between the neighbouring jurisdictions.

When war finally came in the summer of 1277, Edward's ability to mobilize his vastly superior resources, which included the service of Llywelyn's many enemies within Wales, brought it to a swift conclusion. The Four Cantrefs and Anglesey fell into his hands; Llywelyn, stranded in Snowdonia, had no choice but to come to terms. The settlement made in the Treaty of Aberconwy shows that even now the king had no thought of moving beyond the patterns laid down in the past. He imposed stiff penalties, but received Llywelyn into his grace, and does not seem to have considered expropriating the dynasty. The punitive side included the forfeiture of the Four Cantrefs, the loss of the homages of most of the other Welsh lords, and the restoration of Anglesey (which was to be inherited only by the legitimate heirs of the, still childless, prince's body) at a rent of 1,000 marks a year. A provision for oaths to be taken annually by Llywelyn's counsellors and by representatives of each cantref, to abandon him if he withdrew from his allegiance, was a significant extension of royal control into Gwynedd; but it was a conventional arrangement, closely parallel to the 'security' clause of the 1259 Treaty of Paris by which Louis IX had demanded oaths from Henry III's subjects in Gascony. On the other hand, Llywelyn was allowed to retain his princely status, and to hold his lands in Snowdonia without partition; his brother Dafydd was to be rewarded for his service to the king with land in the Four Cantrefs rather than within the rump of Llywelyn's principality.

The Treaty of Aberconwy has been considered radical largely because of the weight historians have accorded to the earlier settlement at Montgomery, which has been regarded as a foundation charter of deep constitutional significance. But the relations between English kings and Welsh rulers had always been fluid, in keeping with the shifting politics of the moment. The 1267 treaty was made at an unusual moment; and, despite the growing habit of precise legal definition, it smacks of wishful thinking to suppose that it was likely to prove more permanent than the Treaty of Worcester of 1218, by which Henry III's minority council had reluctantly accepted the expanded power of Llywelyn the Great. Similarly, the Treaty of Aberconwy can be set beside the Treaty of Woodstock of 1247, by which, after a campaign west of the Clwyd and the death of Dafydd ap Llywelyn, Henry III had kept the Four Cantrefs, taken back direct control of the homages of the Welsh lords, and divided the Gwynedd heartland between Llywelyn ap Gruffydd and his brother, Owain.

In 1277 clashes over jurisdiction had played a part in propelling Edward towards a familiar sort of war, with a familiar conclusion.

The road to the definitive war of 1282–3 was even more richly paved with legal quarrels. The reappearance of English government in the Four Cantrefs aggravated the tensions between royal authority and Welsh custom. The attentions of the king's officials provoked even Dafydd, a chief beneficiary of the war of 1277, into pleading that, since the king was 'lord of divers countries and of divers tongues, and divers laws are administered in them and are not changed',[6] Welsh law should remain unimpaired; Dafydd was to be a prime mover of the rising of 1282. The recovery of royal power also gave Llywelyn's enemies within Wales more assurance. A dispute between the prince and Gruffydd ap Gwenwynwyn over Arwystli, an upland district in central Wales to which both Powys and Gwynedd laid claim, was to prove a *cause célèbre*. The Treaty of Aberconwy had decreed that cases were to be heard according to Welsh law or to March law as appropriate, but had offered no precise guidance for deciding which law should apply in which case. It was impossible to separate the question of laws from that of political power. Llywelyn's assertion that, since Arwystli was a Welsh district, Gruffydd should plead by Welsh law, might be reasonable in theory; but it was hardly neutral. Conversely, Gruffydd's claim that, as the king's subject, he should be tried by English law in the royal courts might seem legally far-fetched; but his belief that he could not have a fair hearing in a region controlled by Llywelyn is hard to gainsay.

Between 1279 and 1282 the Arwystli dispute remained undecided, and there was a distinct possibility that Llywelyn himself would be forced to plead in Edward's court. At the same time judicial commissions, which included Welshmen as well as Englishmen, were endeavouring to sort out this and other cases, and in doing so were amassing information about the legal position in Wales and the marches. Even at this stage, however, it would be wrong to assume that the king was pursuing a malevolent strategy designed to undermine what remained of Llywelyn's principality; indeed in 1279 he had swallowed the most bitter pill of all, and presided over Llywelyn's marriage to Eleanor de Montfort, who was not only daughter and sister to his inveterate enemies, but also his own first cousin. But, as so often at this period, the quarrel over jurisdiction tended to acquire an impetus of its own; and as it went on both parties found themselves taking their stand on principles from which it became increasingly hard to withdraw.

The difficulties were compounded as there developed on the

English side a greater awareness of the actual content of the laws of Wales. The official response was one of distaste. Antipathy was most clearly expressed by John Pecham, the archbishop of Canterbury, who was to play a major part as a negotiator between the king and Llywelyn. For Pecham, a custom that sanctioned blood feud, allowed compensation payments for homicide, and into the bargain did not distinguish between legitimate and illegitimate children for purposes of inheritance, was no quaint survival of an older social order: it was immoral, barbaric, and contrary to natural and divine law. As political relations between the Crown and the Welsh leaders worsened, the tone of official comments departed more and more from that of earlier days, when Henry III had frequently instructed his more officious ministers to respect the laws of Wales when dealing with Welsh leaders and the local communities within the Four Cantrefs.

In his relations with the Crown Llywelyn came constantly to stress Welsh law, and to present himself as its custodian. There was a fair amount of irony in such a stance. He himself had not been slow to set Welsh custom aside when it suited him; the innovatory side of his rule had incurred hostility within the principality, and any suggestion that his voice was that of all Gwynedd let alone native Wales in its entirety was far from the truth. Moreover, the law remained a regional affair both in its details and in its modes of application. But such paradoxes are largely beside the point. As Dafydd's protest suggests, the law had acquired, along with the Welsh language, a symbolic character; by assuming the role of its defender, Llywelyn was striving to forge a connection between infringements of his own jurisdiction and the more widespread sense of oppression that undoubtedly existed in Wales. By responding to the stringency of English claims with the cry 'the laws of Hywel Dda', the prince and his circle were behaving rather as Earl Warenne is said to have done when he protested against the *Quo warranto* proceedings, brandishing a rusty sword before the royal justices and claiming to hold his franchisal rights by virtue of his ancestor's participation in the Norman Conquest.

In 1282 Edward's attitude to Wales broke conclusively with that of his predecessors. When Llywelyn and Dafydd rose in unison, English military and sea power was brought to bear in the usual way to besiege Snowdonia. The aim, however, was no longer mere submission; for the first time the end in view was the territorial conquest of north Wales. When the brothers tried to come to terms through

Pecham's good offices, Edward would have none of it; he was prepared to allow Dafydd to go on crusade and to offer Llywelyn an English earldom and £1,000 a year; but the price (which they refused) was the surrender of Gwynedd to the Crown. As the military net closed on the principality, Llywelyn led a dash into mid-Wales, where he was killed in December 1282; Dafydd remained at large for a further six months, only to be betrayed to the royal forces by some of his own men. By the end of 1283 the death of the old order and the consolidation of Edward's grip on north Wales were already manifest in building work, not just on the great royal castles of Caernarfon, Conway, and Harlech, but at new lordship castles such as Holt and Denbigh and at former strongholds of Llywelyn such as Cricieth and Dolwyddelan.

If the wars of 1277 and 1282–3 were in part the product of the Welsh response to exacting jurisdictional demands of the Crown, the ability to carry the conquest through is a testimony to the wealth and organizational powers of the English state; never before had royal attention and resources been focused so effectively upon a recalcitrant part of the British Isles. Castle-building involved the mobilizing of men, materials, and cash over many years, and detailed planning by Edward's architects and engineers, headed by the Savoyard, Master James of St George. It was accompanied by the founding of boroughs, where the Crown played a direct part in arranging English colonization. A governmental structure was created which equipped north Wales almost at a stroke with an administration that had much in common—despite its smaller scale—with the one that had developed more slowly in Ireland during the generations after 1172. An English justiciar and chamberlain used Caernarfon as their base; Gwynedd west of the Conwy was organized into the shires of Caernarfon, Anglesey, and Merioneth; the sheriffs, who were usually English, were responsible to the exchequer at Caernarfon; the constables of castles were also, naturally, outsiders.

Despite the appearance of abrupt change, the forms of the legal and administrative incorporation were carefully thought out. Its details were set forth in the Statute of Wales, which was published at Rhuddlan in 1284 during a long visit made by King Edward to his conquests. Below the level of the shire, the pattern of commotes was left undisturbed; the local Welsh élites (whose relations with Llywelyn had been uneasy) were harnessed to the service of the new rulers. In the vexed matter of law, the Statute shows evidence of hard

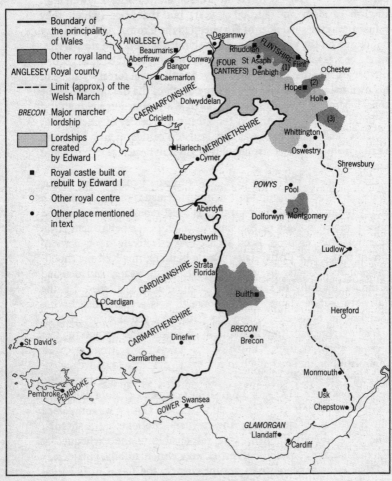

Map 4. Wales, c.1300

reflection; it was of course contemporary with the age of legal reform in England. By outlawing the systems of compensation and feud, Edward rejected aspects of Welsh custom that he, Archbishop Pecham, and God found offensive; instead English and Welsh alike were to accept the English concept of felony and the capital punishment associated with it. On the civil side, however, the Statute was more accommodating. Bastards were disbarred from succession to land, but otherwise the Welsh law of inheritance was left mostly intact, preserving, for example, the convention by which inheritances were shared equally between sons. The king and his advisors were able to tolerate variations of custom that seemed to raise no difficulties of a moral sort; Edward was, after all, the champion of Gascon custom within the broader kingdom of France.

The English conquest may not have involved a blind uprooting of Welsh customs and institutions; but it did of course mark a fundamental break with the past. The process by which princes based in Gwynedd had been establishing their supremacy among the Welsh, and at the same time claiming a place as satellite rulers within the Plantagenet orbit, was halted; with it died a tradition of English overlordship going back to the days of the Mercian and West Saxon kings. Gradual assimilation, mediated through Welsh leaders themselves, gave way to direct rule by the Crown, backed by the advance of English magnates into the Four Cantrefs. By the late thirteenth century the assertiveness of a major European kingship, combined with its superior resources, had left a lesser regime with starker choices than in the past: Llywelyn's principality possessed neither the wealth nor the political coherence to resist incorporation.

Llywelyn's fate is neatly counterpointed by that of one of his bitterest enemies, Rhys ap Maredudd of Deheubarth, the chief heir of the Lord Rhys. Rhys co-operated with Edward I both in 1277 and in 1282–3. He looked forward to royal favour, and Edward seems to have intended that he should have a fitting reward for his loyalty. The English victories in the north were, however, accompanied by the intensification of royal and marcher control in Wales as a whole. Rhys found himself embroiled in disputes with the marchers. He was also denied the prize that meant most to him, the return of Dinefwr, the ancient centre of his dynasty: Dinefwr remained the site of a royal castle which overshadowed his lands in a galling manner. This insult was compounded by the demands of the king's ministers of south Wales, who required his presence at the county court of Carmarthen and tried to insist that he plead in certain cases by English law. In 1287 his frustration led him to attack English castles in south Wales. At first Edward's representatives had problems in containing the outbreak; but within a year the house of Deheubarth had followed that of Gwynedd to political oblivion. It was appropriate that these events should take place during the king's absence in Gascony: royal jurisdiction had acquired its own momentum; and the monarch was needed as much to moderate as to sharpen its impact.

Edward I and the Scots

The conquest of north Wales was followed swiftly by an unexpected crisis in Scotland. Alexander III's son and heir died in 1284. His younger son had already died in 1281, and his only daughter, the wife of Eric II of Norway, in 1283. When Alexander himself, who had recently remarried in the hope of fathering a second family, was killed in a fall from his horse in March 1286, his sole living descendant was an infant granddaughter, Margaret, the Maid of Norway. When Margaret too died, on her journey to Scotland in 1290, not one legitimate descendant of the kings of the three previous generations remained alive, a circumstance that would have presented acute problems to any monarchy of the period.

Edward I was likely to play a major part in determining the future of the neighbouring kingdom, just as his father had been the natural overseer of Scottish affairs during Alexander III's minority. But his attitude and role shifted continually as events unfolded between 1289 (when he returned from Gascony) and 1296. His initial aim was both conventional and predictable: to marry his surviving son, the future Edward II, to Margaret, thus bringing about a dynastic union of England and Scotland and at the same time preventing northern Britain from falling into the hands of a member of a rival royal house. Margaret's death put an end to this strategy, and left the Scottish succession to be contested by distant kinsmen of Alexander, most of them descended from the daughters of Earl David of Huntingdon, the younger brother of William the Lion. Edward heard the claims of the Competitors in courts held at Norham and Berwick in 1291 and 1292; at the close of the latter year he awarded the kingship to John Balliol, who represented the senior line of descent from Earl David. The new king, however, was treated in a way Alexander III had never been. Edward exacted homage specifically for the kingdom of

5. The Scottish succession and the Balliol, Bruce, and Stewart kings, 1286–1406

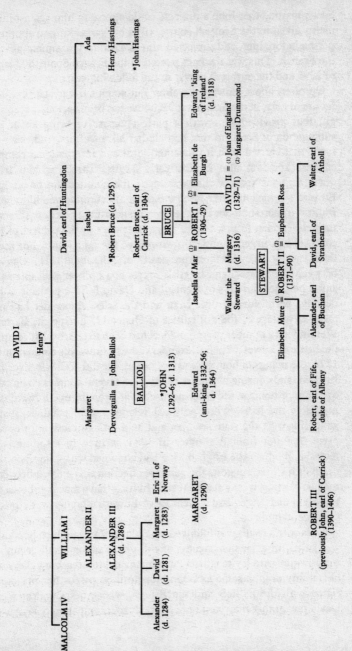

* leading 'Competitors', 1291–2

Scots, insisted that John's subjects could appeal to him against judgments given in the Scottish courts, cited his vassal-king to appear in person before him, and subjected him to a military summons against the French. This was the background to the Franco-Scottish alliance of 1295 and the outbreak of war in the following year.

Opinions about Edward I's aims and actions differ sharply. The failure of heirs in the Scottish royal house has been variously seen as a gift that provided him with a perfect excuse to bring about the subjugation of Scotland that had eluded his ancestors, and as a nuisance that carried with it unwanted local and international complications, and was also by the early 1290s distracting him from organizing the crusade that was to be the culmination of his life. Edward's behaviour after 1292 was certainly abrasive and ill-judged. But it is important to view earlier events against the recent past rather than the hidden future, and to place later ones in the context of the complex and urgent political pressures of the mid-1290s. For more than twenty years before the death of Alexander III relations between the Scottish and English courts had been as amicable as at any time since the days of Henry I and David I. Save perhaps in his dealings with Norway over Man and the Isles, Alexander had not taken advantage of the difficulties of Henry III during the Barons' War; indeed a number of Anglo-Scots had been in the royalist camp at the battle of Lewes. When Alexander came to Edward's coronation in 1274, the matter of homage was not raised. He did do homage for his English lands during a visit in 1278; if (as several sources claim) the question of homage for Scotland itself was brought up, Edward did not force the issue; when personal relations were good, legalistic wrangling over the status of Scotland held little attraction for either party. A letter from Alexander in 1284, written in response to a message in which the English king had condoled with him upon the death of his heir, suggests the genuine affection that existed between the two cousins; it may also be read as hinting that a marriage between the Maid of Norway and a member of Edward's family was already being contemplated.

Alexander's death was followed by a hiatus during which Scotland was ruled, in a manner typical of the period, by a small group of ecclesiastical and lay magnates, who managed to preserve a measure of stability despite some jockeying for position by the factions associated with the Balliols and the Bruces, whose descent from Earl David meant that they could hope for advancement should Margaret die. It was also the task of these Guardians to conduct relations with the outside world. Their authority was seen as arising from the 'community of the realm'. This term, which was familiar in England and elsewhere, embodied a sense of a kingdom that was capable of subsisting even when there was no king. Neither its use nor the reality of the phenomenon it described should occasion surprise in view of the long continuous history of the Scottish monarchy, the territorial definition Scotland had attained over the last century and a half, the presence of a fairly homogeneous (though not entirely self-contained) aristocracy associated with the court, and the antiquity of a Scottish church aware of its rights and liberties. In the years 1289–92 Edward I dealt with the Guardians, never questioned the integrity of the kingdom, and from time to time himself employed the phrase *communitas regni Scotiae*.

It was with the representatives of the kingdom of Scots—'the Guardians, bishops, abbots, earls and barons, and the whole community of the same kingdom'—that Edward in July 1290 made an agreement, known as the Treaty of Birgham, setting out the terms on which his son was to marry the queen of Scots. Though the document insisted that neither England nor Scotland was to see its rights diminished or increased as a result of the dynastic union, its main purpose was plainly to assure the Scots that their kingdom would remain 'separate and apart from the realm of England, and free in itself without any subjection'. It stated resoundingly that 'the rights, laws, liberties and customs of the same kingdom of Scotland . . . shall be fully and inviolably observed for all time throughout the whole of that kingdom and its marches'. Other clauses provided that its new English king (who could be expected to reside mostly in England) would not try his northern subjects south of the border; would not make cathedral chapters travel to England in the course of episcopal elections, or compel new bishops to go south to do fealty; would not demand attendance at parliaments outside Scotland; and would not impose taxes or military service except in the fashion accustomed in Scotland. A royal representative was to be available in Scotland to deal with Scottish business, and the Scots legal system was to continue in the usual way, using writs of the Scottish chancery.[7] The Birgham agreement has much in common with the 1420 Treaty of Troyes, in which Henry V, having married the French king's daughter and been recognized as his heir, undertook to respect the integrity of the kingdom of France. Scotland too was a kingdom of a conventional sort, with its own laws and administrative traditions; these indeed would be entitled to respect even if the English claim to overlordship were to be vindicated. Edward and the Scots saw the position in the same terms; there was none of the uncertainty that overhung relations with a Welsh principality whose territorial boundaries were vague, whose claim to the allegiance of the native nobility was disputed, whose church had long been subject to Canterbury, and whose laws and customs were outlandish in a way that the Common Law of Scotland was not. If clashes arose, they would be between kingdoms and jurisdictions of a similar type.

The prospect of a Plantagenet succession to a kingdom that was coping impressively with the challenge of a royal vacancy is one that has rarely appealed to Scottish historians. Yet in an age when dynastic accident was a more fundamental influence than the modern mind may find comfortable to admit, a union of the sort envisaged in 1290 was by no means far-fetched. Associations of kingdoms were familiar in medieval Scandinavia and in the Iberian peninsula, and the states of central Europe were passed around German princely houses for centuries. A dual monarchy in the hands of Edward I's descendants would have made more geographical and cultural sense than many other European multiple states. The fact that aristocratic families already held property on both sides of the border—though it might have caused friction by blurring the intended legal distinctness of the two realms—was an additional agent of possible coherence. A *regnum Anglo-Scottorum* might appear a natural enough culmination of a process of assimilation that had been under way at least since the marriage of Malcolm Canmore to Margaret of Wessex.

The death of the Maid of Norway put an end to such a possibility, and led to an unparalleled crisis in Anglo-Scottish relations. That it did so cannot be attributed simply to Edward I. Edward has often been accused of hastening to renege on the 1290 treaty. When the Guardians asked him to preside over the settlement of the succession, he insisted on acting, not as good neighbour and friendly arbitrator, but as overlord of Scotland, giving judgment in his own court. And when they declined to surrender the kingdom into his hands as a preliminary step in the process (on the argument that only a king of Scots could do so), he obtained such a surrender from the Competitors, who were only too eager to oblige. His stringent treatment of King John after 1292 was thus foreshadowed in the earlier legal proceedings. It would be naïve to suppose that Edward was reluctant to seize the chance to enlarge his authority when it appeared. But it is unhelpful to view his actions wholly in terms of abstract rights and wrongs. Conditions had changed abruptly with the Maid's death; they were soon to do so again upon the outbreak of the French war. Edward could hardly be expected to view a kingdom over which baronial families were contending in the same light as one that was about to pass to his own heirs; nor could he remain uninfluenced by the fact that Scotland was a natural ally of his Capetian enemies.

Even before the Maid's death the fissure between the Balliol and the Bruce groups was evident. John Balliol was a grandson of the eldest daughter of Earl David, while the aged Robert Bruce (grandfather of the future king) was a son of the second daughter. Balliol's claim by seniority of line looked very strong. Bruce, however, claimed to be the right heir by closeness of degree, and also argued that as long ago as 1238 (before the birth of the future Alexander III) Alexander II had singled him out as his heir presumptive. As the proceedings of 1291–2 drew to a close, and he realized the game was up, he changed tack and urged that the kingdom should be treated as an ordinary landed estate and partitioned among the heirs of David's daughters. In assessing Edward's attitude, it is important to remember that Balliol and Bruce were not merely Scottish lords. Both had substantial lands in England; the Balliols had in addition property in northern France, while Robert Bruce's marriage had brought the family the earldom of Carrick (at present held by his son) and with it contacts and claims to land in Ireland. Edward was faced by a contest, with alarming possible ramifications, between two of his more significant vassals over the succession to a neighbouring kingdom. The need to control it would itself be sufficient to explain his insistence upon treating the proceedings at Norham and Berwick as a formal adjudication, binding on all parties. In accepting that Balliol had the superior case, and in rejecting the mischievous suggestion that the kingdom might suffer partition, he acted in harmony with the legal conventions of the period. And since his overlordship had been accepted throughout the proceedings, there could be no question of homage *not* being required from the new king of Scots. The homage done by King John at Newcastle in December 1292 may have been a humiliation. Edward, however, had reason to see it quite differently. He had awarded the kingship to the rightful heir, even though he was a relatively untried figure. The ceremonial that attended Balliol's installation, far from diminishing him, was a public affirmation of

Edward's favour, and carried a warning to his rivals that they should accept and obey him—for the act of homage placed an obligation on the lord to protect and maintain his vassal.

It was from this point onwards, when the implications of Edward's lordship began to become clear, that things went disastrously wrong. Given contemporary assumptions, a relationship such as that established by John's homage could not be left imprecise; the Birgham treaty itself, by detailing the ways in which the separate status of Scotland was to be safeguarded, shows that the habit of legal definition was shared by both sides. In 1292 Edward forbore to insist on the full feudal right of wardship and marriage; but he was less self-denying in the matter of judicial superiority. Two explanations of his heavy-handedness, which was to prove contrary to his own interests, may be suggested. The first is that by this period it was hard to conceive of overlordship *without* jurisdictional connotations of the sort that soured the Anglo-Scottish relationship: having established that Scotland was a vassal-kingdom, it would have been an unconventional act to desist from making legal demands. The second concerns the whole tenor of Edward's rule amidst the international crisis that arose in 1293. In the earlier years of his reign his dealings with the French, as with the Scots, had been marked by moderation. The war was unsought, and sprang chiefly from French jurisdictional demands. With hindsight it may seem that Edward would have been well advised to treat the Scots gently, for fear of driving them into the arms of the French. Under stress, however, he did not react like that, but instead stepped up the pressure—just as, fiscally and militarily, he was increasing it upon his English, Irish, and Welsh subjects. Indeed the drift towards war with the Scots in 1294–5 took place as Edward coped with a rising in Wales, provoked by taxation and other grievances. His approach, in fact, mirrored that of Philip IV. As Edward forfeited Gascony to Philip, so John Balliol forfeited Scotland to Edward. In a world of closely defined claims, where, furthermore, governments had the machinery and wealth to press them home, disputes had a way of growing beyond the boundaries the main parties may originally have envisaged.

In 1286 Scotland already had the marks of a kingdom; it did not need the experience of war with England to summon them forth. In 1290 the kingdom was on the brink of being absorbed—no doubt with some awkwardness—into a broader, if shallower, political field ruled by a Plantagenet *rex Anglie et Scotie et dominus Hibernie*. The events of 1290-6 ruled out such an anticipation of 1603. Instead Scotland faced a challenge of a more direct sort. After his victory over King John and the Scottish nobles at Dunbar in 1296, Edward treated the kingdom as a fief that had escheated, as the lordship of a rebellious noble might have done, into the hands of its overlord. Its forfeiture was symbolized by the carrying of the emblems of kingship into England. This did not necessarily mean that Edward saw the kingdom of Scots as extinguished for all time; had peace prevailed north of the Tweed and the conflict with France suddenly ceased, a reconciliation might have led to the carts graciously trundling the royal records and Stone of Destiny back to Edinburgh and Perth in favour of Balliol or his son. Actuality, however, was different. The conflict with France reached its peak in 1297-8; it was accompanied by a severe political crisis in England, and by a savage Scottish reaction against English rule.

Feudal rights, as interpreted and applied in the late thirteenth century by a powerful monarch of autocratic temper and legalistic cast of mind, were profoundly inimical—as Gascons, Flemings, and others could testify—to the traditions and interests of lesser political units. Without stepping outside legal proprieties as he and his contemporaries understood them, Edward I in 1296-7 subjected the Scots to a regime that they could only regard as oppressive—for an ancient kingdom was not the equivalent of a mere feudal honor. The seizure of the most precious symbols of the Scottish realm was highly provocative. Similarly Edward's demand in parliament at Berwick for oaths of fealty (which were recorded in writing) from hundreds of lesser as well as greater landholders, while in theory no more than any lord was entitled to from the tenants of a forfeited fief, made the reality of English conquest all too plain to a class of men who hitherto had been little involved in high politics. Scotland was an intimate, conservative kingdom, managed through an alliance between the king and a fairly small group of magnates; its limited size and the restricted ambitions of its rulers meant that there was no tradition of intensive government. The fealties of 1296 heralded the intrusion into the lowlands of an alien political authority of an interventionist and exacting sort. English occupation raised the political awareness of the lairds and freeholders; and the constant warfare from 1297 onwards meant that large numbers of Scots were under arms, and hence in contact with one another and with leaders who were skilled in the arts of propaganda. The first sign of a reckoning came swiftly, when William Wallace, an esquire with Stewart connections, and a force bereft of overt noble leadership defeated the English at Stirling Bridge, celebrating their victory by skinning the corpse of Hugh Cressingham, King Edward's hated treasurer of Scotland.

The vindication of the kingdom by Wallace, and more effectively by Robert Bruce in the years after 1307, echoed the defence of English and Irish franchises by their lords, and of the principality of Wales by Llywelyn ap Gruffydd. Scottish leaders spoke of the community of the realm rather as marchers paraded the custom of the March, or as Llywelyn and Dafydd took their stand on the laws of Wales. In each case demands from a superior jurisdiction forced those who encountered them to define their position, as well as (in some instances) to resort to arms. Where—as in the case of England and Scotland—there was a conflict between political entities neither of which was capable of obliterating or absorbing the other, strife had a habit of clarifying the dimensions of both. In the fourteenth century the Scottish polity was to acquire a sharper focus and a broader appeal, while its English counterpart attracted wider participation and acquired greater self-confidence in the course of the long hostilities against the Scots and the French. The jurisdictional and military clashes of the reign of Edward I heralded an age when rulers were the managers of political communities that had a depth and articulacy unknown a century earlier.

8. Political Communities

In the fourteenth century western Europe was a world of kingdoms and principalities, whose rulers had clearly defined ideas of their authority and were capable of deploying large resources in pursuit of what they regarded as their rights. As royal government grew in scale and ambition, they tended to become involved in direct dealings with an increasing number of their subjects. Political dialogue was thus a feature of the period. Typically, it was conducted in Estates and parliaments, whose frequent meetings were a symbol of political cohesion and could serve to promote a sense of provincial or national identity. On the Continent political units were joined, separated, or passed around by dynastic accident. Several significant levels of authority might lie on top of one another—as in Germany where a shallow royal power was superimposed upon the jurisdictions of lay and ecclesiastical princes and urban oligarchies, which themselves overlapped. With hindsight (for it is easy to forget that more than one outcome of the Anglo-Scottish war was possible) the British Isles seem to present a simpler picture: they were shared between two unitary and effective monarchies, separated by a well-understood frontier. But to present the political life of the period within a simple twofold scheme is scarcely adequate. Since the existence of a parliament is a measure of political significance, it is important to take account of the fact that the British Isles contained three parliaments, not two. The region offers us the opportunity to examine closely related yet contrasting political communities: England, with its long history of unity and royal government; English Ireland, where the Common Law and institutions transplanted from England existed in a very different environment; and Scotland, where unity had come later than in England, and was less bound up with central administration. But to dwell solely on these regnal or quasi-regnal communities is itself to distort more complex realities. The British Isles, like other parts of Europe, included border zones with their own characteristics, and also fringes that lay outside the political mainstream. Such margins deserve a chapter to themselves.

The English Crown and political society

In a Europe where royal power often lay across kingdoms that were highly regionalized, England stands out by reason of its governmental coherence and comparative lack of provincial custom or autonomy. Even before the Norman Conquest, the kingship was a major force to which the higher aristocracy, Church, and lesser landholders alike reacted. After 1066 the kingdom gained clearer definition at its geographical edges, and existing forms of royal government were developed and exploited by the Normans and Angevins. Both these trends are reflected in Magna Carta. The men of the far north, a region only loosely linked with the southern centres of authority in William the Conqueror's time, played a crucial part in the events leading up to Runnymede; and the Charter's clauses about the law and its administration reflected responses to a shared experience of intrusive royal rule on the part of a group much broader than the barons who actually negotiated with King John.

Thereafter these features of the English polity developed further. In 1215 the grievances of the knights and freemen had been articulated on their behalf by the magnates, who were seen as representing the whole realm. But already the lesser landholders were well able to make themselves heard: for example, county élites often bought collective privileges from the Crown. In the disputes that marked the later years of Henry III, the voices of the local communities were more distinctly audible. The baronial leaders of 1258–9 thought it advisable to create machinery to elicit information and complaints from the shires. When Edward I reasserted royal authority, part of his success lay in the care he took to make his justice available to the landed class as a whole, by offering easy access to his courts, and by dealing with petitions in parliaments to which representatives of the shires and boroughs were often summoned. The knights were already accustomed to holding office under the Crown, to attending royal courts as jurors and litigants, and to serving in baronial administrations which had constant dealings with the king's government. The habit of interaction was now reinforced by drawing the leaders of local society to frequent central assemblies.

In the fourteenth century these well-established aspects of English political life acquired additional significance. Central government itself became more weighty and elaborate. Unlike France, England had a single, unquestioned power-centre. The continued growth of

London and the tendency of an ever-larger bureaucracy to settle at Westminster confirmed the political dominance of the south-east. In the early decades of the century the Anglo-Scottish wars had made York a rival focus of royal activity; indeed the central courts migrated there more than once. But from 1337 onwards the war with France had priority, and the south-east became the fulcrum of military and diplomatic operations. The Tower of London was the king's main storehouse of arms. And the capture in 1347 of Calais, where a large garrison was maintained and through which the wool trade came to be regulated, gave London and the southern ports additional significance. Besides this, the period saw the appearance of a larger, more sophisticated court society. The later years of Edward III and the reign of Richard II were marked by the concentration of the king's itinerary on Windsor castle and the palaces and hunting lodges of the Home Counties (where costly building work was undertaken), and the development of the court as a centre of artistic patronage.

The essence of England's political structure remained the close relationship between this powerful centre and the shires, where patterns of landholding were sufficiently complex to prevent most counties from being dominated by a single aristocratic interest. Magnates had of course their zones of influence, or 'countries'; but in most of lowland England these were smaller than the county unit, and might cut across its boundaries. No administration could begin to rival the king's. The character of the links between central and local government marked England off from its continental neighbours. Whereas in France royal power had made itself felt in the regions through paid *baillis* and sénéchaux, who strove to expand the king's jurisdiction at the expense of that of nobles who tended to control large, consolidated lordships, in England much of the Crown's work had long been done by harnessing the services of the lesser landholders. The later thirteenth and fourteenth centuries saw an expansion of the part they played, as two examples may show. The practice of controlling counties through sheriffs associated with the royal household ceased, and the notion—long promoted by shire opinion, which was deeply hostile to curial sheriffs and their exactions—was accepted, that they should be chosen from among the greater gentry, and changed annually. More striking was the ending of the general eyres conducted by the king's justices, and the drift of judicial authority into local hands. Already in the time of Henry III and Edward I more specialized commissions had appeared, to help fill the gaps between the eyres; but these were still staffed by royal judges. In the fourteenth century, however, partly owing to the volume of cases reaching the courts, it was impossible to cope save by using local men. The gentry were given commissions 'of the peace' (which empowered them to deal with felonies and trespasses), or of *oyer et terminer* (allowing them to 'hear and give judgment' in specific cases).

Historians were once apt to assume that the playing of a larger administrative and legal part by local knights and esquires amounted to a loosening of central control over the shires. But it may be more accurate to see the later Middle Ages as a time when the links between the centre and the localities multiplied and became more complex, in keeping with the general growth of government activity. Studies of county societies have made clear the depth of the penetration of the regions by the central government. In the fourteenth century the gentry occupied an impressive range of offices and roles under the Crown—serving as sheriffs, coroners, escheators, assessors of taxes, arrayers of troops, keepers and justices of the peace, commissioners of *oyer et terminer* and gaol delivery, and much else besides. In each of these they were not autonomous but subject to control—for instance by the exchequer or by superior courts. Although the application of the law had passed to a considerable extent into local hands, the king's judges continued to figure in judicial commissions, and the central courts themselves were swamped with business which by definition arose in the localities. There is also evidence of increased involvement by judges and common lawyers in the processes of out-of-court arbitration by which many (perhaps the majority) of cases had always been settled. The wider world of politics and government impinged upon the shires in other ways too. Royal proclamations were made in the county courts. Members of leading county families served the king beyond the shire boundaries: in Gloucestershire twenty-nine of the forty-seven fourteenth-century sheriffs and twenty-one of the thirty-one commissioners of the peace of the years 1300-60 can be traced taking part in the king's military campaigns. Regional contrasts of course existed. But even on the outskirts of the kingdom the relationship with the centre could be close. In the later fourteenth century Lancashire and Cheshire were great liberties with some distinctive customs and a markedly less wealthy gentry than in much of southern and midland England. But they were linked firmly to the centre by their lords (John of Gaunt and King Richard himself); their administrative framework varied only to a limited extent from that of a normal county; and office was the natural perquisite of the landholding class whose members enforced a law that was common to the whole realm.

It is perhaps not surprising, therefore, that—although the preponderant voice in the affairs of the kingdom remained that of the magnates—the county élites came to play a more prominent part in national politics. Their involvement sprang largely from their role in the management of their own areas. But also of fundamental importance was the need of a militarily active monarchy to apply to its subjects for funds. Everybody accepted that taxation required consent. Roman law, which stressed the authority of the sovereign prince, gave him the right to call upon his subjects' resources in an emergency that affected the realm as a whole; but it also contained maxims such as *Quod omnes tangit, ab omnibus comprobetur* ('what touches all must be approved by all'), which confirmed the old feudal assumption that the lord required the assent of his vassals to extraordinary aids. By 1300 it was clear that it was no longer enough to seek consent merely from the baronage—who may indeed have been happy to see the blame for unprecedentedly frequent and heavy taxation more widely spread.

Across Europe the means used to obtain consent varied, largely in accordance with inherited political structures. In France the number and wealth of towns made it natural to involve representatives of the burgesses (the Third Estate) alongside the clergy and nobility, while the decentralized character of the kingdom encouraged the habit of dealing with fiscal affairs in regional Estates. England differed. There too the presence of borough representatives was important when subsidies were under discussion. But the ancient predominance of the county as a governmental unit, and the established practice of summoning its representatives to councils and parliaments, gave the knights of the shire a key role. The habit also emerged of dealing with the lower clergy (whose assent was needed for ecclesiastical taxation) separately through Convocation. The English parliament thus became not so much an assembly of Estates, as a meeting between the king and his ministers, the higher clergy and aristocracy, and the sum total of the local communities. Moreover, England's small size and political unity made it natural to handle fiscal and other great matters in an assembly of the whole kingdom.

Already before the start of the Hundred Years War it had become the normal assumption that both taxation and substantive changes in the law ought to be handled in parliaments in which representatives of the local communities were present. Between 1297 and 1337 fourteen general subsidies had been granted, all in parliaments attended by knights and burgesses. The subsidy of 1334—fixed at one-fifteenth of the value of movable property in the shires and one-tenth in the boroughs—set the normal rate for later taxes. In the 1322 Statute of York Edward II, out of anxiety to shield himself from ordinances made by his baronial opponents, declared that the only binding legislation was that made in full parliament. That the local representatives were increasingly seen as part and parcel of the body politic is also suggested by a shift in the meaning of the phrase *le commune* ('the community [of the realm]'): in the thirteenth century it had referred to the baronage; in the fourteenth it came to be applied instead to the Commons in parliament. New needs were serving to broaden political participation, but the forms of the wider dialogue were heavily influenced by existing governmental patterns.

Up to this point the role of the Commons may chiefly have been to add respectability to the strategies of the king or the magnates. But during the first phase of the Anglo-French war, when the demands of the Crown were large and persistent, they began to play a more prominent part. Between the 1330s and the 1360s Edward III used meetings of parliament to explain and publicize his military ventures. Intervention in Scotland (which involved the cancellation of an Irish expedition which had been discussed in an earlier parliament) was considered in parliament at York in the winter of 1332–3. The beginning of the war with France in 1337 saw the grant of a triennial subsidy in parliament. The knights and burgesses who attended such sessions would have heard from the mouth of the king or his representative the proposals that would later be set forth in local proclamations. Though there was no question of flatly rejecting requests for supply, there was regular debate about the size and nature of grants. Moreover, it is clear that in practice a link was developing between assent to taxation and redress of grievances. The private petitions that had preoccupied Edward I's parliaments were now mostly dealt with elsewhere; instead the king and council received a *commune*, or collective, petition on matters of general import. The parliament roll would note, among other things, the initial royal speech setting out the reasons for the summoning of the parliament, the grant of taxation, and the contents of the *commune* petition, together with the king's answers. Nor was parliament's role limited to considering requests for general subsidies. These decades also saw the drawing of indirect and disguised taxation within the framework of public consent. By the 1360s the king had seen his freedom to exploit purveyance, to assess men for compulsory military service, and to negotiate the taxation of wool with the merchants all curtailed. It would be misleading, however, to regard these events as a simple defeat for the Crown. Edward was in a far stronger position than earlier rulers, who were constantly hampered by their inability to extract consent to taxation from the baronage. Furthermore, at least after 1341, he gained the resources he needed without engendering the friction that had been a feature of the later years of Edward I. His middle decades showed that ambitious and successful rule demanded a dialogue between the king and a broad spectrum of the aristocracy and gentry: Edward was skilled at associating both with his ventures.

Discussions between the Crown and representatives of the shires in parliament were not limited to fiscal matters. On some topics, such as the need to resist papal encroachment on the rights of English lay and ecclesiastical proprietors to appoint clergy to vacant benefices, their views were virtually identical. On others their interests diverged. There were, for example, contrasting attitudes to law and order. In 1340–1 the king, smarting from the failure of his French campaign, had unleashed punitive judicial commissions (nicknamed 'trailbastons') upon the countryside. At this period the commissions of the peace did not always give the keepers of the peace the power to decide cases, making them mere recorders of indictments rather than justices. The Commons were hostile to draconian commissions of outsiders; during the 1350s their pressure succeeded in winning the authority to terminate indictments for the emerging J Ps (whose powers were confirmed by statute in 1361). The fact that lists of commissions of the peace and of *oyer et terminer* were often drawn up after parliamentary sessions hints at the interaction between central politics and local society.

By Edward III's reign parliament was assuming the physical shape familiar in later periods. In the time of Edward I it had taken the form of a meeting between the king and his ministerial council on the one hand, and the magnates on the other, with the shire and borough representatives (on the occasions they had been summoned) making limited appearances in a clearly peripheral role. The troubles of Edward II's reign saw the magnates establish themselves as part of the council in parliament; the frequency of parliaments led to the appearance of a standardized list of magnates who were habitually summoned, so that by the end of the fourteenth century both a House of Lords and a stable and restricted parliamentary peerage had emerged. This process had opened the way for the knights and burgesses to meet separately, a practice that gave rise to a distinct Commons house. These developments among others have led historians to debate the extent to which the Commons carried political weight and were capable of showing independent initiative. In reaction against earlier views, which tended to take their importance for granted (assuming, for example, that the *commune* petition was their unaided work and did not contain items 'planted' by ministers or lords), writers of a generation ago were sceptical. They made much of some undoubted facts: that many knights of the shire were retained by magnates; that magnates can be shown to have influenced shire elections on occasion; or that during parliaments Lords and Commons 'intercommuned'—that is, confabulated with each other—through committees. On these and other grounds they concluded that the Commons were little more than a mouthpiece of their social superiors.

Recent work suggests that both these views are over-simplified. It is true that all the major political crises of the later fourteenth century arose when a segment of the aristocracy, often including royal princes, was hostile to the court: without leadership of this sort, there was no question of the Commons mounting serious opposition. On the other hand the Commons had enough importance for any opposition group to wish to involve them in its strategies. It was not just that they represented the power of the purse and through it in some sense the realm as a whole; individual knights of the shire were often men of substance with extensive experience not just in local but also in national and even, through the war, international affairs. The gap within the Commons between the leading knights and the burgesses was wider than that between those knights and the magnates. What happened in the fourteenth century can only partly be explained as the rise of the Commons as an institution; at least as important was the absorption of the greater gentry, who dominated both the Commons house and many counties, into the ranks of the ruling class.

The crisis associated with the Good Parliament, which met in the spring of 1376, provides a clear view of the main elements that by then made up the English political community. For several years the French war had been going badly. Government was enfeebled by the old age of the king (who had virtually withdrawn from public life into a small, private household), and the prolonged illness of the Black Prince, who died in June 1376 leaving a 9-year-old son as heir to the throne. There were tensions within the inner circle, involving the king's mistress, Alice Perrers, and her associates, the 'reversionary interest' around the dying prince, and John of Gaunt, the eldest of the king's remaining sons. But the problems went far beyond the jockeying of factions. The combination of heavy taxation and military failure made the conduct of the war and fiscal management matters of open debate. Those concerned ranged from younger nobles, such as Edmund Mortimer, earl of March, whose hopes of distinguishing themselves, and making a profit, as commanders had been disappointed, to senior knights who recalled the glories of twenty or thirty years before. The government had further lost support by conceding a tax to the papacy, thus annoying both the Commons and some of the clergy who would have to pay. In a curious way the crisis was a testimony to Edward III's very success in identifying public opinion with his goals; failure and reversals of popular policies were now a matter for general concern.

Anger was concentrated against those who were judged responsible for the mismanagement of the king's affairs, above all Alice Perrers, William Latimer, Edward's household chamberlain, and Richard Lyons, a London merchant who was accused of profiteering amidst the collapse of the Crown's finances. Although the movement was undoubtedly supported by figures such as Mortimer, the Commons played a vital part. They held out against taxation between April and July—'intercommuning' with the Lords, raising questions about the misuse of past grants and the control of future ones, and demanding a purge of what they regarded as a corrupt court. For the first time the procedure of impeachment was used against royal ministers: in their role as petitioners the Commons put forward damning accusations, upon which judgment was given, and Latimer and Lyons were committed to custody. Everything suggests that attacks on the administration arose from widespread dissatisfaction among the entire ruling class. The Commons needed the reassurance of magnate leadership; but, by the same token, aristocratic opposition required the support of the Commons, with their control of the purse-strings, both to be effective without resort to arms, and to appear to rise above the level of faction.

Despite episodes such as 1376, the king and court had an innate strength, not least because they were permanent in a way parliaments were not: the whole political community assumed tangible form only briefly and spasmodically, and could anyway be managed by a competent ruler. It was typical that the current of opposition visible in the Good Parliament should have subsided by 1377, as the Crown regained the initiative. Hated courtiers had been removed in an almost ritual way; the death of the Black Prince and the further deterioration of the king's health had allowed Gaunt to take a firmer hold on affairs; the alliance of Crown and Commons against the papacy had been reconstructed, so removing one source of friction; and the worsening of the war with France had served to concentrate minds wonderfully. As a result taxation was once more forthcoming. Kingly rule was questioned by nobody; the staying-power of the Crown was enough to see it through crises just as it had done in earlier times when its dealings were with a narrower baronial community.

Yet the broadening of the groups with which kings entered into a political dialogue was a change of some moment. Its significance was not lost on Richard II. His attempts to build a secure regime, unsuccessful as they were to prove, went beyond an effort to create a party of noble supporters. His later years saw an expansion in the number of knights associated with the royal household and an unprecedented distribution of the king's badge of the White Hart to supporters in the localities. The policy of retaining echoed the behaviour of the higher nobility, whose power at regional level depended on their ability to attract the service, or ensure the acquiescence, of segments of the county élites: the strategies of king and magnates alike confirm the political importance of the gentry. It comes as no surprise to find Richard also attempting to influence the membership of the Commons. The Crown was locked into a multiple connection with a widening political nation; in a land with a long tradition of administrative unity, their relationship had a strongly integrative effect.

England's political cohesion is visible in many ways. Ironically, the fact that two fourteenth-century English kings were deposed and murdered—a fate suffered by no French (and no Scottish) king of the period—reflects the unity of a polity with a single focus and a tradition of strong and demanding royal government. Politics revolved around a powerful monarchy. Mismanagement, rule in the interests of a clique, or a style of government that was perceived as threatening by the broad ranks of the propertied, was likely to produce a storm at the centre; incorrigible misrule might lead to the downfall of the king himself. Even in 1327 those who masterminded the deposition of Edward II took care to give the representatives of the local communities a part in the accompanying political theatre. In 1399 Richard II's failure to cling on to power was the product, not just of a successful conspiracy by disaffected nobles, but also of a silent withdrawal of support by the gentry. Henry IV did well to give his usurpation a cover of legality through a quasi-parliamentary assembly.

The habit of centralized government, allied with frequent meetings of parliament in an age of constant war, heightened the sense of English national identity. Royal propaganda harped on the threat from the Scots and the French (which from time to time seemed real enough), and found a receptively xenophobic audience. There was as yet no neat correlation between language and nationality; patriotic verse might be written in Latin, and French remained to some extent the language of the court. Nevertheless a sense of Englishness was strong, and was increasingly associated with the mother tongue. As early as 1344 parliamentary proceedings could record Edward III's statement that Philip VI was 'firmly resolved . . . to destroy the English language and occupy the land of England'.[1] Laurence Minot (*c.*1300–*c.*1352) used the native language for the robust, rudimentary verses in which he celebrated the victories of Edward III, stressed the unity of the English, and sneered at his country's enemies. Minot's sentiments may have been less complex than those of princes and great nobles involved in an international chivalric culture, but they were ones to which king and magnates, as well as the county gentry, could respond.

The English of Ireland

Across the Irish Sea the fourteenth century saw the crystallizing of a second English political community with a parliamentary focus, that of the king's subjects in the Lordship of Ireland. By 1400 the 'English of Ireland' (as they called themselves) were a self-conscious group, with a distinctive set of concerns and attitudes formed amidst the stresses created by border war and the general economic difficulties of the period. The Irish parliament had acquired a format and role similar to those of its English exemplar. It was summoned frequently, and was the scene of grants of taxation, and also of dialogue between

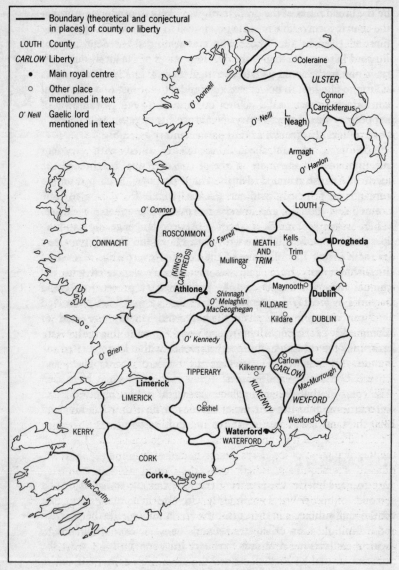

Boundary (theoretical and conjectural in places) of county or liberty

LOUTH County

CARLOW Liberty

● Main royal centre

○ Other place mentioned in text

O' Neill Gaelic lord mentioned in text

Map 5. Ireland, c.1300

the community and the representatives of the Crown, and on occasion the king himself.

The emergence of a political élite in Ireland distinct from that of England was rooted, not in the Hibernicizing of an expatriate society, but in the common institutional structures of England and Ireland, and in the fact that Ireland shared parts of the contemporary English political experience. Almost from the beginning the Lordship was part of the zone of Common Law and was ruled along English administrative lines. In the earlier thirteenth century much of its area was occupied by large, compact lordships. Shires were few in number, and accounted for no more of the settled area than did the great liberties. A large proportion of the knights and freeholders were in consequence primarily members of feudal societies dependent on individual lords. Also characteristic of Ireland at the same period was an aristocracy, many of whose members kept up a role on both sides of the Irish Sea. An assembly of the Lordship's notables in the time of Henry III would have brought together, not a clear-cut provincial community, but a chance assortment of resident barons, transregional lords who happened to be in Ireland, and stewards of such magnates as were overseas. By the fourteenth century these conditions were changing. One part of the background to the emergence of a community of the English of Ireland was the partitioning of the vast lordships of the south-east, and the spread of the scheme of royal counties. Another was the shrinkage of the group of lords who were active in both Ireland and Britain.

Whereas in 1240 Ireland outside Connacht and Ulster contained six counties and the two provincial liberties of Meath and Leinster, in 1300 the same area had nine shires and four county-sized liberties. This change arose from the division of the large county of Munster, the fragmentation of lordships among heiresses, and the keenness of Edward I to acquire jurisdictions for the Crown. Certain counties were to gain liberty status during the fourteenth century, and the demands of border war sometimes led to resident lords being given widespread military authority. But the trend towards smaller units, and a multiplication of the connections between central and local government, was not reversed. In theory Irish counties and liberties were similar to their English counterparts, but in practice there were differences, of which one was of paramount importance: without exception they were incomplete, having fringes and enclaves of upland and bog, which were Gaelic in culture and ruled by native

Irish lords. Such districts, while they might be subject to a form of overlordship, lay outside English law and government as these operated in the core areas. The landholders of English origin were not, of course, sealed off from their Gaelic neighbours: there was every sort of contact, from military alliances to marriages and the movements of minstrels. Even the gentry of the most English areas were affected in as much as they were militarized, rather in the manner of their equivalents in the far north of England. None the less, English law set the knights and esquires of the Irish shires apart from the Gaelic world in important ways: they alone had ready access to the royal courts and security of tenure; only they made up the community that assembled in the shire or liberty court; and they had an exclusive hold on a range of local offices similar to those occupied by the English county gentry.

Though Irish priorities and styles might differ, there is no reason to suppose that county societies were less real in Ireland than England; in some ways they may have been more so. The military aspect of life promoted regional aristocratic supremacies, and gave local offices a distinctive flavour. But in its own way Ireland was familiar with the 'self-government at the king's command' which was a hallmark of English administration. Irish keepers of the peace were arrayers of troops, and commanders and negotiators in border war; their judicial powers were gained more slowly than in England and remained secondary. Yet, just as in England, commissions of the peace gave important duties under the Crown to a broad spectrum of the landed class: in Meath no fewer than ninety families produced commissioners of the peace in the years 1362–1425. Frontier life could give common action extra significance. One of the characteristic features of the fiscal history of the Lordship of Ireland was taxation granted locally, to maintain defences or support a royal army operating in the area. Such grants were made in the courts of counties and liberties. Not only did they involve the leaders of the community in important collective decisions; they also brought a further set of connections between local and central authority, for officials of the Dublin government oversaw their administration. Despite their turbulence and fragmentation, eastern and southern Ireland contained vigorous local societies in which English institutions had struck deep roots; those institutions were manned by local landholders who held offices and performed tasks in the king's name. One responsibility that fell upon the gentry of Louth, Meath, and the Leinster and

Munster counties (together with the burgesses of the major towns) was to represent their communities both in parliament and in the great councils which, because they could be brought together more rapidly than parliaments, were summoned frequently in a land beset by constant emergencies. The habits of discussion and decision familiar at local level were equally appropriate in assemblies of the whole Lordship, where the anxieties of scattered communities found a united voice.

Outside Ulster and Connacht (which passed to the royal family by Lionel of Clarence's marriage to the Burgh heiress, and where English power was anyway fading fast), the summit of colonial society was now occupied by a small group of lords whose interests were concentrated in Ireland. There were some exceptions. Of those based in Ireland, the Butler earls of Ormond held a scattering of land in eleven English counties; while, on the English side, the Mortimers inherited major Irish estates, including eventually those of Lionel. But the Mortimers were plagued by periods of forfeiture and minority, and scarcely filled the shoes of the Marshals, Lacys, Genevilles, Verdons, and the rest. The general pattern, especially in the second half of the century, was one of disengagement by English nobles, who saw little attraction in Irish lands which were outliers of a wider inheritance and produced a declining income that had to be sought in the face of the obstacles presented by distance, disturbed local conditions, and hostility from resident lords. From the 1360s there were numerous sales of land by absentees to resident lords.

This partial withdrawal left space for a more distinctively Irish nobility to blossom. It was led by the Butlers and the Leinster and Munster branches of the Geraldine (FitzGerald) family, who gained earldoms in the early fourteenth century, each at a time when an English regime was anxious to gather or consolidate support in Ireland. John fitz Thomas, the Geraldine lord of Offaly in west Kildare, was made earl of Kildare in 1316, during the Bruce invasion. James Butler was created earl of Ormond, and married to Edward III's cousin, Eleanor Bohun, in 1328 by the Mortimer government. Maurice fitz Thomas, the Geraldine lord of Desmond, was advanced to an earldom of Desmond as part of a deal with Mortimer in the next year. These titles and the new endowments associated with them served to enhance the regional dominance the families already possessed. The earls headed the lay magnates who customarily attended the Irish parliament. Together with second-rank lords, such as the

Barrys of Cork, the Powers of Waterford, or the Prestons of the Dublin Pale, they were in the fifteenth century to form a defined parliamentary peerage.

Against this background it is possible to understand how the English of Ireland could become more clearly delineated and self-aware as a political group. They did so in the course of many-sided dealings with the Irish and English governments, during which they may be said to have marked out a characteristic political agenda. Some of their concerns mirrored those of their counterparts in England. The common experience of the two countries was, above all, that of funding and participating in war. The Lordship of Ireland was organized for war, chiefly to defend itself against the Irish, but also to resist the Bruce invasion and, in the period 1277–1335, to aid the king against the Welsh and Scots. The records of the Dublin administration are packed with evidence of military recruitment, the purveying of supplies, and the raising of taxation; there was, besides, much legislation on matters of internal security and order. English Ireland may have been shrinking in area, but royal management of what remained was intensive.

Although the fragmented nature of Irish warfare encouraged recourse to local subsidies, general taxation was becoming more frequent. Until the 1340s such taxes were normally sought for the king's external wars; thereafter the habit grew of seeking taxes in parliament for the defence of Ireland itself. From the 1290s representatives of the shires and boroughs played a part in giving consent; and, as in England, by Edward III's reign the primacy of the knights and burgesses in fiscal affairs was taken for granted. The question of funding the military activities of the Irish government quickly drew the community of the Lordship into direct dealings with the king. The 1350s saw heavy taxation to counter growing pressure from the Gaelic lords of upland Leinster at a time when the English settlements had been weakened by the Black Death. By the end of the decade help was being sought from England. A great council held at Kilkenny in July 1360 sent a long analysis of Ireland's woes to England, begging for a 'good and sufficient leader' to be sent with troops and money.[3] Among those bearing the petition were knights of the shire deputed by the great council, together with the earl of Ormond. The community of the Lordship will have been well aware that the Treaty of Brétigny had left Edward free to act and also that Lionel, earl of Ulster, was now of age. His appointment as king's lieutenant in 1361 was accompanied, gratifyingly, by a recital of many of the contents of the Kilkenny petition; better still, he brought with him a force of some eight hundred men, whose wages were charged on the English exchequer. With such support he managed to govern without making heavy financial demands upon the locals; the experience of being taxed had taught the English of Ireland the articulacy to escape being mulcted further.

The emergence of what might be called a politics of English Ireland, running alongside, and intertwined with, English politics, is graphically illustrated during the next decade. In 1369 the king appointed William of Windsor, a Cumbrian knight with court associations who had served as a captain under Lionel, as lieutenant, promising him substantial funds from England. With the resumption of the French war Windsor was always likely to find these hard to extract. When his money duly ran out, he was forced to call parliaments and seek subsidies with unprecedented frequency. The outcome was a chorus of vilification which reached Westminster during 1371–2. William was accused of corruption, military incompetence, and of using strong-arm methods to get consent to taxation. As a result, he was withdrawn from Ireland while a lengthy and inconclusive investigation of the complaints against him proceeded. After an interval of some eighteen months Edward decided to send him back to Ireland. Meanwhile the pressures of the French war had grown; and, although Windsor was again promised funding from England, it seems that a decision had been taken to compel the English of Ireland to accept more responsibility for their defence. Further clashes ensued, as the community continued to frustrate William's attempts to raise money. In an attempt to unlock the purses of his subjects, Edward sent special emissaries to address the Irish parliament. When this had no effect, he took the unheard-of step of summoning representatives of the Commons to England, a manœuvre that was resented in the shires and boroughs, where the electors responded by denying their representatives the legal power to assent to taxation. Eventually Windsor was again removed from office, largely because of his association with the court group that was overthrown in the Good Parliament (he was soon to marry Alice Perrers). The whole episode highlights the parallel development of political communities in England and Ireland. Each stood in a relationship with the king to which fiscality was often central, and each sought to use money as a lever to bring about the redress of grievances.

Yet politics in Ireland were no mere echo of those in England; the English community of the Lordship had its own preoccupations. The combination of deteriorating security and reduced involvement by English nobles led to the growth of hostility towards absentees. The more the sense of military crisis in Ireland quickened, the more the outlook of residents and non-residents diverged. For men in Ireland, increasingly required to pay local and general taxes, the sight of treasure flowing out to England (in amounts no doubt greater in their imaginations than in reality) was an affront. The need to compel absentees to see to the defence of their lands became a constant theme of Irish legislation and of collective petitions to the king. It rubbed shoulders with worries about the defence of borderlands, oppression by armed bands maintained by resident magnates, and the need to limit contact with the Gaelic Irish. From the late 1350s it might be accompanied by requests for the king or a member of his family to come to the Lordship. These were not just a stratagem to gain financial assistance; they reflected the desire of a distant and beleaguered élite for reassurance that it was valued, and accepted as part of a broader political society. The insistent clamour was one precipitant of Richard II's visit to Ireland in 1394.

Provincial solidarities and anxieties are perhaps most apparent in recurrent disputes between what the Tudor period was to know as 'new' and 'old' English. It is clear that justiciars and lieutenants arriving from England felt comfortable only with their own kind: more than one petition survives in which they inform the king and council of the unreliability of men of Irish origin, whose local ties they present as threatening to the royal interest, and urge the appointment of judges and even bishops who were 'Englishmen born in England'.[3] The animus was reciprocated. Protests from the English of Ireland lie behind an ordinance of 1357 in which Edward III stressed the common Englishness and worth of both groups, and forbade discrimination and quarrels between them. Historians may sometimes have been too eager to sweep the evidence of such tensions up into discussions of 'colonial nationalism'; they can be compared, more mundanely, to the anger felt by provincial élites in England at insensitive rule by outsiders. Yet the temptation to debunk should not be indulged too far. The English of Ireland lived across the sea; the question of their nationality was given extra point by the existence of the Gaelic Irish; and, above all, they occupied a dominion equipped with regnal institutions, including a parliament closely

modelled on that of England itself. All these things gave their identity
stature and resonance.

There are also intriguing signs that, like other threatened groups,
they were beginning to draw strength from a particular sense of their
own past. In 1317 the Gaelic Irish backers of Edward Bruce had sent
a justification of their behaviour, which contravened the papal grant
of Ireland to Henry II, to Pope John XXII. This document, known
to historians as the *Remonstrance of the Irish Princes*, used as part of
its argument the crimes committed against the Irish by the English of
Ireland. Pope John was unlikely to favour the Bruce cause; but he was
sufficiently struck by the litany of complaint to send it to Edward II
and urge him to take note of its contents. The English of Ireland seem
to have hastened to catch Edward's attention. A contemporary petition, which was accompanied by a copy of Adrian IV's bull
Laudabiliter, reads very much like a riposte to the *Remonstrance*,
which had based much of its case upon the failure of English kings,
and their ministers and subjects in Ireland, to observe Adrian's command to expand the boundaries of the Church, subject the Irish to
law, and 'instruct them in virtue'.[4] The petition dwelt upon the
anarchic state of Ireland before the arrival of the English, the endowment of the Church by Henry and his successors, and the beneficent
role of English law in fostering order. Recent problems, it argued,
sprang from the laxness of judges, and especially the failure to exact
the death penalty for felonies. In short, it presented the historical role
of the English of Ireland as a civilizing mission (of a somewhat
rigorous type). They were stimulated to express their sense of the
legitimacy of their position by a momentary unease about the
Crown's commitment to it. Both the interpretation and the anxiety
endured. There was, for instance, an interest in Gerald of Wales's
writings, which explained how and why the English of Ireland came
to be where they were; and in the early fifteenth century Gerald was to
be used in a forlorn effort to attract the attention of the Lancastrian
dynasty to their other island and its neglected community.

The kingdom of the Scots

In the fourteenth century there was a Scottish political community at
least as real as those of England or Ireland; like theirs, its sense of
identity was heightened by the constant involvement of the population in war. Legally and institutionally the three societies had a good

deal in common. But in its composition and workings the Scottish polity was further removed from its two English counterparts than they were from one another. The Lordship of Ireland, despite its marked political fragmentation, was shaped significantly by English government. But before 1296 Scotland had experienced much less administrative centralization than England. The stresses of the decades that followed were thus bound to affect it in distinctive ways.

Until recently later medieval Scotland was neglected by historians. The period between the death of Robert Bruce in 1329 and the appearance of the supposed 'new monarchy' of James IV (1488–1513) tended to be dismissed as a series of sordid conflicts between feeble or malevolent kings and a factious and brutal nobility. Of domestic political issues there appeared to be few; nor was the reputation of the period redeemed by any marked widening of the political nation in parliament. It is true that the monarchy managed to gain the symbols of authority it had lacked in the time of Alexander II and Alexander III. In 1306 Robert Bruce, upon seizing the kingship by force after murdering John Comyn, did not hesitate to have himself crowned. The supporters of the child David II (who became king while the Treaty of Edinburgh was in force, and was married to a sister of Edward III) succeeded in obtaining the right to both coronation and unction from John XXII. From David's time Scottish inauguration rituals approximated to those of other kingdoms of Christian Europe. But these successes were outweighed by the sorry figures cut by individual monarchs. David II spent eighteen of the first twenty-eight years of his reign in exile in France or captivity in England. When he died in 1371, at the age of 47, he was succeeded by his nephew Robert Stewart, the son of a daughter of Robert Bruce's first marriage. At his accession Robert II (1371–90) was already 55. His main concern seemed to be the aggrandizement of the Stewart kin, and in his later years he signally failed to keep his brood of sons in check. Robert III (1390–1406), who succeeded his father at the age of 53, had a double handicap: he had been born before his parents were canonically married, and an accident had left him impaired physically, and perhaps mentally. In 1400 the kingship could hardly have been at a lower ebb.

Not only did the kings seem personally unimpressive; their rule lacked many of the features that scholars brought up in an age when constitutional and administrative studies were paramount expected to find. Compared with the English monarchy, the Scottish kingship remained a strikingly unbureaucratic affair. Though the kings retained records of their finances, these were infinitely less bulky and varied than those of the English exchequer, wardrobe, and chamber. Whereas English kings had long kept copies of their grants and more important outgoing letters, the kings of Scots had no equivalent of the several series of chancery rolls in which these were recorded: the records of the great seal of Scotland were essentially collections of charters whose recipients had paid for their registration as a legal safeguard.

The income of the Scottish Crown, which hovered somewhere between £4,000 and £10,000 a year, also seemed unimpressive; it was perhaps a tenth part of what Edward III or Richard II could expect to receive. In part of course the discrepancy arose from the smaller size and inferior wealth of Scotland. But it also reflected the fact that the Scottish kings did not raise taxes with anything like the frequency of their southern neighbours. Their income came in the main from traditional sources such as the royal lands, *fermes* of burghs, and the customs. In special circumstances aids might indeed be levied after discussions in Scottish parliaments—as in 1328 when there was a need to find the £20,000 that was the price of the settlement with England. Such grants might receive the assent of burgh representatives and of a concourse of freeholders who had been summoned, alongside the higher nobility, as direct tenants of the Crown. But, unlike the parliaments of England and Ireland, those of Scotland were not attended by representatives of territorial communities; nor did they develop a separate Commons house.

The absence of an elaborate central government engaged in constant fiscal dialogue with elected representatives was paralleled by the lack of a centralized and interventionist legal system of the sort that existed in England, and even to some extent in the Lordship of Ireland. Scottish kings, like all monarchs, heard cases of moment involving their more important subjects; some of these proceeded in parliament, where a certain amount of legislation was also promulgated. But there was no central court of justice in the kingdom until the emergence of the Court of Session in the late fifteenth and early sixteenth centuries, and hence no group of specialist judges and no judicial records to compare with the immense body of rolls of the English courts of King's Bench and Common Pleas. Nor, outside Church circles, was there much in the way of legal education—a curious gap at a time when the rise of the professional lawyer was a feature of other north European states. The influential legal historian Lord Cooper christened the period 1350–1650 'The Dark Age of Scottish Legal History'. For him the evidence of recourse to ecclesiastical courts and to extra-curial arbitration testified to the inadequacy of the public legal system. His opinion harmonized with a more general tendency to dismiss the kingdom of Scots in the late Middle Ages as politically and administratively backward.

This bleak image owed a good deal to fashionable centralist assumptions about political development and the ways in which societies maintain order. It may also be thought to suggest a paradox: for the supposedly underdeveloped Scottish kingdom proved highly successful not only in resisting the attacks of its more advanced neighbour and in exploiting the alliance with France, but also in managing its own affairs during the long periods when its king was under age, absent, or allegedly inadequate. Nor did the scholars who found little to applaud in their country's politics and government doubt for one moment the presence of a profound and articulate sense of national identity. Modern shifts in scholarly perception—not perhaps unconnected with a loss of faith in 'big' government in the wider world—have led to revised estimates of late medieval and early modern Scotland. We are nowadays better able to contemplate the possibility that the limited governmental ambitions and absence of major issues, which historians once deplored, might testify to a kingdom's strength and stability. Scotland's success in defending and cultivating its independent status was not achieved in the face of some imagined political backwardness; the kingdom possessed its own characteristic forms of solidarity which were (ultimately) reinforced amidst the turbulence of the fourteenth century.

To understand the character of the Scottish political community, it may be best to begin in the localities. The Anglo-Saxon legacy of the shires and hundreds, together with a fragmented pattern of landholding, ensured that the English monarchy was linked to local societies by multiple ties. The political geography of most of Scotland was simpler, being marked by consolidated lordships which had more substance than the 'countries' of English magnates. Until the mid-fourteenth century the Scottish higher nobility tended to wield authority over extensive areas: the titles of the earls, for instance, unlike those of their English counterparts, usually signified a real territorial dominance. The endowment of the rising families of Robert Bruce's reign, such as the Randolphs and Douglases, reinforced the pattern of nucleated supremacies in the south, where it had been least evident in the past. Though the late Middle Ages saw a loosening of the connection between title and territory, and the disintegration of certain large traditional units, power came to rest in the hands of some fifty major baronial houses; their continuity—which was enhanced by the growing habit of settling lands on male heirs by entail ('tailzie')—provided a stable focus for regional and local loyalties. Thus the scope, and also the need, for central intervention remained much less than in England. Office-holding in turn tended to reflect landed interests. As in the past, magnates served as provincial justiciars. Sheriffs were chosen from among the local landed élite and many sheriffdoms were in practice hereditary, as was hardly surprising given the concentration of local power in the hands of a small number of kins. Thus Scotland had no real equivalent of the county communities of England and certain parts of Ireland, or of the gentry who competed for office within them. Royal authority had to work through structures of lordship that were well set.

It is against this background that the absence of a centralized judicial system must be viewed. Disputes tended to be settled locally, and in their settlement the power and influence of the magnates was crucial. The lord's influence operated under a variety of guises. As well as acting as royal officials, Scottish earls and barons frequently held high franchises or 'regalities'. They also tended to be heads of widespread kins (for both Gaelic-speaking and English-speaking Scotland were marked by more extended family structures than were normal in most of England). This patriarchal role embraced in addition networks of clients who owed attendance and military service, and could in return expect their lord to offer support and arbitration in their quarrels. In the fifteenth century such matters were to be the subject of written 'bonds of manrent', whose appearance may reflect, besides the spread of literacy, a need to reconstruct lordship amidst the break-up of older provincial patterns. But the relationships themselves were hardly novel. Unfortunately the fourteenth-century evidence rarely allows us to glimpse the realities of regional life; it would be naïve to imagine that monopolistic aristocratic power was wholly benign, or to dismiss the capacity of royal courts and a legal profession to shield the middling against the mighty. Even so there is no reason to suppose that social peace was less well kept in Scotland than in England, despite the absence of a system that clawed cases towards the centre; indeed, as more has been learnt about the importance of informal methods of dispute-settlement in later medieval England itself, the less convincing it is to read the mass of parchment generated by English courts as evidence of their efficiency.

Successful kingship in Scotland, therefore, depended upon the capacity to harness the energies of a limited group of noble families and to provide them with a focal point around which their ambitions could play. It was an intimate and unpretentious sort of rule; the Bruce and Stewart monarchs, whose origins were known to all, moved on terms of rough equality with their leading subjects. Bureaucratic kingship, or high monarchical theories such as those current in the circle of Richard II, were beside the point. When Robert I rewarded his noble supporters with extensive lands and regalities, he was not thereby neglecting his duty to the monarchy or reluctantly doing what was unavoidable, he was playing to one of the monarchy's established strengths. Similarly Robert II's insinuation, both before and after his accession, of his sons into earldoms and regional lordships (mostly by means of strategic marriages) expanded the influence of the new Stewart royal house in a land where the family network was a chief component of political power; it should not be regarded as a failure to pursue an alternative programme of a more bureaucratic sort.

The character of the war against England reflected the nature of the Scottish polity. Whereas the English kings mobilized large and costly armies through what were by the standards of the time complex governmental systems, the war effort of the kings of Scots seems to have demanded relatively little in the way of money or administrative organization. Except during the years immediately after Bannockburn, when their forces penetrated deeply into northern England and Ireland, the Scots were fighting an essentially defensive war. English invasion and occupation of parts of the south had two benefits: it placed the king's right to demand the service of his subjects beyond doubt, and it made a natural appeal to patriotic feelings. The Crown was able to rely on members of the landholding class, who had ready access to local manpower, to raise forces that stayed in the field for short periods only, operated in many instances close to home, and needed no regular payment. When things went well, their reserves of enthusiasm might be replenished by the lure of plunder across the English border: during the heady days of Robert I a fair proportion of the livestock and cash of the north of England was converted to Scottish uses. Accordingly there was little need in

Scotland for the elaborate military and fiscal systems that sprouted in late medieval England and France. The historian may choose to regard Scotland as behind the times; but he should remember that the most 'advanced' states are not necessarily the most stable, and that the kings of Scots avoided some of the political risks courted by rulers who laid heavy burdens on their people.

The Scottish sense of national identity was sharpened, not so much through interaction between a demanding government and those it taxed and drilled, as by the response of a small, conservative society to the sustained threat presented by an external enemy. That society drew strength from a widespread awareness of the antiquity of the native monarchy, which was given clearer focus through the deployment of legendary material by propagandists from the 1290s onwards. The Scottish church had long been the leading proponent of the independence of the kingdom, which was vital to its own freedom from control by York and Canterbury; it felt specially threatened by the intrusion of English clergy during the years when the kingdom lay open to Edward I. The leaders of Scottish resistance, who still regarded John Balliol as their king, did what they could to argue their case at Rome. In doing so they shaped historical and pseudo-historical evidence into a coherent argument against Edward's claim to overlordship. In 1301, for instance, Boniface VIII was informed that the three sons of Brutus had shared Britain as equals (whereas the English claimed that the two younger brothers had been subordinate to the eldest, who was, of course, king of England); that the Britons had anyway been displaced by the Scots, who were descended from Scota, the daughter of the Egyptian pharaoh; that, although King Arthur had subsequently conquered Scotland, his dominion had been temporary; that (moving into historic times) the Saxons had never subjected the kings of Scots, who had held their realm under the direct authority of Rome; and that all homages after 1066 had been solely for lands in England, save for the submission of William the Lion to Henry II, which had been exacted under duress. This argument managed not only to blend myth and history with a good deal of skill, but also to make use of two origin-legends, the Brutus and Scota tales, which plainer minds might have regarded as mutually incompatible.

By 1310, when Robert Bruce's grip was closing on the kingdom, recent history was also neatly rehandled as the Scottish church publicly identified itself with the new order. John Balliol, churchmen declared, had never been the rightful king, but had been foisted upon the Scots by English might. His reign had led to tribulations which had ended only when the people, 'being unable any longer to endure injuries so many and so great, and more bitter than death, which were being continually inflicted on their property and persons for lack of a captain and faithful leader, agreed, by divine prompting, on Lord Robert who now is king'.[5] The law book *Regiam Majestatem* (c.1318) may be similarly connected with the propaganda drive of a new, vulnerable regime. It lays heavy stress on the supposed association of Scots law with David I, the epitome of Scottish kingship, whose legitimate successor Robert I claimed to be. And it can be viewed as an attempt, not dissimilar (despite the very different political contexts of Scotland and Gwynedd) to Llywelyn ap Gruffydd's championing of the laws of Wales, to link king and people together through the bond of a national history and custom.

There is no doubt—despite the manipulation of history, the insecurities of Robert Bruce, or the unseemly eagerness of Scottish churchmen to disembark from the foundering Balliol ship—that the propaganda of the period echoed the genuine feelings of the broad class of landholders, not least those of southern Scotland, who had since 1296 experienced continual war and episodes of English rule. The clerical publicists were, moreover, in many cases bound to that class by family ties. Some members of the higher nobility had, it is true, English interests to consider. But the main difficulty in the early fourteenth century lay, not in any want of patriotic feelings, but in the fact that it was less clear to contemporaries than to modern historians whether the Bruces or the Balliols embodied the Scottish cause. Those Scots who did not at once accept the Bruce version of the past deserve a more sympathetic hearing than they have often been granted. If one part of the story of the period is the growing evidence of a collective political identity, rooted in a shared belief in the free status of the kingdom and in hatred of English domination, another is the impudent success of the Bruce and Stewart dynasties in seizing the national past for themselves.

Until the 1350s there remained a discrepancy between Scottish sentiment and practical politics. The tension is evident, for example, in the circumstances surrounding the most famous of all documents of medieval Scottish history, the Declaration of Arbroath of 1320. This was a letter sent in the name of the Scottish earls, barons, and leading freeholders, whose seals were affixed to it, to Pope John

XXII. It contained an impassioned statement of the kingdom's ancient right to independence, based on the Scota story and other legendary matter, and roundly condemned Edward I's oppressions. Thus far it articulated what were undoubtedly the feelings of most of those living in Scotland. The Declaration's purpose was, however, to support Robert Bruce's case at Avignon against the representations of the English, and to persuade the pope to accept his kingship as legitimate. When its signatories went on to explain that Robert had become king by 'divine providence, the succession to his right according to our laws and customs which we shall maintain to the death, and the due consent and assent of us all',[6] they skated on some very thin ice. Even in 1320 Robert could not count on universal support. His agents had been successful in getting wide endorsement for the document. But not only were there dispossessed magnates (such as the earls of Mar and Atholl) in exile in England; several of the signatories, led by William Soules, who came from an old Balliol family, actually rose against him before the year was out. It was only with the military failure of Edward Balliol and his supporters after 1333–5 that national sentiment and political realities began to come into full accord.

In the later fourteenth century the English were only gradually ousted from the areas of southern Scotland taken by Edward III in the 1330s; there remained some English lords (notably the Percies) eager to maintain or resurrect claims to Scottish lands; occasionally too a Scottish renegade might turn to the English court for assistance. But in general the English and Scottish kingdoms, like their aristocracies, were now distinct. Even during the years 1346–57, when David II was a prisoner in England, the natural leaders of the Scottish clergy and laity co-operated with one another. Parliaments were held in the name of the absent king, and diplomatic relations conducted with outside powers. After the childless David's release, Scottish opinion (no doubt carefully nurtured by the Stewart and his supporters) proved well able to frustrate any scheme to designate an English prince as his heir. The kingdom was dominated by a small but tenacious ecclesiastical and baronial community, bound tightly together by practical interests and by shared political memories and assumptions.

It is no coincidence that this period should have seen the first flowering of a Scottish tradition of historical writing. Before the 1370s the scholar in search of narratives can turn only to two or three exiguous and conventional monastic chronicles, and must indeed find much of his information in works written in England or Ireland. During that decade, however, the silence was broken by John Barbour's *The Bruce*, a verse biography recounting the heroic deeds of Robert I. *The Bruce* was a validation of the current political order. Written in the time of Robert II, it did more than crystallize the collective memory of the founding events of the recent past; Barbour took pains to celebrate the part played in them by the noble houses that were dominant in his own day (especially of course the Stewarts and Douglases), while displaying various degrees of amnesia about those who had since fallen from grace or (like the Randolph earls of Moray) become extinct. His role as the recorder of martial deeds in verse was continued by Andrew Wyntoun, whose long *Origynal Cronykyl* dealt with Scottish history down to 1408. During the 1380s another genre of historical writing was developed by the antiquarian John Fordun. Fordun used earlier annals (now lost), which gave a sober enough account of many episodes of the twelfth and thirteenth centuries. But he shaped the whole of his material into a sustained account of Scottish history from its earliest beginnings to his own time. He used king-lists that took the royal house back into the mysterious days of the Caledonian equivalents of Geoffrey of Monmouth's British kings. This long past reached its climax in the steadfast stand of the fourteenth-century kingdom against the English enemy. Fordun's work was revised, expanded, and extended in the vast *Scotichronicon* of Walter Bower (d. 1449). Between them these works purveyed an orthodox version of the Scottish past that was to become enshrined in the national psyche. But they were no artificial growth; they gave perspective and proportions to stories, opinions, and experiences with which contemporaries were familiar.

By the time of the first Stewart kings, Scotland had a firmly drawn corporate identity, which was fortified by the French alliance, nourished by a general awareness of a national past, and expressed in action either by the king or by an aristocratic and clerical junta supplying his place. If high politics saw the direct participation of a smaller segment of the population than was the case in England, this was in accordance with the traditions and needs of an intimate kingdom managed by the royal house, higher clergy, and a limited number of noble kins, whose periodic quarrels did not disturb the underlying consensus; it was not a sign of arrested development. Nor should Scottish parliaments be underestimated merely because they differed in composition from their English counterparts, and served less frequently as a fiscal instrument. Parliament was an important political focus in a kingdom that had gained solidarity through the shearing away of cross-border ties and was led by men whose families had weathered, and in many cases benefited from, the turbulence of the fourteenth century.

The differences between the polities of England, Scotland, and English Ireland in the fourteenth century arose from complex patterns of interaction between their earlier development and present circumstances. England had a long history of political coherence and of government through direct relations with both magnates and lesser landholders. An assertive, militaristic monarchy, which demanded much from its subjects, thus led to the development of a single national politics, characterized by breadth of participation and frequent clashes over the directions, conduct, and funding of royal policy. In Scotland, which had a tradition of less intrusive central authority and management of the regions by entrenched aristocratic interests, political life involved a more restricted spectrum of the population; major questions of government were relatively few, and politics normally amounted to the quarrels and reconciliations of kings and a limited number of noble kins. Yet there was one overriding issue, that of relations with England, which provided the kingdom (whatever its divisions) with a common agenda. Resistance to English claims deepened the sense of national identity and bound the active political groups together with those below them in a sense of a shared cause and a common past. The English population in Ireland for their part built a political identity upon two distinct foundations. One was a local variant of the English institutional tradition, allied to the fiscal and other demands English rule entailed in the later Middle Ages. The other was the particular problems of a colonial ruling class which felt itself trapped between the pressures of its own environment and the forgetfulness or insensitivity of its masters on the other side of the Irish Sea. But, despite the different experiences of the three countries, each had by 1400 a vocal political community with a developed sense of its identity, rights, and worth.

9. On the Margins

LIKE all attempts to portray central developments, the previous chapter pushed much of significance to one side. The political communities with which it was concerned embraced some regions less effectively than others; certain groups they shut out almost wholly. To discuss the various marginal and excluded elements—as this final chapter tries to do—involves gathering up a set of topics that may appear to have little direct connection with one another. But the act of viewing them together reveals comparisons and contrasts that would otherwise remain hidden; it also shows the limitations of contemporary regnal structures, and may highlight some general political features of the British Isles in the later Middle Ages.

One sort of margin was economic and social. It need hardly be said that the institutions with which the political historian is concerned gave most of the population no voice; in that sense the vast bulk of the inhabitants of the British Isles were always non-participants. Their views are rarely recorded, though the actions of their betters were no doubt shaped by an awareness of what would or would not be tolerated by them. The period saw only one significant challenge to this state of affairs. During the Peasants' Revolt of 1381 parts of southern and eastern England were disturbed by episodes of violence, accompanied by demands for the abolition of serfdom, that shook the governing classes. These risings—which involved artisans, clergy, and minor gentry as well as peasants—seem to have sprung from a combination of long-term and more immediate circumstances. From 1348 repeated outbreaks of plague had reduced the population dramatically, leaving those who survived in a position to hope for improvements in their lot. Rising wages, and in places the availability of more options, made the remaining legal disabilities of serfdom harder to bear; it was no accident that disturbances affected, not the poorest regions of England, but those where expectations had risen most. To such long-term tensions were added others created by the three poll taxes granted between 1377 and 1381. By replacing the usual rough-and-ready assessments according to wealth in movable goods with a levy (in 1377 and 1381 a flat-rate levy) on the entire adult population, these heightened feelings of inequity. At the same time the military and diplomatic failures in France came very close to home with attacks on the south coast and a fear of invasion. In the end, however, the uprising, while it put a stop to experiments in taxation, did not upset the existing political order. During the later thirteenth and fourteenth centuries the gentry of the shires had gained a place in the political firmament; those beneath them (who anyway had demanded redress of their grievances by the king, not admission to the ruling groups) remained on the outside. The main effect of the events of 1381 was probably to consolidate an identity of interests between the higher and lesser nobility that had been visible ever since the Black Death presented unexpected problems to all landlords.

The troubles of 1381 found few echoes in the far north and the west of England; in Wales, Scotland, and Ireland the silence of the popular voice is deafening. In these regions, it may be suggested, threats to the social order tended to be smothered by relative poverty, by the prevalence of pastoralism and dispersed settlement, and by vigorous aristocratic power manifested in compact, jurisdictionally privileged lordships. But it was here that political margins of a different sort were to be found. They included geographical zones that were managed lightly and indirectly by central government, whether English or Scottish, and also (in Wales and Ireland) native élites who were at best incompletely absorbed into the dominant political structure.

Border societies

In the fourteenth century the Welsh marches—the border area that figures most prominently in accounts of earlier ages—was losing some of its political significance. In important respects of course it remained distinctive: the lords of the March continued to wield judicial powers unmatched elsewhere in the king of England's dominions, and the communities of their lordships did not send representatives to parliament or normally come within the field of royal taxation. But more peaceful conditions in Wales tended to weaken the military justification of marcher lordship, while accidents and devices of inheritance brought accumulations of marcher property into the hands of a small group of English noble families, to whom the unfettered profits afforded by Welsh lordships were attractive. Thus the March, although not assimilated to county society, was tightly bound to the English polity. In the later years of Edward III its leading lords—who included the Mortimer earls of March, the Fitz-Alan earls of Arundel, the Bohun earls of Hereford, and the Hastings earls of Pembroke—could hardly have been closer to the centre of affairs.

If the Welsh March was fading as a real military and political borderland, in other areas of the British Isles frontier characteristics were becoming more prominent. Between England and Scotland there had long been a border line, disputed in places even after the 1237 Treaty of York, but minutely traceable on the ground by contemporaries. The Anglo-Scottish wars did not lead to formal alterations of the Tweed–Solway frontier; none the less, the fourteenth century saw periods when parts of southern Scotland were occupied by the English, as well as a phase when Robert Bruce's raids on northern England diverted much of its wealth into Scottish coffers. The main impact of war was twofold: it provoked common responses and entrenched shared social patterns on both sides of a frontier that cut through what was still in many ways a single region; and it presented similar political problems to the English and Scottish monarchies. The English dominion in Ireland also had its marches, which were enlarging as the grip of government by the king and English magnates loosened in the face of war and pestilence. The Irish borderland is less easy to depict: rather than forming a single belt, it was made up of the discontinuous fringes of individual counties and lordships. But, despite this difference, it had at least two things in common with the Anglo-Scottish border. In both areas, central authority had little choice but to depend heavily on a resident aristocracy, a fact that was bound to have political consequences. Both also shared in the irony that—unlike the more amenable marches of Wales—they lay in theory within the regular framework of English or Scottish law and local government.

For nearly eighty years after 1217, the Tweed–Solway line marked the frontier between two kingdoms which were at peace. Cross-border landholding was commonplace, and increasing; lords in northern England were more likely to have property in Scotland than south of the Trent, while Scottish lords, such as the earls of Dunbar and Strathearn, held lands in Northumbria of the English king. In such circumstances the region, despite its distance from Westminster and the inaccessibility of parts of it from Edinburgh, presented few political problems; indeed the spread of landed interests across the frontier produced a group of families with an interest in keeping Anglo-Scottish relations on an even keel. The border country itself, with its expanses of hill and moor, harboured a stock-rearing society which was prone to violence, often sparked off by competition for grazing land. But during the thirteenth century, in the absence of conflict between kings, this had only local significance. Border infractions, which arose for the most part in the course of cattle-rustling and routine criminality, were handled by the courts or through the body of local custom known as the 'Laws of the Marches', which had assumed written form by 1249.

The fourteenth century transformed the borders. National war raised questions of allegiance that had hitherto lain dormant, and also interacted with, and stimulated, private vendettas. Quite apart from that, the combination of destructive military activity with the effects of famine and plague had by 1400 led to a decline in population and a significant retreat of arable farming. Pastoralism became even more dominant, while insecurity seems to have enhanced the importance of ties of extended kinship which must always have been strong in the uplands. The result was the development of the cattle-reiving (rustling) kins, later known as 'surnames'. They do not emerge into the full light of documentary day until the appearance of the State Papers of the Tudor period; but there is enough evidence to confirm that their world of raids, feuds, parleys, and compensation payments existed in the later Middle Ages. The borders were a region where definitions of order and disorder, and the balance between formal legal process and self-help, differed from those in districts that central governments controlled in more detail.

This area of turbulence and constant military emergency provided fertile soil for the growth of noble power. On the Scottish side the favour of Robert Bruce had enlarged the holdings of the Stewarts in southern Scotland and also made the fortunes of the Douglases and Randolphs. The extinction of the Randolphs in the mid-fourteenth century, and the passage of the Crown itself to the Stewarts in 1371, meant that the house of Douglas emerged pre-eminent, sharing power with older lords such as the earls of March (Dunbar). On the English side aristocratic dominance became more marked after the outbreak of the Hundred Years War reduced direct royal involvement in the north. As the attention of Edward III passed elsewhere, magnate kins, above all the Percies and Nevilles, assumed a new importance. The Percies, a Yorkshire family, had become lords of

Alnwick in 1309, and had received grants of land in Scotland during times of English success. They continued to amass property and influence throughout the north, gaining, for example, the lordships of Cockermouth in Cumberland and Prudhoe in Northumberland during the 1380s. The Nevilles, who were leading tenants of the bishop of Durham, likewise expanded their lands and network of clients. The reputation earned by Ralph Neville when he led the forces of Yorkshire and Durham that defeated the Scots at Neville's Cross in 1346 materially assisted their rise; it also highlights the conditions that led aristocratic power to flourish.

The situation in the border region meant that it came to have an important part in English and Scottish politics. Magnate ambitions often appear to have had free play, and to have taken precedence over national concerns. The border lords, with their rival claims to property in both realms, now had an interest in perpetuating war, not peace. The Scottish victory at Otterburn in 1388, for instance, was as much an episode in the feud between Douglas and Percy over the possession of Jedburgh as an event in the war between England and Scotland. Just as to Scottish historians the Douglases have seemed to epitomize the over-mighty subject, so the role played by the northerners in the downfall of Richard II and the early troubles of Henry IV have prompted similar judgements. Richard's attempts to insinuate his own men into the north during the 1390s alienated the northern lords; and Henry Percy, earl of Northumberland, proved to be a key supporter of the Lancastrian coup in 1399. Then, when Henry IV disappointed the Percies' expectations of reward, they proceeded to pose a major threat to his regime. The Anglo-Scottish wars had given the north a political significance it had not possessed since the time of King John.

It would be easy to conclude that the borders had emerged as a zone beyond the control of the English and Scottish monarchies, where magnates lorded it over societies that had closer associations with what lay on the other side of the frontier than with their own national communities. But such a judgement is over-simplified. While it is true that conflict between the two kingdoms gave their respective margins a distinctive character and enhanced importance, there was in reality little danger of their detachment from the interiors to which they belonged. The ambitions of magnates—as the events of the late fourteenth and early fifteenth centuries show—were pursued primarily within the context of national politics. On the Scottish side, the activities of the Douglases and others had by 1400 resulted in the recovery of almost all the areas occupied by Edward III in the 1330s; and the nobles of southern Scotland played an important part in guarding the integrity of the kingdom during the feeble rule of Robert III and the long English captivity of James I (1406–24). In England the advancement of the Percies and Nevilles had taken place through service to the Crown, on whose patronage they fed. The English military system in the north was complex and expensive, and it was to all intents and purposes devolved into the hands of the magnates; they and their men held offices and commands, from constableships of castles to wardenships of the March itself, and depended on the wages and profits that went with them. They blended the roles of landholders, military captains, and political managers, all of which derived from the king.

Although the experience of war deeply affected the society of the borders, serving to distance it further from that of the Home Counties or Fife, the political implications of this should not be exaggerated. The region was dominated by nobles whose allegiances were, when it came to the pinch, clear-cut, and whose membership of the noble communities of their kingdoms was not in doubt. The border ballads of a later age may seem to suggest that the denizens of the areas on either side of the Tweed–Solway line felt they had more in common with one another than with their supposed compatriots to the north or south of them; but even if this was so, the magnates who ruled the borders were strong enough to keep their 'countries' in line; in the fifteenth century, when there was little open war between the kingdoms, cross-border contacts were effectively reduced. The border zones, while socially, and to some extent administratively, distinctive, remained firmly wedded to the heartlands of their respective kingdoms through men whose allegiances had been clarified by the war itself.

The crucial role of a small number of nobles in northern England and southern Scotland has strong parallels in Ireland, where broad areas, whose inhabitants lay neither fully within nor wholly outside the king's allegiance, were given cohesion and linked to Dublin through aristocratic lordship. The nature and significance of these borderlands may have been obscured by the habit of dividing Ireland too neatly into English and Irish areas. Scholars have tended to be expert either in the records of English administration in Ireland (which bring us into contact with shires, liberties, towns, Common

Law, parliaments, and the alarmist rhetoric of officials looking out upon a scene they could not control), or in the literary remains of a self-conscious Gaelic culture (which introduce us to a world of Irish dynasties conscious of their royal past, a deceptively changeless customary law, and bards who were expert in the perpetuation of traditional forms). The dichotomy was real enough; but it may be regarded as representing two poles, between which large elements in the population oscillated. It was the task of the magnates to span contrasting social environments, and to exercise a lordship flexible enough to incorporate, at one extreme, English burgess communities and, at another, Irish upland clans for whom the cattle-raid was a way of life.

From centres such as Maynooth in the manorialized hinterland of Dublin, the fourth earl of Kildare (1342–90) wielded an authority that stretched towards the Wicklow Hills to the south-east and into the boggy central lowlands to the west. In 1350 he made an agreement with two Gaelic lords, Maurice Shinnagh (Muirchertach Sionnach) and Fergal MacGeoghegan (Fearghal Mág Eochagáin), who occupied an area on the borders of Kildare and Meath (where the Mortimer lordship of Trim lay). The deed records

that Maurice and Fergal have become [the earl's] men from this day forth for the rest of [their] lives, and are obliged to give him counsel and aid with all their power against all men, our lord the king and the lord Mortimer alone excepted, following and attending [his] banners, expeditions and wars throughout all Ireland at the cost of [the earl]. . . . And [the earl] has agreed that he will aid and assist the said Maurice and Fergal by means of his justice against all other Irishmen.[1]

The terms are in some ways reminiscent of Scottish bonds of manrent; but they belong to a society where the military element in lordship and cultural divergences were both more conspicuous. The document shows an area which was wholly Irish in character being drawn within a hierarchy at whose summit lay the king of England himself. Nor was the link with royal authority merely theoretical: the earl of Kildare had served Edward III at the siege of Calais in 1347, received knighthood at his hands, and married the daughter of one of his household stewards; he was also to serve as justiciar of Ireland on several occasions over the next thirty years.

Further south the Butler earls of Ormond fulfilled a similar role. They controlled extensive lands in Kilkenny, Tipperary, Waterford, and Limerick, with outlying properties in Connacht, Kildare, and Dublin. Their scattered and diverse possessions meant that they exercised power in a remarkable variety of settings and forms. They dominated stretches of the valleys of the rivers Barrow, Nore, and Suir, which reach the sea at Waterford, protecting and exploiting English-speaking communities. They also acted as patrons of English and Irish kins of north Kilkenny and Tipperary, from whom they drew much of their military manpower. These kins had a good deal in common with the 'surnames' of the Anglo-Scottish borders (though the borderers did not have the satisfaction of hearing their cattle-raids celebrated in stylized Irish bardic poems). The mingled environments in which the Butler earls operated are nicely caught in 1358, when the second earl took Edmund O'Kennedy (Éamonn Ó Ceinnéidigh), a north Tipperary lord with whom he was at odds, to England with him. The terms of Edmund's rehabilitation were set out in a document witnessed by the earl's mother, Eleanor Bohun, at the family manor of Aylesbury. They included arrangements for the delivery of hostages by O'Kennedy, his attendance at Ormond's courts, and his military service both within and beyond his own region. But the most revealing clauses are those that set out his duty to discipline his own people, to compensate the earl and his English tenants for any offences committed against them, and to look to the earl and his officers for justice against the English.

The styles and significance of Irish border lordship varied from region to region and from decade to decade, reflecting the shifting balances between English and Irish culture and custom. In the north the Burgh earls of Ulster and lords of Connacht had exercised a real dominance over a largely Gaelic society, whose leaders owed them tribute and military attendance. Their empire had crumbled by the middle of the fourteenth century, after the Bruce occupation and the murder of the last earl in 1333. But one small part of their role was inherited by the archbishops of Armagh, who from 1346 were invariably of English blood. The archbishops resided in the Anglicized areas of eastern Meath and Louth, but were skilled at exercising influence over the Gaelic parts of their diocese and province, a task that involved them in continual dealings with the O'Neills, O'Hanlons, and others. Their activities had political overtones, for not infrequently they acted as diplomatic agents of the Crown. At the other extremity of English Ireland the earls of Desmond, who were lords of Kerry and had property distributed across much of the south-west, were the most turbulent of the nobles, and culturally furthest removed from English styles. The first earl (1329–56) clashed repeatedly with royal ministers; and his younger son, the third earl (1358–98), was a passable poet in the Irish tongue. But it is misleading to assume that they were losing sight of their English identity, or abandoning their role as political agents of the Crown. Their recalcitrance was closely related to territorial disputes with absentees and resident lords; and their marriages (the mother of the first earl was a Berkeley, and the wife of the second earl a daughter of the earl of Stafford), devotion to knighthood, and service as justiciars of Ireland all suggest that they should be viewed as marcher lords, albeit of a remote and awkward type, rather than as Gaelic princes. They formed a stable centre in a world that contained, not just O'Brien and MacCarthy renegades, but also citizens of Limerick and families who provided sheriffs, coroners, and keepers of the peace in the south-western counties.

In Ireland as in England there existed borderlands where royal government relied on nobles whose power was unusually extensive and concentrated. Whereas the English border shires formed a readily identifiable marchland of limited size, in Ireland the fringes were broken, and associated with numerous small administrative cores, called by contemporaries 'the land of peace'; the Irish marches also, of course, harboured a richer mixture of language and custom than the Anglo-Scottish borders. Yet the parallels are striking. The Dublin government, like the English and Scottish kings, had to reckon with militarized zones where the risks attendant on disturbing settled patterns of aristocratic rule were very great: earls of Desmond could be brought down, as the first earl was in 1345; the difficulty was to replace them. The governing of Ireland was not merely to do with administering, protecting, and taxing regions where Common Law was effective; it was also about managing lords who were the main link between central government and local populations who stood outside the conventional scheme of English administration. In that sense the Lordship of Ireland was a good deal larger than a map of the cramped areas of effective shire ground would suggest.

The leaders of the Welsh

Britain and Ireland also contained leaders whose links with the political mainstream were problematical in ways those of even the most outrageous border magnates were not. The closer binding of Wales to England after 1282 presented the Welsh élites with opportunities as well as difficulties, and their position in the post-conquest age was not wanting in paradoxes. Among the native leaders two groups may be distinguished: surviving members of the old princely houses, and a rising office-holding class who were to form a Welsh squirearchy. The line between them should not be too firmly drawn. Cadets of the royal lineages could sink to ministerial level, while the dynasties founded by newer men could acquire the trappings of nobility, including celebration by the bards. The most influential leaders of the Welsh in the time of Edward II, Sir Gruffydd Llwyd and Sir Rhys ap Gruffydd, were descendants of Llywelyn the Great's steward, Ednyfed Fychan; while Owain Glyn Dŵr, though merely a squire, was of doubly royal ancestry. But the division has enough reality to serve as a rudimentary analytical tool.

For the royal kins the late thirteenth and fourteenth centuries were a period of decline. In many cases this was no more than the continuation of an established trend, since the supremacy of the house of Gwynedd had grown at the expense of its rivals elsewhere in Wales. But it should not be seen as an automatic outcome of the conquest: after all Edward I defeated Llywelyn ap Gruffydd with the assistance of other Welsh lords; and for men such as Rhys ap Maredudd of Deheubarth or Gruffydd ap Gwenwynwyn of Powys his victory may have seemed to herald a fresh dawn. In fact the new dispensation proved to be fraught with perils; it was one thing to turn to the English for support against the arrogance of a fellow Welsh ruler, quite another to maintain status in the face of the demands of an infinitely superior power which was now located within native Wales, not just around its edges.

There was more than one road to ruin. The rising of 1282–3 had been provoked partly by the demands of Edwardian government and the intrusiveness of its local agents. Its defeat resulted in the death or expropriation of the chief members of the house of Gwynedd and those who had thrown in their lot with them. Very similar pressures soon came to play upon the Welsh lords who had taken the side of the English. In 1287–8 Rhys ap Maredudd, angered by the limitations placed upon him by royal government in south Wales, led a rebellion whose failure signalled the end of the power of the descendants of the Lord Rhys. In 1294–5 a more widespread Welsh revolt took place, sparked off by the very heavy taxation of the principality by Edward I in 1292-3, and by fears of further fiscal and military demands arising from the war with France. Its leader was Madog ap Llywelyn, head of a cadet branch of the house of Gwynedd based in Merioneth, where high tax-assessments had been imposed upon an impoverished rural society. With the failure of the rising, traditional aristocratic leadership was all but extinguished in north Wales. A similar pattern may be discerned in the revolt of Llywelyn Bren, a descendant of minor royalty in upland Glamorgan, in 1316. It took place after the death of the earl of Gloucester at Bannockburn had brought Glamorgan into the custody of royal agents, and at a time of famine when the demands of lordship seemed specially insufferable. The realities of English rule proved incompatible with the aspirations of a class of men who desired scope and recognition, and needed to appear as effective protectors and patrons of their own people.

An alternative path to oblivion lay through assimilation. The proximity of southern Powys to England, and the immediacy of the threat it faced from Gwynedd, had long ensured that its rulers developed strong ties with the marcher families of Shropshire and with the Crown; even before 1282 Gruffydd ap Gwenwynwyn and his sons had as much in common with the Corbets and Lestranges as with Welsh lords. After the conquest Gruffydd's successors abandoned their native customs of naming, and became known as 'de la Pole [Welshpool]'. Their integration was such that by the reign of Edward II their lordship—which under Welsh law would have passed in the male line only—had been inherited by an heiress, who carried it to the English family of Charlton. Once John Charlton established himself, the process by which southern Powys became just one more marcher lordship was complete; adaptation had proved as treacherous a course as resistance. By 1327 only vestigial remnants of the old aristocratic order survived.

The rising ministerial group in Welsh society had fewer problems in coping with the new political environment. This is not surprising. The English had long subscribed to the truism that the Welsh were best controlled through Welshmen. During the thirteenth century an official class had emerged whose members served in the administrations not just of the princes of Gwynedd and other Welsh rulers but also of marcher lords and the Crown. The fluid quality of native politics had long accustomed such men to changes of allegiance: the *uchelwyr* ('chief men') of Powys, for example, had maintained their position as the pendulum swung from their own lords to the house of

Gwynedd, and back again; while those of the Four Cantrefs had experienced both native and English rule between 1240 and 1282. After 1284 royal government offered employment to members of the native élite, and many individuals pursued their careers successfully across what appears to us a deep political chasm.

In the post-conquest age there was a strong demand for Welshmen of substance to act as administrators and political intermediaries, not just in the old marcher lordships and the royal lands in south Wales but also in the new lordships which occupied much of the Four Cantrefs, and of course in the conquered principality of north Wales itself, where Welsh structures of local administration were incorporated rather than demolished. Throughout Wales, for instance, landholders with a position in their communities could add to their wealth and status by serving as rhaglaws in the commotes. In the royal lands of the north, governed under the Statute of Wales, offices such as coroner and deputy sheriff were also open to them. For those at the top of the tree, such as Gruffydd Llwyd, greater things were available. Gruffydd acted as an arrayer and leader of Welsh troops serving Edward I in Scotland, and also as sheriff of Merioneth. More personal links with the Crown were also possible: Edward of Carnarvon, who held the principality as prince and king from 1301 to 1327, had Welshmen among his household knights and esquires, so allowing a small group access to a wider stage. The *uchelwyr* were, moreover, emerging as effective rural capitalists; new legal devices —above all that of *prid*, or 'Welsh mortgage'—circumvented the traditional fragmentation of holdings among heirs and facilitated investment in land. By the late fourteenth century a native class of middling landholders had emerged.

Yet it is too simple to conclude that the conquest, while sounding the death-knell of the old princely houses, created conditions in which a lesser élite flourished and became harmoniously involved with their English superiors. Alongside co-operation and opportunism was an acute sense of alienation and oppression. An episode in Gruffydd Llwyd's career well illustrates the underlying tension. In 1316–17 Gruffydd's record of service to the Crown was interrupted, and he found himself in prison, accused of communicating with the king's enemies. Edward Bruce had sent letters from Ireland, seeking support for the extension of his war into Wales. Significantly, he stressed the dispossession of the Welsh by the English, and held out the bait of a pan-Celtic movement to throw off the Saxon yoke for ever. Gruffydd's reply was studiously vague, but was couched in the same apocalyptic terms. His action in responding is probably to be explained by very specific grievances: he was at odds with the Mortimers, who held the justiciarships of north and south Wales, and he had recently been deprived of his position as sheriff of Merioneth. None the less the nature of the appeal and the answer is revealing. The themes they emphasized—a Welsh identity rooted in a heroic British past, the sense of present humiliation and loss, the yearning for a day of reckoning when English rule would be cast aside—are common in the Welsh prophecy and poetry (some of it written for, and indeed by, members of the *uchelwyr* class) of the fourteenth century. Such sentiments seem at odds with the compromise and self-advancement so noticeable in the careers of leading Welshmen. But they are not to be dismissed as mere froth, irrelevant to the 'real' world in which the Welsh squirearchy lived. They suggest the dilemma of a subordinate group, trying to preserve its sense of itself while making its way in an alien environment; and the feeling of being an outsider in one's own country gave them a special bitterness. The reality was that the collaborator and the protestor frequently inhabited the same body. Memories of past greatness and hopes for the distant future helped to preserve a national identity that present conditions threatened to obliterate.

Resentment sprang from the inescapable fact that even for the Welsh élite the possibilities of advancement were limited; in general their milieu was the relatively humble one of commote and manor. Gruffydd Llwyd was unusual in holding a shrievalty; the vast majority of sheriffs, and all constables of royal castles, were English. The main offices in central administration, such as those of justiciar and chamberlain of north and south Wales, were also closed to Welshmen. Although in 1322, when he needed support wherever he could find it, Edward II summoned representatives of north and south Wales to the York parliament, normally Welshmen had no place in such assemblies. In other ways too their situation contained much that was likely to frustrate those who sought to thrive: the difficulty of gaining legal redress against Englishmen; the economic advantages enjoyed by English borough communities within Wales; and the profiteering face of marcher lordship and the administration of the Black Prince, who held the principality from 1343 to 1376.

Welsh feelings of alienation were normally held in check by the sheer weight of English dominance and denied a focus by the geographical and administrative fragmentation of Wales. In special circumstances, however, they could assume an unwonted political importance. The fall of Richard II in 1399 was one such moment. Like Edward II before him, Richard had held the principality in his own hands, so bringing about a closer connection between Crown and Welsh leaders than was usual; his abrupt removal thus left a vacuum of control. It was exacerbated by forfeitures and minorities in key marcher lordships (including the vast complex of Mortimer holdings), and by the early weakness of Henry IV. These political difficulties came after half a century of social and economic change in Wales in the wake of the Black Death. Falling population and the gradual abandonment of demesne farming by English landowners had created a climate of expectation yet also of uncertainty amongst the Welsh squirearchy who might hope to benefit from the opening up of the land-market.

Against this background Owain Glyn Dŵr led a rising in 1400 which over the succeeding six years attracted the backing of native squires, clergy, and commoners. Owain himself encapsulates the ambiguities of Welsh society at this period. He was a landholder in northern Powys, a man of local note, but not wealthy enough to achieve knighthood. His grandmother came from the marcher family of Lestrange, and he married a daughter of Sir David Hanmer, a descendant of English settlers in Flintshire. He seems to have spent a period at the Inns of Court in London, and in 1385 he served on Richard II's Scottish campaign. So described, his origins and career seem little different from those of other Welsh squires. But, unlike many of his counterparts, Owain could claim a distinguished ancestry: he sprang from a branch of the old ruling house of Powys that had retained a portion of its lands despite 1282; what is more, his mother was descended from the Lord Rhys of Deheubarth. His own consciousness of this royal heritage seems to have made him an active patron of the bards, who celebrated his lineage and deeds long before 1400. During his rising political activity and national feeling, so often at odds with each other, briefly came together. In the years 1403–6 he dominated much of Wales, styled himself Prince, and conducted diplomacy with the kings of Scotland and France and with the Avignon papacy. While doing so he assiduously presented himself as heir to the British past and as the fulfilment of the Welsh messianic tradition; like Edward Bruce, he tried to involve the other Celtic peoples in his rising, sending letters to Ireland

and reminding the aged Robert III of their common descent from Brutus.

Owain's supremacy could not last once English government recovered its equilibrium. Much of his support had arisen from the simple fact that he possessed the military initiative; as that faded he rapidly lost his command of men's allegiances, and by 1410 he was a hunted fugitive. Welsh resentment of English rule once again became a matter to be aired by consenting squires and bards in private. It was now, moreover, voiced in less relaxed conditions. The shock of the rising made the authorities exceedingly suspicious of the Welsh, and their exclusion from office, English law, and urban privileges became more stringent. In the aftermath of the Edwardian conquest the *uchelwyr* had in many ways come to terms with, and benefited from, their association with England; but they had remained aware of their identity as leaders of a subject people. The English, secure in their own superiority, had held them at arm's length, and had found no wholly satisfactory place for a group who, despite many points of contact, remained alien.

The lords of the Irish

In the later Middle Ages native leadership in Ireland differed from its Welsh equivalent in two fundamental respects. The absence of a royal conquest in the thirteenth century meant that the traditional dynasties were still in place. Secondly, although in 1300 the area under their control was much smaller than it had been a century before, in many parts of the country the balance of territorial advantage had already begun to tip in their favour once again. The Gaelic lords of the later Middle Ages may be distinguished in important ways from their royal ancestors. The Anglo-Norman conquests had broken the provincial kingships of the twelfth century; and, apart perhaps from that of the O'Neills in the north, the reviving lordships of the fourteenth century were on a smaller scale. Though annalists and bards continued to stress the royal attributes of their patrons, by 1400 they themselves used kingly styles sparingly, usually contenting themselves with the titles 'lord', 'prince', or 'chieftain' (*capitaneus*), or simply with the unadorned family name in the manner of the head of a clan. Their rule also betrays new features of a practical sort—from the occupation and building of stone castles, to the imposition of a complex range of dues designed to maintain armed retinues which in the north and west included Scottish gallowglasses. In the south the need to adapt to the continuing reality of English power was a significant influence. Art MacMurrough (Art Mór Mac Murchadha), the Leinster lord who proved a thorn in Richard II's side, was married to the heiress of the Kildare barony of Norragh; his power was nourished by regular fees from the Dublin exchequer and by blackmail extorted from towns; and his followers included men with English and Welsh as well as Irish patronymics.

The sheer number of Irish lords, together with the wide variations in their power and setting, makes it difficult to generalize about their political position. For most of the fourteenth century they impinged little on the consciousness of English kings, with whom they rarely had direct dealings until Richard II's arrival in Ireland in 1394. So far as the royal government within Ireland was concerned, the picture is complicated. By the later fourteenth century, of the descendants of the provincial kings, the O'Briens of Thomond and MacCarthys of Desmond encountered English authority spasmodically when a governor led an armed expedition to Munster, perhaps offering backing to one dynastic claimant against another; the O'Neills of Ulster met it only indirectly, in the form of the archbishop of Armagh or an occasional emissary of the Mortimer earls of Ulster; the O'Connors of Connacht and, still more, the O'Donnells in the far north-west remained largely beyond its scope. On the other hand many lesser Irish leaders in the midlands and south lived within the orbit of magnates who were themselves still firmly linked to Dublin and Westminster. More than that, especially in the south-east, the king's representatives engaged in constant military and diplomatic activity, in the course of which they took hostages and imposed tributes, awarded gifts and retaining fees, and sometimes installed favoured candidates as clan leaders. The language of royal documents, with its formal references to 'warlike expeditions' against 'Irish felons and enemies', can obscure the fact that the government, as well as conducting a defensive war, was ruling in a manner that would have been recognized instantly by a Gaelic overlord or a border magnate.

While many Irish lords may be said to have been, to a greater or lesser degree, in contact with the English dominion, they were not integrated into its political structures; they ruled over their own people, and entered into relations, by turns friendly or hostile, with magnates or royal ministers on an *ad hoc* basis. Socially and culturally they might differ little from some of the minor border lords of English origin, but, in the matter of formal status, a gulf remained.

Irishmen held no offices, central or local, under the Crown; with rare (and in practice irrelevant) exceptions, they did not hold lands by titles that could be defended in the royal courts; they were not summoned to parliaments and great councils. In effect they shared the disabilities of the Irish population at large, who remained outside the English legal (and hence political) system. The English of Ireland were a provincial aristocracy and gentry, holding lands in the same way as their fellows in England, and having a corporate existence, locally in shire and liberty courts, and centrally in parliaments. Their management might present problems to the Crown, but they were ones of a familiar type. The Gaelic lords, standing apart from the Lordship's institutions and lacking collective political structures of their own, could not be handled in the same way.

To the Irish historian this division is so much part of the daily landscape that he tends to take it for granted. Yet in Scotland a blending of native and newcomer had taken place, so that by the time of Alexander III a single aristocracy of mixed descent had emerged; even in fourteenth-century Wales the gap between English and Welsh rural landholders was less impassable. The solidity of distinctions in Ireland arose from the political circumstances of the Lordship and the chronology of its development. Among the initial difficulties were the lack of a resident king who might have helped to resolve differences; the hardening of the English legal system, which meant that even in the early thirteenth century there was a set of official norms to which native lords could not adhere without revolutionary changes in their own society; and the protracted and piecemeal nature of the conquest which led to the entrenchment of a class of English landholders who might favour individual Gaelic lords under their power but would not wish to see the Irish as a whole brought within the protection of the courts. In the late thirteenth and early fourteenth centuries this exclusion was viewed as morally wrong by the clergy, and was to figure in the argument against English rule which Irish supporters of Edward Bruce sent to the pope in 1317. But by then the renewed vitality of Gaelic lordship and the increasingly defensive outlook of the settler population formed unpromising ground for the extension of Common Law to the Irish. Indeed the barriers between the two nations grew firmer, just as they were to do in Wales after the Glyn Dŵr rebellion. The Statute of Kilkenny (1366) enshrined a programme designed to protect the Englishness of the English of Ireland, outlawing the use of the Irish language and modes of dress amongst them, and confirming earlier legislation that had placed obstacles in the way of social contacts (including marriage) between English and Irish. Among those affected by it was Art MacMurrough, whose wife was judged to have forfeited her barony of Norragh by marrying him.

Only once before the reign of Henry VIII were the assumptions on which the politics of the Lordship of Ireland were founded seriously challenged. In October 1394 Richard II landed at Waterford at the head of a substantial army. It seems unlikely that he arrived with a clear programme of action decided in advance; he probably expected to have to fight much harder against the 'Irish enemies', of whom the English authorities had heard so much from Irish councils and parliaments, than in the event proved necessary. But by the early months of 1395 he seems to have identified the grievances of the Gaelic lords, the uncertainty of their legal position and the extent of their territories, and (at least by implication) their exclusion from the official structures of the Lordship as basic flaws. His presence in Ireland had faced the Irish lords with an unfamiliar situation. Richard overawed MacMurrough and the other Leinster lords very quickly, accepting their submissions and taking them into his protection. This success, followed by diplomacy, and the application of some limited force in the south-west, soon led those in other regions—including the O'Neills, O'Connors of Connacht, O'Briens, and MacCarthys—to submit. The rapid 'conquest' (as Richard presented it in England) meant that an attitude had to be struck towards the lords who had accepted his authority, sometimes with loud protestations that they had never denied it in the first place.

The terms of the submissions were recorded in notarial documents which show that Richard and his advisers were concerned to clarify the relationship between the Irish lords and the Crown. Since they could no longer be accommodated as sub-kings within a Plantagenet empire that included others of their kind, the obvious alternative was to view them as subjects in a more conventional sense. Accordingly they took oaths of liege homage and fealty to the king as their sovereign lord and agreed to obey his laws and orders. Richard's intention that they should be brought within the political fold in a way they had not been in the past is suggested by a clause in which each undertook to 'come to the said lord my king and his heirs, being kings of England, and to his or their parliament or council or otherwise whensoever he or they shall send for me or whenever I shall be required, called or summoned on his or their part or on the part of their lieutenants'.[2] Even in theory these arrangements did not remove the distinction between the Irish and English aristocracies of Ireland: Gaelic lordship could not be reduced to the usual formula of exact units of land held in return for precise amounts of military service, nor were Irish successions as predictable as English primogeniture. Even so the king, by taking submissions on identical terms from most of those who mattered and by contemplating the attendance of the Irish at parliaments, seemed to sketch a future in which the native lords might form part of a polity that took in all the powerful elements in the island. More than that, Richard sought to entice the Irish towards the chivalric culture of which his court was a notable centre. Before he left for England in May 1395 he knighted O'Neill, O'Brien, and others, an act whose impact may be glimpsed in O'Neill's description of himself in a letter to the king as 'knight by your creation'.[3] Though the details of Froissart's tale of the king's attempts to school these 'wild Irish' in polite behaviour are probably apocryphal, there is no reason to doubt the general message: that a settled place in the formal life of the reconstructed Lordship of Ireland might be dependent on social re-education.

Regarded in this somewhat abstract way, the king's policy appears coherent and imaginative. But its practical application presented so many problems that it is of interest chiefly as an illustration of the firmness with which the exclusion of the Irish lords was now embedded in the political fabric of Ireland. The effect of Richard's presence was momentarily to rewrite the rules to which all were accustomed; hopes were raised, not just on the part of the Gaelic Irish, and stones that had long lain undisturbed suddenly turned over. The result was to uncover a mass of conflicting claims whose resolution required nothing less than the re-drawing of the tenurial map of Ireland, together with a reformation of political attitudes, which could only have been brought about, if at all, by kings prepared to give priority to the Lordship for decades. Ulster provides the clearest example of the difficulties that ensued. In 1300 the Burgh earls had controlled the whole coastal belt from Carlingford Lough round to the Foyle, from which they wielded direct lordship over the Irish of the interior. By 1394 the English area had shrunk to a few small enclaves, and the allegiances of the Irish lords had been collected in by the O'Neills. A settlement with O'Neill thus raised the perplexing question of what areas and services he legitimately held; and his view of the matter differed sharply from that of Roger Mortimer, earl of March and Ulster, who came to Ireland with Richard, remained as lieutenant after his departure, and was intent on recovering what was his. Richard did not, and no doubt could not, offer a solution to a quarrel that arose from the existence of two wholly incompatible rights. Nor was O'Neill's position challenged only by Mortimer: several of the Irish lords whom he had subordinated saw the king's visit as their opportunity to escape from his tutelage, just as Welsh lords had once fled to the English from the exacting rule of the princes of Gwynedd. All over Ireland Richard's presence was to throw into high relief both the tensions within the segmented Gaelic polity, and the irreconcilable claims of English and Irish to land and lordship.

The failure of the Ricardian settlement, despite the king's brief second visit on the eve of his deposition in 1399, is thus scarcely to be wondered at. It left Ireland as before, a land marked by fundamental paradoxes. On the one hand there was many-sided interaction between English and Irish: in practice English royal and magnate lordship developed an extra dimension that enabled it to accommodate and manage Gaelic leaders, while at the same time native styles of lordship were influenced by the outside world. Yet on the other hand formal barriers between the English and Irish ruling groups survived, and were even reinforced. Their additional thickness was in part the product of the anxieties of a colonial society that felt itself more and more under threat; it also sprang from a wider climate in which Englishness—defined by a set of linguistic, legal, and cultural norms—was seen as synonomous with the civility the 'wild Irish' so conspicuously lacked. The legal barriers cannot be dismissed as merely theoretical and of little importance. Crown authority and that of magnates of English status was still widespread and significant in Ireland. So long as this remained the case the Irish lords were stranded politically, having lost their royal rank, yet also having failed to acquire the lineaments of an aristocratic community: for it was in concert with such communities that kings were accustomed to rule.

Gaelic Scotland and the Lordship of the Isles

The little that has been said about Scotland in this chapter has tended to confirm the image of a kingdom where the diverse elements in the nobility were peacefully amalgamating under the presiding genius of a monarchy that itself successfully combined 'native' and 'foreign' attributes. Certainly in 1286 the obstacles in the way of an integrated kingdom might well have seemed to be more of distance and communications than of linguistic and ethnic division; although regional differences remained marked, the kingdom of Scots always showed a greater capacity to combine unity with diversity than did England, with its long history of administrative centralization. Typically, the recent acquisition by Alexander III of the Western Isles seems to have been followed, not by assertive attempts at governmental incorporation, but by a gradual drawing of the noble kins of the region into the orbit of the Scottish court and aristocratic society.

In the fourteenth century this picture of a kingdom, where outlying districts and their nobilities were being woven together by a national kingship, is disturbed. There was an obvious practical reason for the change. Disputed successions, civil war, and war with England loosened the grasp of the monarchy on the areas furthest from its heartlands in the south and east. Galloway, for instance, was a region where the Balliols had interests, and it was open to English interference both from across the Solway and from Ireland. Argyll and the Isles were even more vulnerable. Feuds among the descendants of Somerled, especially the MacDonalds and MacDougalls, were readily exploited by the English, who kept up an active diplomacy in the western approaches to Scotland. The result was to give the lords of the west a—sometimes risky—freedom of manœuvre that they had not enjoyed since the withdrawal of Norway in the 1260s. One of the strategic advantages possessed by the English in the earlier fourteenth century was the Burgh earldom of Ulster, which formed a Saxon salient in what would otherwise have been a wholly Gaelic region. Yet the collapse of the earldom after 1333 did not prove as advantageous to the Scots as might be thought. What remained of it was in the hands of the Crown or a member of the royal family; and the castle of Carrickfergus on the shores of Belfast Lough remained a key centre from which the seaways were monitored and diplomatic contacts maintained. More important, the ebbing of English power from the north of Ireland coincided with the period of David II's minority, exile, and captivity when Scottish royal authority was at its weakest. It is no accident that it was at this time that John MacDonald (d. 1387), having emerged as victor in the quarrels of the Islesmen, began to establish what was to prove a powerful and enduring lordship in an area that not so long before had seemed destined to become a peaceful frontier between the dominions of Alexander III and Edward I.

The retreat of Scottish royal authority from the west by the middle of the fourteenth century was followed by the first appearance of a consciousness of what may seem the most familiar distinction in Scottish geography, history, and culture: that between the English-speaking lowlands and the Gaelic-speaking highlands. John Fordun, writing under the first Stewart kings, is the earliest commentator for whom this was a basic datum: he and his successors, though fervent nationalists, made a sharp contrast between the civility of the south where English (known, confusingly, as 'Scots') was the language of the inhabitants, and the north, which was inhabited by a barbarous people, now commonly referred to as 'wild Scots'. The image of the Gael as outlandish and uncivilized may be connected with the growing perception of a threat emanating from outlying regions at a time of royal weakness: the late fourteenth century saw magnate feuds in which troops recruited beyond the highland line intruded into the lowlands. A similar fear of what lay beyond the unstable frontiers contributed to the currency of the stereotype of the 'wild Irish' in Ireland. There is a second possible parallel, in the increasing confidence among the lowlanders as to what constituted civility—for the fourteenth century saw the spread of lay literacy and the beginning of a courtly literature in Scots, of which Barbour's *Bruce* was an early example.

The Lordship of the Isles was the largest and most stable power to emerge in the highland zone. John MacDonald is known to have used the title *dominus Insularum*, which may have been an echo of the long-defunct Norse petty kingship, as early as 1336. He held much of Argyll, and in the later fourteenth and fifteenth centuries the authority of his descendants expanded to take in the earldom of Ross, while a segment of the kin created a lordship in Ulster, based in the Glens of Antrim. This seaborne realm was the most impressive piece of Celtic state-building since that of the house of Gwynedd a century before. The societies of the Isles and of northern Ireland were in many ways one. Members of Irish learned families moved to and fro; and the style of the Lordship—with, for example, its inaugurations where the lord was 'elected' by his kinsmen, had his genealogy declaimed by a bard, and was invested with a wand of office in an open-air ceremony at a traditional site—had much in common with those of Gaelic lordships in Ireland. Yet, like Gwynedd (and indeed like the Irish lordships themselves), the late medieval Lordship of the Isles shows the capacity of Celtic lordship to change and absorb foreign customs and techniques. It was passed from father to son without division, avoiding the grosser instabilities of Gaelic succession customs. The power of the lord was expressed in ways little different from those employed in principalities elsewhere in northern Europe: the Lord of the Isles occupied impressive stone fortresses; he issued Latin charters in conventional form; he presided over councils attended by the heads of the leading kins and regional officials, where justice was done and financial matters were handled; and he conducted an effective diplomacy with outside powers—above all, of course, with the king of England. His rule might be described more accurately as 'hybrid', than as 'Gaelic', in character.

Historians have sought to define the position of the Lordship of the Isles in relation to the kingdom of the Scots. Should the Lord be viewed primarily as a Scottish magnate, however unruly and overblown? Or was he to all intents and purposes an independent prince? To pose the question in such stark and theoretical terms is probably unhelpful. Lords of the Isles attended the king's court from time to time, and indeed the Lordship occupied parts of the very region where the Scottish kingdom had itself been born centuries earlier: total detachment from the realm was not a goal that is likely to have occurred to them. On the other hand they undoubtedly behaved in ways normally associated with the possession of sovereign attributes. In fact, of course, later medieval Europe was full of princes whose status and conduct were, to the modern eye, equally ambiguous. The Lordship of the Isles has been compared with the Duchy of Brittany, which was one of a number of principalities that occupied the extensive peripheries of the kingdom of France. Its rulers, like the MacDonalds of the Isles, conducted a sinuous diplomacy in the profitable, though often dangerous, borderland of French and English power. The parallel is close in another sense. Just as Breton statebuilding ultimately worked to the advantage of the king of France, so the Lordship of the Isles was to be taken over by James IV in the 1490s.

The British Isles in 1400

The history of the Lordship of the Isles offers a useful starting-point for reflection upon the political make-up of the British Isles in the late

Middle Ages. If the Lordship prompts unfamiliar questions, that may be significant. The development of the British Isles tends to present itself as the story of the emergence of two national monarchies which appear by 1400 to have had few rivals besides each other. The English may have purveyed much 'bigger', more bureaucratic government than the Scottish; none the less the kings of Scots were effective rulers after their own fashion. Between them the two monarchies and their respective political communities have a way of monopolizing the historian's attention.

It must be admitted that there is a good deal of justification for this. Even in 1100 the English kingship was an ancient, powerful, and (by the standards of the time) centralized concern. During the twelfth and thirteenth centuries it incorporated, through the expansion of its aristocracy and administrative systems, the far north of England, Wales, and much of Ireland. The matter might be put another way: starting from a wealthy and organized core, the English kings spread their power into the peripheries, where they established a position so firm as to be virtually unchallengeable. Margins remained, of course; in Ireland they even enlarged in the fourteenth century. But they were scattered and poor, and the powers that occupied them were too diverse and fragmented to mount a sustained or severe threat to the English Crown. Even in the darkest days of Edward II, the Scots were defeated in Ireland by a local army levied there, not by an expeditionary force from England; and they signally failed to spread their campaign into Wales. In the fourteenth century there is little sign that Wales and Ireland struck the kings of France as promising routes for an attack on Edward III, in the way that he could threaten the French through Flanders or Brittany. French forces were to land at Milford Haven in 1405 in the unusual circumstances of the Glyn Dŵr rising; but the same year saw Henry IV call on the justiciar of Ireland to launch an attack on Anglesey from Dublin.

The Scottish kingship for its part, alone among the many lesser royalties that existed in Britain and Ireland in 1100, proved to have the solidity to draw more than temporary nourishment from the new men, techniques, and resources available in the twelfth and thirteenth centuries. In the years 1296–1305 and again for a moment in the 1330s Scotland appeared to have succeeded only in adorning herself for an English bridegroom. But from the perspective of 1400 her stability and recuperative qualities are striking. Of course the kingdom was much less wealthy and administratively centralized than its neighbour to the south. Yet the monarchy of the early Stewarts, little threatened from within or without, is impressive in its very lack of assertiveness. The existence of the kingship was unchallenged; loyalty was sustained by a generally accepted set of national myths, to which the years of English oppression had given wider currency; and Scottish churchmen and nobles, for all their quarrels, provided the kingdom with effective political and governmental articulation.

But, if it is reasonable that primacy should be accorded to the development of two relatively coherent kingdoms and their respective political communities, that is by no means the whole story. English history in particular has traditionally been written with a heavy metropolitan bias; generalizations have been based upon study of the heartlands of royal authority in southern and midland England, leaving the rest of the English dominions to be viewed as a set of (discrete) 'exceptions', available for exploration by historians of Wales, Ireland, or 'the North'. One result has been to obscure aspects of the wider English polity. Compared to France, it is true, England had a disproportionately powerful centre of regnal gravity, and little or no equivalent of the principalities that made up much of the complex realm presided over by the Valois. Yet in its own way the late medieval Plantagenet state was also a complicated affair, in which different modes and intensities of government are evident. It is too easily forgotten that more than half the geographical area of the English dominions in the British Isles was far from being reduced to the condition of the regions that lay south of the Humber and east of the Severn.

The English kings sought to rule a realm that contained devolved administrations—at Caernarfon and Carmarthen, to some extent in the north, and above all at Dublin. They dealt not with one parliament and political community, but two. They had to manage border magnates of varied social complexion, who had links across the Scottish border or stretching deep into Gaelic Ireland. Into the bargain their dominions contained Welsh and Irish élites, neither of which can be dismissed as insignificant. These peripheries (which—thanks to the expansion of the twelfth and thirteenth centuries—amounted to an English as much as a 'Celtic' fringe) may have been too dispersed to offer themselves as a political 'problem'; their fragmentation and comparative poverty, together with the degree to which they were controlled by aristocratic interests, may have made them appear less than promising as a source of revenue. But to marginalize them historiographically is to forswear part of the richness of late medieval English history. To do so seems the more misguided at a time when hard questions are being asked about the character and effectiveness of government within the English heartlands themselves. Forms of law-enforcement or patterns of lord–client relations—to take just two examples—deserve to be considered in the varying settings of the regions of England, together with Wales and Ireland.

The historian of the individual periphery has in turn much to gain from viewing his region in the broader context of the English lands as a whole. Studies of the Lordship of Ireland in particular have not been helped by the assumption that Irish conditions were so peculiar as to make the wider setting and the comparisons it can open up irrelevant. Yet the political community of the English of Ireland may be better comprehended when it is set beside its English counterpart, as well as being located in the particular circumstances of Ireland. English lords in Ireland were not so detached from the metropolis and its standards as has sometimes been thought; their behaviour makes more sense when it is set in a continuum extending outwards from the Home Counties, and one in which the Welsh March and the northern borders also have a place. The border magnates of Ireland, moreover, attached at least some of the native lords to the outskirts of English authority; and the position of the native élite in Ireland offers obvious points of comparison and (more especially) contrast with that of the Welsh in Wales: the development of English official attitudes to both may reasonably be regarded as one subject.

Scottish historians, conscious of the cultural diversity of the kingdom of Scots and of the power of nobles who dominated broader areas and commanded more exclusive bundles of allegiances than was normal in most of England, are perhaps less likely to adopt an exclusively metropolitan viewpoint. Nevertheless it is only quite recently that the Scottish aristocracy have ceased to be presented primarily as a force for disruption in a kingdom whose superficial turbulence has pained many conscientious scholars. And given the scanty documentation and the royal provenance of much that does survive, it remains easier, certainly before the mid-fifteenth century, to proclaim the importance of nobles as agents of order and social peace than to dissect their regional empires.

Above all much is to be gained by bringing together the English and Scottish orbits, in all their individual complexity, in order to make the British Isles as a whole a possible object of study. Through doing so, of course, the zones where the two overlapped are better understood—whether the world of the borders (where interaction was intensive), or that of northern Ireland and the western highlands and islands (where the sprouting of alternative political structures, in the shape of the Lordship of the Isles and the impressive O'Neill lordship in Ulster, suggests the lightness with which those orbits touched). But more than that, there is the opportunity to find illuminating contrasts between two very different kingdoms; to compare three parliaments and the political communities that found their voices in them; to follow the development of law and its administration across England, Wales, Ireland, and Scotland, all of which in their different ways were affected by the custom that had crystallized in the courts of the English kings during the twelfth and thirteenth centuries; or to look at the aristocracies which throughout the British Isles were, ultimately, offshoots of the same period of Anglo-Norman enterprise. Only by viewing Britain and Ireland as a whole do these and other themes become visible.

While it would be idle to deny that the British Isles by 1400 were dominated by two powerful monarchies, each presided over dominions that amounted to both more and less than a neatly delineated national unit. The kingdoms of England and Scotland were of course in territorial terms more defined and 'complete' than they had been three hundred years before, and also more tautly organized. They had absorbed much of the arc of multiple kingship that had once existed in the west and north of the British Isles, and had extended their political and administrative systems accordingly. That phenomenon, together with the responses of peripheral societies to it, must be the chief theme in any account of the period. But uniformity of control was far out of reach; moreover barely assimilated fringes remained, and were capable of sustaining their own political growths. In 1400 the English and Scottish realms were composite, uneven affairs, and had much about them that was still tentative.

Notes

Chapter 1. The British Isles in 1100: Political Perceptions and the Geography of Power

1. *Brut y Tywysogyon: The Chronicle of the Princes (Red Book of Hergest Version)*, ed. T. Jones (Board of Celtic Studies, History and Law Series; 2nd edn., Cardiff, 1973), 87.
2. *English Historical Documents, c.500–1042*, ed. D. Whitelock (London, 1955), 505–8.
3. Ibid. 527, 529, 531.
4. A. A. M. Duncan, 'The Earliest Scottish Charters', *Scottish Historical Review*, 37 (1958), 103.
5. J. A. Watt, *The Church and the Two Nations in Medieval Ireland* (Cambridge, 1970), 217.

Chapter 2. Empires, Continental and British

1. *The Ecclesiastical History of Orderic Vitalis*, ed. and trans. M. Chibnall (Oxford, 1969–80), vi. 13.
2. *Chronica Magistri Rogeri de Houdene*, ed. W. Stubbs (London, Rolls Series, 1868–71), ii. 133–6.
3. *Close Rolls, 1259–61* (London, 1934), 64.
4. *Annála Connacht: The Annals of Connacht*, ed. A. M. Freeman (Dublin, 1944), 72–3.
5. Tewkesbury Annals, in *Annales Monastici*, ed. H. R. Luard (London, Rolls Series, 1864–9), i. 115.
6. *Chronica Regum Manniae et Insularum*, ed. P. A. Munch (Christiana, 1860), 23.
7. *The Flowers of History by Roger of Wendover*, ed. H. G. Hewlett (London, Rolls Series, 1886–9), iii. 113–14.

Chapter 3. The Aristocratic Nexus

1. D. Crouch, *The Beaumont Twins: The Roots and Branches of Power in the Twelfth Century* (Cambridge, 1986), 127.
2. *Song of Dermot and the Earl*, ed. G. H. Orpen (Oxford, 1892), ll. 2185–90.
3. *Calendar of the Gormanston Register*, ed. J. Mills and M. J. McEnery (Dublin, 1916), 177.

Chapter 4. The Expansion of Royal Government

1. *Statutes and Ordinances and Acts of the Parliament of Ireland, King John to Henry V*, ed. H. F. Berry (Dublin, 1907), 20.
2. *Rolls of the Justices in Eyre for Gloucestershire, Warwickshire and Staffordshire, 1221, 1222*, ed. D. M. Stenton (Selden Society, 59; London, 1940), no. 1133.
3. *Regesta Regum Scottorum*, ii. *The Acts of William I*, ed. G. W. S. Barrow (Edinburgh, 1971), 178–9.

Chapter 5. Kings and Princes

1. R. R. Davies, *Conquest, Coexistence, and Change: Wales, 1063–1415* (Oxford, 1987), 56 (quoting an observation by James Campbell on Anglo-Saxon 'kingliness').
2. *Song of Dermot and the Earl*, ll. 2191–2: 'En yrland erent reis plusur | Cum alures erent les cunturs.'
3. Quoted in B. Webster, *Scotland from the Eleventh Century to 1603* (London, 1975), 14 n. 3.
4. *The Annals of Inisfallen*, ed. S. Mac Airt (Dublin, 1951), 204–5.
5. *The Historical Works of Master Ralph de Diceto*, ed. W. Stubbs (London, Rolls Series, 1876), i. 397–8.

Chapter 6. The British Isles in an Age of War

1. *The Annals of Inisfallen*, 398–9.
2. *Calendar of Documents Relating to Scotland*, ed. J. Bain (Edinburgh, 1881–8), ii. 537. Other translations are to be found in ibid., no. 1926, and G. W. S. Barrow, *Robert Bruce and the Community of the Realm of Scotland* (2nd edn., Edinburgh, 1976), 245.
3. J. B. Smith, 'Gruffydd Llwyd and the Celtic Alliance, 1315–18', *Bulletin of the Board of Celtic Studies*, 26 (1976), 478.
4. 'Papers Relating to the Captivity and Release of David II', ed. E. W. M. Balfour-Melville, *Miscellany of the Scottish History Society*, ix (1958), 42.

Chapter 7. Jurisdiction and Conquest: The Reign of Edward I

1. E. L. G. Stones (ed.), *Anglo-Scottish Relations, 1174–1328* (Oxford, 1970), 250–1.
2. *Irish Historical Documents, 1172–1922*, ed. E. Curtis and R. B. McDowell (London, 1943), 31–2.
3. *The Annals of Connacht*, 212–13.
4. *The Chronicle of Pierre de Langtoft*, ed. T. Wright (London, Rolls Series, 1866–8), ii. 266–7.

5. *Calendar of Ancient Correspondence Relating to Wales*, ed. J. G. Edwards (Board of Celtic Studies, History and Law Series; Cardiff, 1935), 86.
6. Ibid. 73.
7. *Documents Illustrative of the History of Scotland, 1286–1306*, ed. J. Stevenson (Edinburgh, 1870), i. 162–73, at 167.

Chapter 8. Political Communities

1. *Rotuli Parliamentorum* (London, Record Commission, 1783), ii. 147.
2. H. G. Richardson and G. O. Sayles (eds.), *Parliaments and Councils of Mediaeval Ireland*, i (Dublin, 1947), no. 16.
3. *Documents on the Affairs of Ireland before the King's Council*, ed. G. O. Sayles (Dublin, 1979), no. 209.
4. Ibid., no. 136; echoing *Laudabiliter* (*Irish Historical Documents, 1172–1922*, ed. Curtis and McDowell, 17–18).
5. Stones (ed.), *Anglo-Scottish Relations, 1174–1328*, no. 36, at p. 283.
6. A. A. M. Duncan, *The Nation of Scots and the Declaration of Arbroath* (London, 1970), 34–7.

Chapter 9. On the Margins

1. *The Red Book of the Earls of Kildare*, ed. G. Mac Niocaill (Dublin, 1964), no. 168.
2. E. Curtis, *Richard II in Ireland, 1394–5, and Submissions of the Irish Chiefs* (Oxford, 1927), 150–1.
3. Ibid. 214.

Further Reading

THE political and institutional history of England and Wales in this period has generated a vast literature, much of it of high quality; Scotland and Ireland are less well served, though they have attracted more attention since the 1960s. The suggestions that follow are highly selective. They concentrate for the most part on recent work, and often indicate what I have found specially helpful. Except where otherwise stated, the books mentioned were published in London.

Part One: Ascendancy and Assimilation, 1100–1270

General

G. W. S. Barrow, *Feudal Britain, 1066–1314* (1956), is inevitably dated in places but remains a useful introduction to English, Scottish, and Welsh history; Ireland figures little. R. R. Davies's 1988 Wiles Lectures, *Domination and Conquest: Ireland, Wales and Scotland, 1100–1300* (Cambridge, forthcoming), are a brilliant and original discussion of English expansion and its impact. On **England**, F. Barlow, *The Feudal Kingdom of England, 1042–1216* (3rd edn., 1972), has worn much better than most textbooks. M. T. Clanchy, *England and its Rulers, 1066–1272: Foreign Lordship and National Identity* (1983), is stimulating. The Anglo-Saxon background may be approached through P. H. Sawyer, *From Roman Britain to Norman England* (1978), and J. Campbell, E. John, and P. Wormald, *The Anglo-Saxons* (Oxford, 1982). M. Chibnall, *Anglo-Norman England, 1066–1166* (Oxford, 1986), is a good introduction to the century after the Conquest. On **Scotland**, G. W. S. Barrow, *Kingship and Unity: Scotland, 1000–1306* (1981), is a work of mature reflection. A. A. M. Duncan, *Scotland: The Making of the Kingdom* (Edinburgh, 1975), is learned, tough, and indispensable. A. P. Smyth, *Warlords and Holy Men: Scotland, AD 80–1000* (1984), ventures boldly into dark areas. B. Webster, *Scotland from the Eleventh Century to 1603* (1975), though primarily about the sources, is a good introduction to many topics. On **Wales**, R. R. Davies, *Conquest, Coexistence, and Change: Wales, 1063–1415* (Oxford, 1987), is both scholarly and immensely readable. The second volume of J. E. Lloyd, *A History of Wales from the Earliest Times to the Edwardian Conquest* (3rd edn. 1939), is still the essential narrative. W. Davies, *Wales in the Early Middle Ages* (Leicester, 1982), is searching and measured. D. Walker, *The Norman Conquerors* (Swansea, 1977), is a useful brief introduction. For **Ireland**, A. J. Otway-Ruthven, *A History of Medieval Ireland* (2nd edn., 1980), remains the standard account of the centuries after 1167; it has a valuable introduction on Gaelic Ireland by Kathleen Hughes. A. Cosgrove (ed.), *Medieval Ireland, 1169–1534: A New History of Ireland*, ii (Oxford, 1987), is a gigantic lucky dip. J. F. Lydon, *The Lordship of Ireland in the Middle Ages* (Dublin, 1972), and R. Frame, *Colonial Ireland, 1169–1369* (Dublin, 1981), are briefer surveys. The pre-Norman period is best approached through D. Ó Corráin, *Ireland before the Normans* (Dublin, 1972), and M. Richter, *Medieval Ireland: The Enduring Tradition* (1988).

Chapter 1. The British Isles in 1100: Political Perceptions and the Geography of Power

Many of the topics discussed in this chapter may be pursued further in the general works mentioned above, and in those listed below, under Chapters 2 and 5. The concept of the English people is explored in P. Wormald, 'Bede, the *Bretwaldas* and the Origins of the *Gens Anglorum*', in Wormald *et al.* (eds.), *Ideal and Reality in Frankish and Anglo-Saxon Society: Studies Presented to J. M. Wallace-Hadrill* (Oxford, 1983). On the imperial face of the Anglo-Saxon monarchy, see M. Wood, 'The Making of King Aethelstan's Empire: An English Charlemagne?', in the same volume, and E. John, *Orbis Britanniae* (Leicester, 1966). On the north, the following are useful: D. Whitelock, 'The Dealings of the Kings of England with Northumbria in the Tenth and Eleventh Centuries', in P. Clemoes (ed.), *The Anglo-Saxons: Studies presented to Bruce Dickins* (1959, reprinted in Whitelock, *History, Law and Literature in Tenth- and Eleventh-Century England* (1981)); G. W. S. Barrow, 'The Anglo-Scottish Border', in his *The Kingdom of the Scots* (1973); and W. E. Kapelle, *The Norman Conquest of the North: The Region and its Transformation, 1000–1135* (1979). P. Holm, 'The Slave Trade of Dublin, Ninth to Twelfth Centuries', *Peritia*, 5 (1986), contains much of interest on the Irish Sea province. Chronicles are surveyed in A. Gransden, *Historical Writing in England, c.550 to c.1307* (1974); see also Webster, *Scotland from the Eleventh Century to 1603*, ch. 2. M. Chibnall, *The World of Orderic Vitalis* (Oxford, 1984), and R. Thomson, *William of Malmesbury* (Woodbridge, 1987), are scholarly studies of individual historians. E. J. Cowan, 'Myth and Identity in Early Medieval Scotland', *Scottish Historical Review*, 63 (1984), deals with the idea of Scotland, and G. A. Loud, 'The *Gens Normannorum*—Myth or Reality?', *Battle Anglo-Norman Studies*, 4 (1981), with the Norman myth. Notions of Wales and the Welsh are analysed in Davies, *Conquest, Coexistence, and Change*, ch. 1; on the narrative sources, see R. I. Jack, *Medieval Wales* (1972), ch. 1. K. Hughes, *Early Christian Ireland: Introduction to the Sources* (1972), ch. 9, surveys Irish writings of the eleventh and twelfth centuries. M. Richter, 'The First Century of Anglo-Irish Relations', *History*, 59 (1974), traces the history of Canterbury's claims. On the wider matter of national identities, B. Guenée, 'État et nation en France au Moyen Âge', *Revue historique*, 237 (1967), and K. F. Werner, 'Les Nations et le sentiment national dans l'Europe médiévale', ibid. 244 (1970), are interesting.

Chapter 2. Empires, Continental and British

The theme of 'empires' is developed in the writings of J. Le Patourel, many of whose papers are collected in *Feudal Empires: Norman and Plantagenet* (1984): see, in particular, 'Normandy and England, 1066–1144', 'The Plantagenet Dominions', and 'Angevin Successions and the Angevin Empire'. C. W. Hollister, 'Normandy, France and the Anglo-Norman *Regnum*', *Speculum*, 51 (1976), is also valuable. Le Patourel's *The Norman Empire* (Oxford, 1976), is the classic account of its subject; on the Norman background, see D. Bates, *Normandy before 1066* (1982). The dynamics of royal power are explored in J. O. Prestwich, 'The Military Household of the Norman Kings', *English Historical Review*, 96 (1981). Consolidation on the fringes of England is described in Kapelle, *The Norman Conquest of the North*, ch. 7, and R. R. Davies, 'Henry I and Wales', in H. Mayr-Harting and R. I. Moore (eds.), *Studies in Medieval History presented to R. H. C. Davis* (1985). For the disasters under Stephen, see R. H. C. Davis, *King Stephen* (1967). Angevin power is surveyed in W. L. Warren, *Henry II* (1973), which has an excellent chapter on the lordship of the British Isles. J. Gillingham, in *Richard the Lionheart* (1978) and *The Angevin Empire* (1984), presents a very positive picture of the Angevin regime; on its retreat, see F. M. Powicke, *The Loss of Normandy* (2nd edn., Manchester, 1960), and J. C. Holt, 'The End of the Anglo-Norman Realm', *Proceedings of the British Academy*, 61 (1975). Two essays by W. L. Warren offer a thought-provoking view of expansion into Ireland: 'John in Ireland, 1185', in J. Bossy and P. Jupp (eds.), *Essays Presented to Michael Roberts* (Belfast, 1976), and 'King John and Ireland', in J. F. Lydon (ed.), *England and Ireland in the Later Middle Ages: Essays in Honour of Jocelyn Otway-Ruthven* (Dublin, 1981). See also M. T. Flanagan, 'Strongbow, Henry II and Anglo-Norman Intervention in Ireland', in J. Gillingham and J. C. Holt (eds.), *War and Government in the Middle Ages: Essays in Honour of J. O Prestwich* (Woodbridge, 1984), and R. Frame, 'England and Ireland, 1171–1399', in M. Jones and M. Vale (eds.), *England and her Neighbours, 1066–1453: Essays in Honour of Pierre Chaplais* (1989). G. H. Orpen, *Ireland under the Normans, 1169–1333* (4 vols.; Oxford, 1911–20), remains the fullest account of the spread of Anglo-Norman power in the Irish regions. Henry III's reign is covered in F. M. Powicke's monumental *King Henry III and the Lord Edward* (Oxford, 1947), one of whose virtues is the ease with which it ranges across national boundaries; R. C. Stacey, *Politics, Policy, and Finance under Henry III, 1216–45* (Oxford, 1987), includes discussion of the aftermath of the loss of Normandy; while J. R. Studd, 'The Lord Edward and Henry III', *Bulletin of the Institute of Historical Research*, 50 (1977), considers the make up of the royal lands in the mid-thirteenth century.

The expansion of the effective Scottish realm may be followed in Barrow, *Kingship and Unity*, chs. 3 and 6, and in Duncan, *Scotland: The Making of the*

Kingdom, chs. 7–9, 20–1. B. E. Crawford, 'The Earldom of Caithness and the Kingdom of Scotland, 1150–1266', in K. J. Stringer (ed.), *Essays on the Nobility of Medieval Scotland* (Edinburgh, 1985), and R. I. Lustig, 'The Treaty of Perth: A Re-examination', *Scottish Historical Review*, 58 (1979), are useful on the incorporation of the peripheries. Other relevant writings are listed below, under Chapter 5.

Chapter 3. The Aristocratic Nexus

The spread of the new aristocracy is discussed in J. Le Patourel, 'The Norman Colonization of Britain', in *I Normanni e la loro espansione in Europa nell'alto medioevo. Settimane di Studio del Centro Italiano di Studi sull'alto medioevo*, 16 (Spoleto, 1969), and *The Norman Empire*. Le Patourel, *Norman Barons* (Historical Association, 1971; reprinted in *Feudal Empires*), illustrates the geographical ramification of particular families, while in 'The Norman Conquest of Yorkshire', *Northern History*, 6 (1971), he sets one area in a broad canvas. Anglo-Norman links are analysed in a number of studies, including W. E. Wightman, *The Lacy Family in England and Normandy, 1066–1194* (Oxford, 1966); D. Crouch, *The Beaumont Twins: The Roots and Branches of Power in the Twelfth Century* (Cambridge, 1986); and D. Matthew, *The Norman Monasteries and their English Possessions* (Oxford, 1962). Thirteenth-century baronial empires are described in S. Painter, *William Marshal* (Baltimore, 1933), and M. Altschul, *A Baronial Family in Medieval England: The Clares, 1217–1314* (Baltimore, 1965).

F. M. Stenton, *The First Century of English Feudalism, 1066–1166* (2nd edn., Oxford, 1961), is the classic study of aristocratic institutions. Feudal society is examined in articles by J. C. Holt: 'Politics and Property in Early Medieval England', *Past and Present*, 57 (1972), and 'Feudal Society and the Family in Early Medieval England, I–IV', *Transactions of the Royal Historical Society*, 5th ser., 32–5 (1982–5). The same author's 'The Introduction of Knight Service in England', *Anglo-Norman Studies*, 6 (1983), revisits an old topic, and even deploys some Irish evidence.

Aristocratic colonization in Scotland is anatomized in G. W. S. Barrow, *The Anglo-Norman Era in Scottish History* (Oxford, 1980). Several of the papers reprinted in Barrow's *Kingdom of the Scots* are also important, notably 'The Royal House and the Religious Orders', 'The Beginnings of Military Feudalism', and 'Scotland's "Norman" Families'. The subject is also extensively discussed in Duncan, *Scotland: The Making of the Kingdom*, chs. 7, 8, 15, 16. K. J. Stringer, *Earl David of Huntingdon, 1152–1219: A Study in Anglo-Scottish History* (Edinburgh, 1985), like its subject, profitably criss-crosses the border, as do several of the papers edited by Stringer in *Essays on the Nobility of Medieval Scotland*, and D. E. R. Watt, 'The Minority of Alexander III of Scotland', *Transactions of the Royal Historical Society*, 5th ser., 21 (1971).

The lords of the Welsh March are examined in R. R. Davies, *Conquest, Coexistence, and Change*, chs. 4 and 10. See also L. H. Nelson, *The Normans in South Wales, 1070–1171* (Austin, Texas, 1966). Two recent articles are also very useful: I. W. Rowlands, 'The Making of the March: Aspects of the Norman Settlement in Dyfed', *Battle Anglo-Norman Studies*, 3 (1981), and C. J. Spurgeon, 'Mottes and Castle-Ringworks in Wales', in J. R. Kenyon and R. Avent (eds.), *Castles in Wales and the Marches: Essays in Honour of D. J. C. King* (1987). The ethos of the marchers is captured in R. J. Bartlett, *Gerald of Wales, 1146–1223* (Oxford, 1982), ch. 1.

Aspects of aristocratic settlement in Ireland are discussed in A. J. Otway-Ruthven, 'Knight Service in Ireland', *Journal of the Royal Society of Antiquaries of Ireland*, 89 (1959); J. R. S. Phillips, 'The Anglo-Norman Nobility', in J. F. Lydon (ed.), *The English in Medieval Ireland* (Dublin, 1984); and C. A. Empey, 'The Settlement of the Kingdom of Limerick', in Lydon (ed.), *England and Ireland*. R. Frame, 'Aristocracies and the Political Configuration of the British Isles', in R. R. Davies (ed.), *The British Isles 1100–1500: Comparisons, Contrasts and Connections* (Edinburgh, 1988), is a general view, from an Irish standpoint. Recent archaeological work is harvested in T. B. Barry, *The Archaeology of Medieval Ireland* (1987).

Questions of territorial and institutional continuity are addressed in several of the works already mentioned, notably those by Le Patourel and Stringer. They are a central theme of J. G. Edwards, 'The Normans and the Welsh March', *Proceedings of the British Academy*, 42 (1956); G. W. S. Barrow, 'The Pattern of Lordship and Feudal Settlement in Cumbria', *Journal of Medieval History*, 1 (1975); and R. R. Davies, 'Kings, Lords and Liberties in the March of Wales, 1066–1272', *Transactions of the Royal Historical Society*, 5th ser., 29 (1979).

Chapter 4. The Expansion of Royal Government

The literature on English government is vast. W. L. Warren, *The Governance of Norman and Angevin England, 1086–1272* (1987), is the best starting-point. S. B. Chrimes, *An Introduction to the Administrative History of Mediaeval England* (3rd edn., Oxford, 1966), remains a useful, though dry, account of central government. The discussion of the impact of literacy in M. T. Clanchy, *From Memory to Written Record: England 1066–1307* (1979), is more exhilarating. C. W. Hollister and J. W. Baldwin, 'The Rise of Administrative Kingship: Henry I and Philip Augustus', *American Historical Review*, 83 (1978), offer a broad view. J. Campbell, 'Observations on English Government from the Tenth to the Twelfth Century', *Transactions of the Royal Historical Society*, 5th ser., 25 (1975; reprinted, with other significant paper, in his *Essays in Anglo-Saxon History* (1986)), and P. Stafford, 'The Laws of Cnut and the History of Anglo-Saxon Royal Promises', *Anglo-Saxon*

England, 10 (1981), are stimulating on the Anglo-Saxon background. R. W. Southern, 'King Henry I', in his *Medieval Humanism and other Studies* (Oxford, 1970), is a deservedly famous article, though its conclusions need to be modified in the light, for instance, of J. A. Green, *The Government of England under Henry I* (Cambridge, 1986). The development of the Common Law is traced in D. M. Stenton, *English Justice between the Norman Conquest and the Great Charter* (1965), A. Harding, *The Law Courts of Medieval England* (1973), and D. W. Sutherland, *The Assize of Novel Disseisin* (Oxford, 1973). S. F. C. Milsom, *Historical Foundations of the Common Law* (2nd edn., 1981), is demanding but essential; P. Hyams, 'The Common Law and the French Connection', *Battle Anglo-Norman Studies*, 4 (1981), is thought-provoking. The impact of government on the governed is a preoccupation of J. C. Holt's studies of John's reign, in particular *The Northerners* (Oxford, 1961), and *Magna Carta* (Cambridge, 1965); the theme is also pursued in J. R. Maddicott, 'Magna Carta and the Local Community, 1215-1259', *Past and Present*, 102 (1984). Local government is still best approached by way of H. M. Cam, *The Hundred and the Hundred Rolls* (1930). W. A. Morris, *The Medieval English Sheriff to 1307* (Manchester, 1927), remains useful; but see also D. A. Carpenter, 'The Decline of the Curial Sheriff in England, 1194-1258', *English Historical Review*, 91 (1976).

Otway-Ruthven, *History of Medieval Ireland*, ch. 5, is a clear introduction to the history of English institutions in Ireland. Fuller accounts are to be found in the earlier parts of H. G. Richardson and G. O. Sayles, *The Irish Parliament in the Middle Ages* (2nd edn., Philadelphia, 1964), the same authors' *The Administration of Ireland, 1172-1377* (Dublin, 1963), and G. J. Hand, *English Law in Ireland, 1290-1324* (Cambridge, 1967). P. Brand, 'Ireland and the Literature of the Early Common Law', *The Irish Jurist*, new ser. 16 (1981), provides illumination on both sides of the Irish Sea. A. J. Otway-Ruthven, 'Anglo-Irish Shire Government in the Thirteenth Century', *Irish Historical Studies*, 5 (1946-7), traces the growth of institutions of local government.

Webster, *Scotland from the Eleventh Century to 1603*, chs. 5 and 6, is a lucid introduction to Scottish government and its records; the maps and accompanying text in P. McNeill and R. Nicholson, *An Historical Atlas of Scotland, c.400-c.1600* (St Andrews, 1975), are another useful starting-point. Duncan, *Scotland: The Making of the Kingdom*, chs. 7, 8, 22, is basic, as are G. W. S. Barrow's papers, 'Pre-feudal Scotland: Shires and Thanes', 'The Judex', and 'The Justiciar', in his *The Kingdom of the Scots*. Detailed accounts of twelfth-century government are to be found in the introductions to Barrow's editions of the Scottish royal charters in the first two volumes of *Regesta Regum Scottorum: The Acts of Malcolm IV, 1153-1165* and *The Acts of William I, 1165-1214* (Edinburgh, 1960, 1971). The growing body of work on Scots law is well represented by H. L. MacQueen, 'Dissasine and Mortancestor in Scots Law', *The Journal of Legal History*, 4 (1983), and W. D. H. Sellar, 'The

Common Law of Scotland and the Common Law of England', in Davies (ed.), *The British Isles*.

Chapter 5. Kings and Princes

Old and new facets of kingship are perceptively treated in K. J. Leyser, 'Some Reflections on Twelfth-century Kings and Kingship', in his *Medieval Germany and its Neighbours, 900–1250* (1982). G. W. S. Barrow surveys kingship in the British Isles in 'Das Mittelalterliche Englische und Schottische Königtum: Ein Vergleich', *Historisches Jahrbuch*, 102 (1982); the theme recurs, in English, in his writings on Scotland mentioned below. D. A. Binchy, *Celtic and Anglo-Saxon Kingship* (Oxford, 1970), is a classic essay.

English successions and coronations are considered in H. G. Richardson and G. O. Sayles, *The Governance of Mediaeval England from the Conquest to Magna Carta* (Edinburgh, 1963), ch. 7. J. E. A. Jolliffe stresses the authoritarian face of monarchy in *Angevin Kingship* (2nd edn., 1963). The writings of J. C. Holt suggest a more nuanced picture: see, for example, *Magna Carta*, and many of the essays reprinted in *Magna Carta and Medieval Government* (1985). M. T. Clanchy emphasizes the Roman features of Henry III's kingship in 'Did Henry III have a Policy?', *History*, 53 (1968); D. A. Carpenter, with his eye on practical politics, dissents, in 'The Personal Rule of King Henry III, 1234–1258', *Speculum*, 60 (1985). The political ideas in *Bracton* are considered by B. Tierney, 'Bracton on Government', *Speculum*, 38 (1963).

On Scotland, Barrow, *Kingship and Unity*, ch. 2, is the readiest starting-point, and there is valuable discussion in Duncan, *Scotland: The Making of the Kingdom*, chs. 5–8 and 20–2; but D. P. Kirby poses some pointed questions about the emergence of a unitary kingship when reviewing Duncan in *English Historical Review*, 91 (1976). Two studies by Barrow of individual kings contain important reflections: *David I of Scotland (1124–1153): The Balance of New and Old* (University of Reading, 1985), and 'The Reign of William the Lion, King of Scotland', in J. C. Beckett (ed.), *Historical Studies VII* (1969). The habitat of the peripheral rulers is depicted in A. A. M. Duncan and A. L. Brown, 'Argyll and the Isles in the Earlier Middle Ages', *Proceedings of the Society of Antiquaries of Scotland*, 90 (1956–7); on the Norse background, see B. E. Crawford, *Scandinavian Scotland* (Leicester, 1987). R. J. Bartlett sets the 'modernizing' Scottish kingship in a European context in 'Technique militaire et pouvoir politique, 900–1300', *Annales: Économies, sociétés, civilisations*, 41 (1986).

Early Irish kingship is tersely delineated by D. A. Binchy, 'Secular Institutions', in M. Dillon (ed.), *Early Irish Society* (Dublin, 1954). On political developments from the ninth to twelfth centuries, see Binchy, 'The Passing of the Old Order', in B. Ó Cuív (ed.), *The Impact of the Scandinavian Invasions on the Celtic-speaking Peoples, c.800–1100 A.D.* (Dublin, 1975); F. J.

Byrne, *Irish Kings and High-Kings* (1973), ch. 12; D. Ó Corráin, *Ireland before the Normans*, ch. 4, and 'Nationality and Kingship in Pre-Norman Ireland', in T. W Moody (ed.), *Nationality and the Pursuit of National Independence: Historical Studies XI* (Belfast, 1978). Ecclesiastical change is discussed in the early chapters of J. A. Watt, *The Church and the Two Nations in Medieval Ireland* (Cambridge, 1970); in D. Bethell, 'English Monks and Irish Reform in the Eleventh and Twelfth Centuries', in T. D. Williams (ed.), *Historical Studies VIII* (Dublin, 1971); and in H. Pryce, 'Church and Society in Wales, 1150–1250: An Irish Perspective', in Davies (ed.), *The British Isles*. The post-invasion retreat of individual native dynasties may be traced in Orpen's *Ireland under the Normans* and Otway-Ruthven's *History of Medieval Ireland*; but the impact of the Anglo-Normans on Irish kingship received little analysis until the publication of K. Simms, *From Kings to Warlords: The Changing Political Structure of Gaelic Ireland in the Later Middle Ages* (Woodbridge, 1987), which provides a guide to Simms's important articles in Irish journals. The fate of a leading dynasty is considered in R. D. Edwards, 'Anglo–Norman Relations with Connacht, 1169–1224', *Irish Historical Studies*, 1 (1938–9), and J. F. Lydon, 'Lordship and Crown: Llywelyn of Wales and O'Connor of Connacht', in Davies (ed.), *The British Isles*.

Welsh kingship has generated an extensive literature of high quality, which throws light on 'Celtic' kingship in general. The subject is now best approached through Davies, *Conquest, Coexistence, and Change*, chs. 3, 5–9, 12. Big claims for the thirteenth-century Welsh polity are made in T. Jones Pierce, 'The Age of the Princes', in his *Medieval Welsh Society* (Cardiff, 1972); rather abstract and linear views of its development are presented in J. G. Edwards's introduction to *Littere Wallie* (Cardiff, 1940), and M. Richter, 'The Political and Institutional Background to National Consciousness in Medieval Wales', in Moody (ed.), *Historical Studies XI*; while J. B. Smith explores theories in 'The Succession to Welsh Princely Inheritance: The Evidence Reconsidered', in Davies (ed.), *The British Isles*. The practicalities and uncertainties of princely rule are illustrated in G. A. Williams, 'The Succession to Gwynedd, 1238–47', *Bulletin of the Board of Celtic Studies*, 20 (1962–4), and in three studies by D. Stephenson: *The Governance of Gwynedd* (Cardiff, 1984); 'Llywelyn ap Gruffydd and the Struggle for the Principality of Wales', *Transactions of the Honourable Society of Cymmrodorion* (1983); and 'The Politics of Powys Wenwynwyn in the Thirteenth Century', *Cambridge Medieval Celtic Studies*, 7 (1984). Aspects of change are sensitively portrayed by H. Pryce in 'The Prologues to the Welsh Lawbooks', *Bulletin of the Board of Celtic Studies*, 33 (1986), and in his paper on the church, mentioned above.

Part Two: Incorporations and Divisions, 1270–1400

General

Recent surveys of politics and government in later medieval **England** include
M. Keen, *England in the Later Middle Ages* (1973); M. Prestwich, *The Three
Edwards: War and State in England, 1272–1377* (1980); and A. Tuck, *Crown
and Nobility, 1272–1461* (1985). The most substantial study of **Scotland** is
R. Nicholson, *Scotland: The Later Middle Ages* (Edinburgh, 1974); A. Grant,
Independence and Nationhood: Scotland, 1306–1469 (1984), presents a more
optimistic view of the Scottish polity. On **Wales**, Davies, *Conquest, Coexist-
ence, and Change*, continues fundamental. Likewise for **Ireland**, the general
works remain those listed in **PART ONE**, save for two useful brief surveys:
J. F. Lydon, *Ireland in the Later Middle Ages* (Dublin, 1973), and A.
Cosgrove, *Late Medieval Ireland, 1370–1541* (Dublin, 1981).

Chapter 6. The British Isles in an Age of War

On general developments in European warfare, see P. Contamine, *War in the
Middle Ages*, trans. M. Jones (Oxford, 1984). War and its impact on England
in the time of Edward I are considered in M. Prestwich, *War, Politics and
Finance under Edward I* (1972). On the Welsh wars, see also J. E. Morris, *The
Welsh Wars of Edward I* (Oxford, 1901). The Anglo-Scottish wars are consid-
ered, from a Scottish point of view, in G. W. S. Barrow, *Robert Bruce and the
Community of the Realm of Scotland* (3rd edn., Edinburgh, 1988); later peri-
ods are dealt with in R. Nicholson, *Edward III and the Scots, 1327–1335*
(Oxford, 1965), and J. Campbell, 'England, Scotland and the Hundred Years
War in the Fourteenth Century', in J. R. Hale, J. R. L. Highfield, and B.
Smalley (eds.) *Europe in the Late Middle Ages* (1965). The impact of war on
the north of England and southern Scotland is traced in J. Scammell, 'Robert
I and the North of England', *English Historical Review*, 73 (1958); E. Miller,
War in the North (University of Hull, 1960); and G. W. S. Barrow, 'The
Aftermath of War: Scotland and England in the Late Thirteenth and Early
Fourteenth Centuries', *Transactions of the Royal Historical Society*, 5th ser.,
28 (1978). On the extension of the war into Ireland, see J. F. Lydon, 'The
Bruce Invasion of Ireland', in G. A. Hayes–McCoy (ed.), *Historical Studies
IV* (1963), and in Cosgrove (ed.). *Medieval Ireland, 1169–1534*, chs. 7, 9, 10;
and R. Frame, 'The Bruces in Ireland, 1315–18', *Irish Historical Studies*, 19
(1974–5). The repercussions of the war in Wales are considered in J. B.
Smith's two articles, 'Gruffydd Llwyd and the Celtic Alliance, 1315–18',
Bulletin of the Board of Celtic Studies, 26 (1976), and 'Edward II and the
Allegiance of Wales', *Welsh History Review*, 8 (1976–7). For the Hundred
Years War, see now C. T. Allmand, *The Hundred Years War: England and
France at War, c.1300–c.1450* (Cambridge, 1988), and also the essays in

K. Fowler (ed.), *The Hundred Years War* (1971). The nature of the war effort is analysed in H. J. Hewitt, *The Organization of War under Edward III* (Manchester, 1966). The pressures of war may be glimpsed in, for instance, E. B. Fryde, 'Parliament and the French War, 1336–40', in Fryde and E. Miller (eds.), *Historical Studies of the English Parliament* (Cambridge, 1970), i, and J. R. Maddicott, *The English Peasantry and the Demands of the Crown, 1294–1341 (Past and Present*, Supplement 1, 1975). On English armies in Ireland, see P. Connolly, 'The Financing of English Expeditions to Ireland, 1361–76', in Lydon (ed.), *England and Ireland*, and J. F. Lydon, 'Richard II's Expeditions to Ireland', *Journal of the Royal Society of Antiquaries of Ireland*, 93 (1963). Edward III's dynastic policy is assessed in W. M. Ormrod, 'Edward III and his Family', *Journal of British Studies*, 26 (1987). R. W. Kaeuper, *War, Justice, and Public Order: England and France in the Later Middle Ages* (Oxford, 1988), is an interesting comparative study, but it appeared too late to be of use to me.

Chapter 7. Jurisdiction and Conquest: The Age of Edward I

On Edward I's reign, see now M. Prestwich, *Edward I* (1988). Aspects of his rule in England are examined in J. R. Maddicott, 'Edward I and the Lessons of Baronial Reform: Local Government, 1258–80', in P. R. Coss and S. D. Lloyd (eds.), *Thirteenth Century England*, i (Woodbridge, 1986); K. B. McFarlane, 'Had Edward I a "Policy" towards the Earls?', in his *The Nobility of Later Medieval England* (Oxford, 1973); T. F. T. Plucknett, *Legislation of Edward I* (Oxford, 1949); and D. W. Sutherland, *Quo Warranto Proceedings in the Reign of Edward I, 1278–1294* (Oxford, 1963). The nature of liberties is skilfully explained in H. M. Cam, 'The Evolution of the Medieval English Franchise', in her *Law-finders and Law-makers in Medieval England* (1962). The marcher lordships and Edward's handling of them are considered in A. J. Otway-Ruthven, 'The Constitutional Position of the Great Lordships of South Wales', *Transactions of the Royal Historical Society*, 5th ser., 8 (1958), and R. R. Davies, *Lordship and Society in the March of Wales, 1282–1400* (Oxford, 1978), ch. 12. On Irish parliaments, finances, law, and liberties, see Richardson and Sayles, *The Irish Parliament in the Middle Ages*, ch. 5; *The Administration of Ireland*, by the same authors; and Hand, *English Law in Ireland*, chs. 6–8.

For the breakdown of relations with Llywelyn and the conquest and encastellation of north Wales, see Davies, *Conquest, Coexistence, and Change*, Part IV, and the same author's 'Law and National Identity in Thirteenth-century Wales', in R. R. Davies *et al.* (eds.), *Welsh Society and Nationhood: Historical Essays Presented to Glanmor Williams* (Cardiff, 1984); J. G. Edwards, 'Edward I's Castle-building in Wales', *Proceedings of the British Academy*, 32 (1946); and A. J. Taylor, *The Welsh Castles of Edward I* (1986). The subsequent settlement, and reactions to it, are discussed in W. H.

Waters, *The Edwardian Settlement of North Wales in its Administrative and Legal Aspects, 1284–1343* (Cardiff, 1935); J. G. Edwards, *The Principality of Wales, 1267–1967: A Study in Constitutional History* (Caernarvon, 1969); R. R. Davies, 'Colonial Wales', *Past and Present,* 65 (1974); L. B. Smith, 'The Statute of Wales, 1284', *Welsh History Review,* 10 (1980–1); R. A. Griffiths, 'The Revolt of Rhys ap Maredudd, 1287–8', ibid. 3 (1966–7); and the wide-ranging introduction to *The Merioneth Lay Subsidy Roll, 1292–3,* ed. K. Williams-Jones (Cardiff, 1976).

Scottish responses to Edward I are traced in Nicholson, *Scotland: The Later Middle Ages,* chs. 2–4; Barrow, *Robert Bruce;* and N. Reid, 'The Kingless Kingdom: The Scottish Guardianships of 1286–1306', *Scottish Historical Review,* 61 (1982). The elaborate commentary by E. L. G. Stones and G. G. Simpson on their edition of the records of the Great Cause, *Edward I and the Throne of Scotland, 1290–6* (2 vols; Oxford, 1978), offers a more sympathetic view of Edward's behaviour, as does Prestwich, *Edward I.* The impact of English rule on Scottish society is a main subject of A. A. M. Duncan, *The Nation of Scots and the Declaration of Arbroath* (Historical Association, 1970). Important documents are edited and translated in E. L. G. Stones, *Anglo-Scottish Relations, 1174–1328* (2nd edn., Oxford, 1970).

Chapter 8. Political Communities

On late medieval polities in general, see S. Reynolds, *Kingdoms and Communities in Western Europe, 900–1300* (Oxford, 1984), ch. 8; and B. Guenée, *States and Rulers in Later Medieval Europe,* trans. J. Vale (Oxford, 1985). Two recent books by C. Given-Wilson contain broader discussions of the structure of the English kingdom than may be apparent from their titles: *The Royal Household and the King's Affinity: Service, Politics and Finance in England, 1360–1413* (Yale, 1986), and *The English Nobility in the Late Middle Ages: The Fourteenth-century Political Community* (1987). Fiscality, military service, parliament, propaganda, and nationalism are examined, from various angles, by G. L. Harriss, J. R. Maddicott, and A. L. Brown, in R. G. Davies and J. H. Denton (eds.), *The English Parliament in the Middle Ages* (Manchester, 1981); G. L. Harriss, *King, Parliament, and Public Finance in Medieval England to 1369* (Oxford, 1975); G. Post, *Studies in Medieval Legal Thought* (Princeton, 1964); J. Barnie, *War in Medieval Society: Social Values and the Hundred Years War, 1337–99* (1974); B. C. Keeney, 'Military Service and the Development of Nationalism in England, 1272–1327', *Speculum,* 22 (1947); and M. Prestwich, 'Parliament and the Community of the Realm in Fourteenth-century England', in A. Cosgrove and J. I. McGuire (eds.), *Parliament and Community: Historical Studies XIV* (Belfast, 1983). Local communities and their relations with the centre are discussed in J. R. Maddicott, 'The County Community and the Making of Public Opinion in Fourteenth-century England', *Transactions of the Royal Historical Society*, 5th ser., 28 (1978); N. Saul, *Knights and Esquires: The Gloucestershire Gentry in the Four-teenth Century* (Oxford, 1981); and M. J. Bennett, *Community, Class and Careerism: Cheshire and Lancashire Society in the Age of Sir Gawain and the Green Knight* (Cambridge, 1983). Legal developments are considered in Harding, *The Law Courts of Medieval England*; B. H. Putnam, 'The Trans-formation of the Keepers of the Peace into the Justices of the Peace, 1327–80', *Transactions of the Royal Historical Society*, 4th ser., 12 (1929); and E. Powell, 'Arbitration and the Law in England in the late Middle Ages', ibid. 5th ser., 33 (1983). The literature on particular political episodes is very large. I made much use of G. Holmes, *The Good Parliament* (Oxford, 1975). Other valuable works include J. R. Maddicott, *Thomas of Lancaster, 1307–1322* (Oxford, 1970); J. R. S. Phillips, *Aymer de Valence, Earl of Pembroke, 1307–1324* (Oxford , 1972); W. M. Ormrod, 'Edward III and the Recovery of Royal Authority in England, 1340–60', *History*, 72 (1987); A. Tuck, *Richard II and the English Nobility* (1973); C. M. Barron, 'The Tyr-anny of Richard II', *Bulletin of the Institute of Historical Research*, 41 (1968); and F. R. H. du Boulay and C. M. Barron (eds.), *The Reign of Richard II: Essays in Honour of May McKisack* (1971).

English Ireland is still neglected. Apart from the general histories, the following may be found useful: Richardson and Sayles, *The Irish Parliament in the Middle Ages*, chs. 6–11; R. Frame, *English Lordship in Ireland, 1318–1361* (Oxford, 1982); J. F. Lydon, 'William of Windsor and the Irish Parliament', *English Historical Review*, 80 (1965); S. Harbison, 'William of Windsor, the Court Party and the Administration of Ireland', in Lydon (ed.), *England and Ireland*; A. Cosgrove, 'Parliament and the Anglo-Irish Commu-nity: The Declaration of 1460', in Cosgrove and McGuire (eds.), *Historical Studies XIV*; R. Frame, 'Military Service in the Lordship of Ireland, 1290–1360: Institutions and Society on the Anglo-Gaelic Frontier', in R. Bartlett and A. MacKay (eds.), *Medieval Frontier Societies* (Oxford, 1989).

Views of the Scottish polity have been undergoing revision, as a compari-son of Nicholson, *Scotland: The Later Middle Ages*, and Grant, *Independence and Nationhood*, will reveal. Grant's article 'Crown and Nobility in Late Medieval Britain', in R. A. Mason (ed.), *Scotland and England, 1286–1815* (Edinburgh, 1987), pin-points important contrasts between Scotland and England. Other relevant articles include A. A. M. Duncan, 'The Early Par-liaments of Scotland' and 'The Community of the Realm and Robert Bruce', both in *Scottish Historical Review*, 45 (1966); B. Webster, 'David II and the Government of Fourteenth-century Scotland', *Transactions of the Royal His-torical Society*, 16 (1966); and A. Grant's papers on the nobility: 'Earls and Earldoms in Late Medieval Scotland, c.1310–1460', in Bossy and Jupp (eds.), *Essays Presented to Michael Roberts*; 'The Development of the Scottish Peerage', *Scottish Historical Review*, 57 (1978); and 'Extinction of Direct Male Lines among Scottish Noble Families in the Fourteenth and Fifteenth

Centuries', in Stringer (ed.), *Essays on the Nobility of Medieval Scotland*. Fundamental to recent shifts in perception has been the work of Jenny Wormald, which, though focused on the fifteenth century, has implications for the earlier period. See, in particular, 'The Exercise of Power', in J. M. Brown [Wormald] (ed.), *Scottish Society in the Fifteenth Century* (1977); 'Bloodfeud, Kindred and Government in Early Modern Scotland', *Past and Present*, 87 (1980); and *Lords and Men in Scotland: Bonds of Manrent, 1442-1603* (Edinburgh, 1985). Myth, history, propaganda, and national identity are considered in E. L. G. Stones, 'The Appeal to History in Anglo–Scottish Relations', *Archives*, 9 (1969); Duncan, *The Nation of Scots and the Declaration of Arbroath*; G. G. Simpson, 'The Declaration of Arbroath Revitalised', *Scottish Historical Review*, 56 (1977); Webster, *Scotland from the Eleventh Century to 1603*, chs. 1–2; and R. A. Mason, 'Scotching the Brut: Politics, History and National Myth in Sixteenth-century Britain', in Mason (ed.), *Scotland and England*, which glances helpfully backwards.

Chapter 9. On the Margins

On the Peasants' Revolt, see R. H. Hilton and T. H. Aston (eds.), *The English Rising of 1381* (Cambridge, 1984), and R. B. Dobson (ed.), *The Peasants' Revolt of 1381* (2nd edn., 1983).

Useful on Anglo-Scottish border society are D. Hay, 'England, Scotland and Europe: The Problem of the Frontier', *Transactions of the Royal Historical Society*, 5th ser., 25 (1975); J. A. Tuck, 'Richard II and the Border Magnates', *Northern History*, 3 (1968), and 'Northumbrian Society in the Fourteenth Century', ibid. 6 (1971); and A. Goodman, 'The Anglo-Scottish Marches in the Fifteenth Century: A Frontier Society?', in Mason (ed.), *Scotland and England*. Two papers by R. Frame deal with the Irish marches: 'Power and Society in the Lordship of Ireland, 1272–1377', *Past and Present*, 76 (1977), and 'War and Peace in the Lordship of Ireland', in Lydon (ed.), *The English in Medieval Ireland*.

On the Welsh in post-conquest Wales, see Davies, *Conquest, Coexistence, and Change*, Part V. The subject is also considered in a number of excellent articles, including G. Roberts, 'Wales and England: Antipathy and Sympathy, 1282–1485', *Welsh History Review*, 1 (1960–3; reprinted in his *Aspects of Welsh History* (Cardiff, 1969)); R. R. Davies, 'The Twilight of Welsh Law', *History*, 51 (1966), and 'Race-Relations in Post-Conquest Wales: Confrontation and Compromise', *Transactions of the Honourable Society of Cymmrodorion* (1974–5); A. D. Carr, 'An Aristocracy in Decline: The Native Welsh Lords after the Edwardian Conquest', *Welsh History Review*, 5 (1970–1); and G. Williams, 'Prophecy, Poetry and Politics in Medieval and Tudor Wales', in his *Religion, Language and Nationality in Wales* (Cardiff, 1979). J. E. Lloyd, *Owen Glendower* (Oxford, 1931), is still useful.

Native Irish society is surveyed in K. Nicholls, *Gaelic and Gaelicised Ireland in the Middle Ages* (Dublin, 1972). Simms, *From Kings to Warlords*, is fundamental for the development of Gaelic lordship. See also J. A. Watt, in Cosgrove (ed.), *Medieval Ireland, 1169–1534*, ch. 12, and A. Nic Ghiollamhaith, 'Dynastic Warfare and Historical Writing in North Munster, 1276–1350', *Cambridge Medieval Celtic Studies*, 2 (1981). The legal status of the Irish is considered in A. J. Otway-Ruthven, 'The Native Irish and English Law in Medieval Ireland', *Irish Historical Studies*, 7 (1950–1); Hand, *English Law in Ireland*, ch. 10; and B. Murphy, 'The Status of the Native Irish after 1331', *The Irish Jurist*, new ser., 2 (1967). Relations between the Gaelic lords and royal and baronial authority are analysed in the articles by R. Frame referred to above, and also in R. Frame, 'English Officials and Irish Chiefs in the Fourteenth Century', *English Historical Review*, 90 (1975); E. Curtis, *Richard II in Ireland, 1394–5, and Submissions of the Irish Chiefs* (Oxford, 1927); D. Johnston, 'Richard II and the Submissions of Gaelic Ireland', *Irish Historical Studies*, 22 (1980), and 'The Interim Years: Richard II and Ireland, 1395–1399', in Lydon (ed.), *England and Ireland*; and K. Simms, 'The Archbishops of Armagh and the O'Neills, 1347–1471', *Irish Historical Studies*, 19 (1974–5).

The Scottish highlands and islands are explored in G. W. S. Barrow, 'The Highlands in the Lifetime of Robert the Bruce', in his *The Kingdom of the Scots*; Grant, *Independence and Nationhood*, ch. 8, and 'Scotland's "Celtic Fringe" in the Late Middle Ages: the MacDonald Lords of the Isles and the Kingdom of Scotland' in Davies (ed.), *The British Isles*; and J. W. M. Bannerman, 'The Lordship of the Isles', in Brown (ed.), *Scottish Society in the Fifteenth Century*.

Index

Clare (Ireland), 113
Clare, Richard de ('Strongbow')
    (d.1176), 35, 37, 38, 45, 67
Clarendon, Assize of (1166), 83
Clarendon, Constitutions of (1164), 73
Cloyne, bishopric of, 46
Cnut, King of the English (1016–35),
    8, 23, 74, 81
Cockermouth, 202
Coety, 67
coinage, coins: in England, 14, 75, 77,
    136, 137; in Ireland, 87; in Scotland,
    91, 93; in Wales, 117, 119
Coldingham Priory, 60
Coleraine, 36
Columba, St, 10
Commons, the: in English parliaments,
    137, 173–8; in Irish parliaments,
    184–5
commotes, 68–9, 120, 157, 209, 210
Comyn family, 62–3
Comyn, John, of Badenoch (d.1306),
    188
Comyn, Walter, earl of Menteith
    (d.1258), 62
Conan IV, duke of Brittany (d.1171),
    105
Connacht, 20, 35, 114, 181, 183, 205;
    county of, 88; kings of, *see* O'Connor;
    lords of, *see* Burgh, Lionel,
    Mortimer
Connor, bishopric of, 46
Constantinople, 16, 143
Convocation of the Clergy, 173
Cooper, T.M., Lord, 190
Copeland, 65
Corbet family, 208
Cork, 38, 93, 114, 118; county of, 88,
    151, 184
Cornwall, dukes of, 138
coronations, *see* royal inaugurations
Costentin family, 58
county communities: in England, 170,
    172–4, 179; in Ireland, 182–3;
    absence of in Scotland, 191
county courts, *see* sheriffs
Cowal, 43, 71
Crécy, battle of (1346), 132
Cressingham, Hugh, 168

Cricieth, 157
Cumberland, 63, 79
Cumbria, 15, 26, 29, 59, 66, 69; king-
    dom of, 9, 14, 68; *see also* Strathclyde
Cunningham, 40, 66
Cuthbert, St, 10, 11, 146
Cymer, abbey of, 120

Dafydd ap Gruffydd (d.1283), 140,
    143, 152, 154, 155, 156–7, 168
Dafydd ap Llywelyn (d.1246), 46, 48,
    119, 120, 121, 124, 143, 154
Dafydd ab Owain Gwynedd (d.1203),
    39, 117
David I, King of Scots (1124–53): his
    Anglo-Normans, 50, 58–9, 92, 93,
    107; and Henry I, 26, 28, 94, 162;
    inauguration of, 107; 'Laws of
    King David', 142, 194; and northern
    England, 28–9, 33, 40; and religious
    reform, 106; rule of, in Scotland, 40,
    89, 90, 91, 94–5, 105; and the suc-
    cession, 106–7
David II, King of Scots (1329–71),
    131, 132, 133, 137, 138, 140, 188,
    195, 218
David, earl of Huntingdon (d.1219),
    33, 34, 42, 60, 64, 66, 69, 70, 96,
    160, 162, 165
Declaration of Arbroath (1320), the,
    194–5
Degannwy, 46
Deheubarth, 15; kings, princes of, 10,
    15, 37, 39, 67, 117–8, 159, 160, 207,
    211; *see also* Gruffydd ap Rhys, Rhys
    ap Gruffydd, Rhys ap Tewdwr,
    Wales (south)
Denbigh, 58, 157
Desmond: earls of, 205–6; lords of, *see*
    MacCarthy
Desmond, Gerald, earl of (d.1398),
    206
Desmond, Maurice, earl of (d.1356),
    183, 206
Desmond, Maurice, earl of (d.1358),
    206
Desmond, Thomas, lord of (d.1298),
    151
Dialogue of the Exchequer, 80

(d.1190), 105
Holt, 157
honorial courts, 65–6, 67, 70, 82, 83, 84
households: baronial, 62; royal, 24–5, 30, 38, 78, 92, 136
Howden, Roger of, 39
hundred, hundred court, 75–6, 146, 148; Hundred Rolls, the, 145
Hundred Years War, *see* Anglo-French wars
Huntingdon, honor of, 26, 33, 34, 48, 59, 64, 66, 70
Huscarl, Roger, 87
Hywel Dda (d.949/50), 16; 'Laws of Hywel Dda', 120, 156

Iberia, 129, 164
Idwal, Welsh king, 16
Inverness, 42, 43, 93, 97
Inverurie, 66
Iona, 10
Irish, the: legal status of, 142, 187, 213–14, 215–16; lords of, 204–6, 212–17, 220, 223
Irish Sea Province, the, 12, 23, 37, 61
Isabella, wife of Edward II, 131, 132
Islam, 74, 80
Isles of Scotland, the, 10; *see also* Lordship of the Isles, Northern Isles, Orkney, Western Isles
Italy, 8, 23

James I, King of Scots (1406–37), 203
James IV, King of Scots (1488–1513), 188, 220
Jedburgh, 202
Joan, wife of Llywelyn the Great, 119, 124
John, King of England (1199–1216), 32, 48, 56, 100, 118, 136, 202; government of, 20–2, 45, 79–80, 100–2, 130, 170; and Ireland, 32, 36, 38, 39, 50, 59, 60–2, 67, 86–8, 100; loses Normandy, 30, 44–5, 53, 129–30; and Scotland, 34; and Wales, 119, 123–4
John II, King of France (1364–80), 133, 137, 139

John, King of Scotland (1292–6), 131, 140, 143, 160, 164–6, 193–4
John of Gaunt, duke of Lancaster (d.1399), 138, 139, 172, 177–8
John of Scotland, earl of Huntingdon and Chester (d.1237), 48, 121
John, bishop of Glasgow (c.1114–47), 106
John of Hexham, 11
Joinville, Jean de, 57
justices: in England, 79, 82, 83, 84, 86, 87, 96, 149, 171–2, 175; in Ireland, 86–7, 96, 182, 206; in Scotland, 95, 96, 191

Kells (Meath), 70; Synod of (1152), 110
Kendal, 65
Kenneth mac Alpin, King of Scots (c.843–58), 10, 17, 98
Kent, 14, 57
Kerry (Ireland), 36; county or lordship of, 88, 205
Kildare, 62, 67; county or lordship of, 57, 148, 204, 205, 213
Kildare, John, earl of (d.1316), 183
Kildare, Maurice, earl of (d.1390), 204
Kilkenny, 67, 150, 184, 185; county or lordship of, 57, 138, 204, 205
Kilkenny, Statute of (1366), 214–15
Kilkenny, William of, 101
King Arthur, 13, 193
kingship: English, 3, 8, 13–14, 99–102; general development of, 15–16, 98–9, 124–5, 129, 224; Irish, 8–9, 108–15; Scottish, 3, 10–11, 15, 102–8, 188, 192, 221–2; Welsh, 9–10, 15–16, 115–25, 151; *see also* government, Irish lords, overlordship, royal inaugurations, royal succession, royal titles
Kintyre, 50

La Rochelle, 30, 44
Lachlan, lord of Galloway, *see* Roland
Lacy family, 58, 61, 66, 71, 113, 147, 148
Lacy, Hugh de (d.1186), 35, 58, 69–70
Lacy, Hugh de, earl of Ulster (d.1242), 61

OXFORD

MORE OXFORD PAPERBACKS

Details of a selection of other Oxford Paperbacks follow. A complete list of Oxford Paperbacks, including The World's Classics, Twentieth-Century Classics, OPUS, Past Masters, Oxford Authors, Oxford Shakespeare, and Oxford Paperback Reference, is available in the UK from the General Publicity Department, Oxford University Press (RS), Walton Street, Oxford, OX2 6DP.

In the USA, complete lists are available from the Paperbacks Marketing Manager, Oxford University Press, 200 Madison Avenue, New York, NY 10016.

Oxford Paperbacks are available from all good bookshops. In case of difficulty, customers in the UK can order direct from Oxford University Press Bookshop, 116 High Street, Oxford, Freepost, OX1 4BR, enclosing full payment. Please add 10 per cent of the published price for postage and packing.

THE OXFORD BOOK OF SHORT POEMS

Chosen and Edited by P. J. Kavanagh and James Michie

A collection of short poems (less than fourteen lines), from medieval times to the present day. The sonnet is excluded; and epigrams and epitaphs, of which adequate anthologies exist, have been avoided. The result is a collection of more than 650 poems which draw attention to the short works of the great poets which are sometimes overlooked, whilst giving extended room to established masters of the short poem. From Chaucer and Shakespeare, to Philip Larkin and Ted Hughes, this wide-ranging collection demonstrates the gradual change in style, subject-matter, and tone, from one generation of poets to the next.

'[the editors] are both scrupulous poets with a liking for clean, clear craftsmanship' *P N Review*

THE OXFORD BOOK OF LATE MEDIEVAL VERSE AND PROSE

Edited by Douglas Gray

In this illuminating anthology the late medieval period—from the death of Chaucer to the early years of Henry VIII's reign—emerges as an age of great literary achievement. The works of familiar authors such as Malory, Henryson, Skelton, and More are well-represented, along with well-known styles such as songs and lyrics, ballads and romances. The Testament of Cresseid, Mankind, and Everyman are given in full, and the anthology also includes some works never before published.

'The range of texts is astonishing . . . Gray writes with all the sharp and authoritative asservation of a C. S. Lewis.' *Times Literary Supplement*

THE OXFORD BOOK OF CONTEMPORARY VERSE, 1945–1980

Compiled by D. J. Enright

This anthology offers substantial selections from the work of forty British, American, and Commonwealth poets who have emerged and confirmed their talents since 1945.

'There is more pithy and Johnsonian good sense in his short introduction than in all the many books that have been written about modern poetry . . . one of the best personal anthologies I have come across.' John Bayley, *Listener*

THE NEW OXFORD BOOK OF EIGHTEENTH-CENTURY VERSE

Chosen and Edited by Roger Lonsdale

'a major anthology: one of the best that Oxford has ever produced' *The Times*

'a major event . . . forces a reappraisal of what 18th-century poetry is' *Sunday Times*

'the most important anthology in recent years' *The Economist*

'indispensable' Kingsley Amis

THE OXFORD BOOK OF SATIRICAL VERSE

Chosen by Geoffrey Grigson

'one of the best anthologies by the best modern anthologist' *New York Review of Books*

'An immense treasury of wit, exuberance, controlled malice and uncontrolled rage' *Times Literary Supplement*

POEMS 1962–1978

Derek Mahon

Derek Mahon is widely regarded as one of the most important Irish poets of his generation. *Poems 1962–1978* brings together a selection of his best-known poems, plus a number of previously uncollected and more recent ones.

Oxford Poets

CLASSIC IRISH SHORT STORIES

Selected and introduced by Frank O'Connor

Good Irish short stories will always be a delight. In this marvellous selection by Frank O'Connor, himself a distinguished short-story writer, the richly varied Irish tradition of spinning a yarn is triumphantly displayed. James Joyce, George Moore, and Sean O'Faoláin are just a few of the authors included.

'a wealth of characteristically "Irish" writing . . . as good a collection of stories as you could find anywhere' *Books and Bookmen*

THE HUNT BY NIGHT

Derek Mahon

This is Derek Mahon's first full-length collection since *Poems 1962–1978* and is probably his most exuberant and authoritative single volume to date. The remarkable depth and range of poems in this book show a rare excitement and lyrical beauty.

Oxford Poets

SELECTED LETTERS OF OSCAR WILDE

Edited by Rupert Hart-Davis

When Sir Rupert Hart-Davis's magnificent edition was first published in 1962, Cyril Connolly called it 'a must for everyone who is seriously interested in the history of English literature—or European morals'. That edition of more than 1,000 letters is now out of print; from it Sir Rupert has culled a representative sample from each period of Wilde's life, 'giving preference', as he says in his Introduction to this selection, 'to those of literary interest, to the most amusing, and to those that throw light on his life and work'. The long letter to Lord Alfred Douglas, usually known as *De Profundis*, is again printed in its entirety.

'In Mr. Hart-Davis's *The Letters of Oscar Wilde*, the true Wilde emerges again for us, elegant, witty, paradoxical and touchingly kind . . . I urge all those who are interested in the contrasts between pride and humiliation, between agony and laughter, to acquire this truly remarkable book.' Harold Nicolson, *Observer*

MAIN CURRENTS OF MARXISM

Volume 1: The Founders

Leszek Kolakowski

In this first volume, Leszek Kolakowski examines the origins of Marxism, tracing its descent from the neo-Platonists through Hegel and the Enlightenment. He analyses the development of Marx's thought and shows its divergence from other forms of socialism.

'The most commanding, the most decisive, the most properly passionate and yet also . . . the most accessible account of Marxism that we now have. It is a work of surpassing lucidity and power, of the sharpest and most sensitive judgement, of a far finer quality than almost all of that with which it deals. It is, in short, a masterpiece.' *Times Higher Education Supplement*

BLAKE

Complete Writings

Edited by Geoffrey Keynes

This definitive edition of Blake's writings—a volume which, the *Times Literary Supplement* observed, 'might serve as a model of how a great editor is able to efface himself from his work'—was first published by the Nonesuch Press in 1957, and reissued in 1966, with substantive corrections and additions, in the Oxford Standard Authors series.

The writings are printed in chronological sequence, with a section of Blake's letters at the end, followed by Notes, and a supplement containing a small amount of new material. Peculiarities of spelling, frequent use of capitals, and abbreviations in Blake's original manuscripts and etched texts are preserved, but certain eccentricities of his punctuation have been regularized. Lines are numbered, and Blake's designs reproduced where they are essential to an understanding of the text.

JAMES JOYCE

Richard Ellmann

Winner of the James Tait Black and the Duff Cooper Memorial Prizes

Professor Ellmann has thoroughly revised and expanded his classic biography to incorporate the considerable amount of new information tht has come to light in the twenty-two years since it was first published. The new material deals with most aspects of Joyce's life: his literary aims, a failed love affair, domestic problems, and his political views.

'The greatest literary biography of the century.' Anthony Burgess

'Richard Ellmann's superb biography . . . [is] a great feat of twentieth-century literary scholarship.' Christopher Ricks

'A superlatively good biography of Joyce.' Frank Kermode, *Spectator*

Oxford Lives